AUTISM ASPERGERS:

SOLVING THE RELATIONSHIP PUZZLE

A NEW DEVELOPMENTAL PROGRAM
THAT OPENS THE DOOR
TO LIFELONG SOCIAL & EMOTIONAL GROWTH

Steven E. Gutstein, Ph.D.

FUTURE HORIZONS INC.
Arlington, Texas

All marketing and publishing rights guaranteed to and reserved by

FUTURE HORIZONS INC.

Future Horizons, Inc.
721 W. Abram Street
Arlington, TX 76013

800.489.0727 Toll Free
817.277.0727
817.277.2270 Fax

www.futurehorizons-autism.com
email: info@futurehorizons-autism.com

ISBN   1-885477-70-8

*I dedicate this book to the memory of
Arle, Abe and Dave,
who gave me the gift and curse of my crazy male dances.*

*And, to Rachelle, Rachel, Esther and Hannah,
who taught me how to properly dance with ladies.*

Contents

Acknowledgments

Preface   **xi**

Introduction   **xv**

1   **Isaac**   **1**

2   **Experience Sharing**   **7**

3   **Autism: Life Without Experience Sharing**   **33**

4   **Relational Development Intervention**   **47**

5   **Principles of Treatment**   **67**

6   **Laying the Foundation for Relational Development**
      Level One   **81**

7   **Becoming an Apprentice**
      Level Two   **93**

8   **You & Me: Working Together as Partners**
      Level Three   **113**

9   **Sharing Our Worlds**
      Level Four   **127**

10   **Sharing Our Minds: The Inner Game**
      Level Five   **139**

11   **True Friends**
      Level Six   **155**

Afterword   **169**

Appendix I: Glossary   **173**

Appendix II: Six Levels of Experience Sharing   **177**

Appendix III: Research on Social Development in Autism   **181**

References   **183**

Acknowledgements

*T*his book would never have gone from more than a collection of ideas to its final form, if it weren't for the patience, dedication and clinical genius of my wife, Dr. Rachelle Sheely. Rachelle is my vision of the perfect blend of artist and clinician. If I have provided the science for this book, there is no doubt that Rachelle has provided the dance, not to mention excellent editing. I would also like to express thanks to my daughters Hannah and Esther who have graciously forgiven the frequent mental absences of their father over the past five years, as I labored with this volume. Thanks also to my mother-in-law, Rachel, for her constant prayers and endless support, which made this work possible. I wish to gratefully acknowledge the efforts of my editor, Veronica Palmer, whose faith, excitement and skill provided the final push I needed to complete this journey. Finally, I want to acknowledge the help of Dr. Iris Rosenzweig, who aided me so much with her encouragement and editing.

This work stands directly on the shoulders of many others. Most, if not all the theoretical ideas and clinical methods put forth, are either elaborations or direct contributions of gifted theorists and clinicians like R. Peter Hobson, Alan Fogel, Daniel Stern, Barry Prizant, Gary Mesibov, Peter Mundy and others too numerous to mention.

Some of our results are harder to quantify...like the reactions we sometimes get from audiences who see videotapes of our patients and—noticing the spontaneity, the flexibility and readiness to compromise and the emotional spark, insist that they were not really autistic to begin with.

Or, the hilarity in our hallways when our dyads and groups laugh and run and do all of the things we expect typical children to do. Or the way that their eyes light up when their buddies come into the waiting room.

Parents' depression lifts and joy fills them instead. They tell us things like "My child has become someone who desires to play with me and doesn't care that much which game I choose. My child looks at me from across the room and gives me a smile to reassure me that all is well. He notices my face and comes up to me wondering if I am sad."

These are scenes that our parents had come to believe would never occur in their lifetimes...

*A*s any parent of a typical infant knows, acquiring the rules and formulas for social functioning is only a small part of the experience of early development. A much more critical element unfolds during the thousands of hours of mutual joy, absurd silliness and creative excitement of parent-infant play, characterizing the first year of life. The brilliant developmental researcher Daniel Stern uses a metaphor of dance to describe the earliest relationship as "...a human happening, conducted solely with interpersonal 'moves,' with no other end in mind than to be with and enjoy someone else."

For children with Autism, something goes drastically wrong during their first year of life, interrupting the natural joyful dances of parent and child that form the base for all future development. Despite parents' best efforts, infants with Autism do not comprehend the predictable patterns embedded in our constantly changing facial expressions and gestures. Children with Autism do not learn to run alongside their partners, share their unique perceptions, or wonder about the differences of other people's minds. Instead of wanting to expand their social universe and make new discoveries, they contract their social world until it fits into their limited ability to understand it.

The greatest tragedy of the disorder of Autism is that it robs children of thousands of hours of joy, wonder and creative excitement that relationships provide the rest of us. The social world of children with Autism too often becomes an overly scripted, or chaotically mystifying setting. Relationships do not become the center of safety, excitement and novelty. Rather, social encounters are a major source of stress and confusion. It is no wonder that most children and adults with Autism have little motivation to become more proficient in their social worlds. It is no surprise that so many people with Autism develop fascinations with computers, videotapes and other objects that provide them predictable stimulation, even at the price of social isolation.

Should we attempt to treat this core deficit of the disorder? Is it reasonable to hope that people with Autism can experience the same yearning for emotional relationships that most of us take for granted? Can individuals with Autism learn to coordinate their emotions with others? There are those who would argue that people with Autism are not neurologically constructed with the capacity to engage in these activities and that trying to treat this deficit is a fruitless, or even improper endeavor.

We have hopefully progressed past the point of believing that people with Autism are "happier in their own worlds." However, many professionals and even some parents implicitly, or explicitly believe that the best we should hope for is for people with Autism to learn social "scripts" and rote behavioral responses, with the purpose of helping them "get by" on a superficial level. Others believe that giving persons with Autism a repertoire of appropriate social behaviors will allow them to be better accepted by peers and ensure that they fit into their social environments. This is undoubtedly true and no minor feat.

But what is lost when we accept this limited definition of success? If we remove the spontaneity, improvisation, joy and silliness from our social encounters, as we do when we teach social skills in rote fashion, we fail to convey the rationale for working so hard at making interpersonal connections. We present an empty, barren picture of our social worlds. We omit our lifelong drive for someone to share our innermost thoughts and fears, become our ally and create an "us" that joins together against the world, and all the other unique moments that make us feel worthwhile. In short, we fail to convey the very reasons why a person with Autism would choose to struggle against the great obstacles their disorder presents them with, to attempt to master this confusing world. Before we inundate autistic people with skills, we must first make sure they have experienced enough of the reasons for using them—the payoffs—for operating in the social world.

When people with Autism learn social skills in a "scripted" manner, they do not understand the most important part of the relational dance. It is as if they are being taught the steps of a dance like the Tango or Foxtrot without any comprehension of what it means to dance with a partner on a crowded dance floor. They present their behavior to the world, without any awareness of whether it fits with what has just come before, without any means of judging how it will be received and without the capacity to instantly adjust their actions based on the response of their partner. There is an "out of synch" quality to their actions—a lack of timing.

This strange and sometimes tragic nature of interacting, observed even with "high functioning," intelligent people with Autism, is striking. Others have to do all the work to keep the encounter balanced to any degree, like continually moving away, as they relentlessly encroach upon your personal space. The emotions that people with Autism express may be directed at no one in particular. They may take actions and make statements without regard to the reactions of those around them.

Even after all these years as psychotherapist, father and husband, I sometimes tend to forget the most critical part of relationships. When I'm not careful, I lapse into my own version of an autistic existence. Or, I get so involved in the highly complex, "important," but empty scripts of "responsible parenting," "dutiful husbanding" and "professional psychologizing," that I lose sight of the joy derived from simple shared moments. Luckily, Life offers me reminders. I'm seated at a restaurant, when quite by chance my eyes meet those of a baby at a nearby table and

I am "captured"—no other word describes the power of that event—by the baby's gaze. Instantly and without the slightest self-consciousness, I find myself making faces so odd and gestures so strange, that in any other context I would be committed to a mental hospital. I know myself well enough to realize that these moments are insufficient to maintain my emotional "hold" in the world of relationships. A few seconds after such an encounter, I return to whatever problem or topic preoccupies me and I am surprised by how quickly I forget about the more important discovery right in front of me.

Fortunately for me, I spend time each day with children and teenagers who have Autism. They never let me forget our basic need to connect with others. I watch in wonder as they cast adrift into the open ocean on a solo voyage to nowhere. I experience their desperation, as they are unable to build even the simplest bridges with others and must cling to their few precious islands of attachment for dear life, fearful of letting go and never finding their way back. And, I know they are the ones who fully appreciate the awesome chasms that exist between us in ordinary life. They are the ones who cherish each precious bridge they must build with such methodical, deliberate effort.

This book is dedicated to them.

Steven E. Gutstein, Ph.D.
Houston, TX
December 2000

Preparing for the Journey

How do you teach someone, born without the proper tools, to overcome severe neurological barriers and fully participate in the world of emotional relationships? Over ten years ago, I started on a journey to answer this question. At the time, I had resigned my position as a Medical School Professor. I had given up my research grants and team of assistants when I chose to depart academics for private practice. But, despite the obstacles and all the good reasons I gave myself for leaving this problem alone, I was driven to pursue an answer. I just could not accept the consequences of waiting for others to do something about the tragedy I saw unfolding around me every day.

A child with Autism may never get invited over to a pal's house to play. Friendships, if they occur at all, are scarce and superficial. Teenagers with Autism do not date, or hang out with their peers. Few get to go to the prom. Outside of contact with immediate family, the vast majority of adults with Autism spend their lives in isolation. They do not get married and have families. Even for those with high intelligence, employment opportunities are severely curtailed by their inability to work as part of a collaborative team and their lack of sensitivity to co-workers' feelings and needs.

Whatever help and treatment we provide people with Autism, if we cannot help them overcome their inability to make emotional connections, we condemn them to empty lives. I was determined to make a difference and develop a method that would enable people with Autism to build emotional bridges with others.

Early on, I realized that I would need to battle against some prejudices and misconceptions I too frequently encountered among the non-autistic population. People with Autism are not happy living in their own world. They can love and show affection to parents and family members. They are not trapped behind a wall that can be "broken through." *They are social beings.* Many, even without treatment, develop a wide range of social behaviors and interests. They may or may not suffer from a variety of other symptoms such as impaired language development, profound sensory impairments and obsessive and compulsive behavior. They might possess high intelligence, or suffer severe cognitive limitations.

Autism is a complex disorder. No two individuals manifest the same characteristics in the same way. Once thought to be rare, incidence rates in the last few years have been increasing at almost epidemic proportions. Despite the attention Autism has attracted in the professional and lay communities, there remains a great mystery attached to this disorder, one that deprives an individual of the capacity to share his emotional world with those he loves. Despite their many differences, these people all share a common deficit, one that takes root early in life and results in devastating consequences.

More than twenty years ago, as a young medical school Assistant Professor, I could never have predicted that I would spend the second half of my career obsessively pursuing new ways of treating Autism. I had almost no experience or training in the disorder. I was a highly trained family therapist and clinical researcher, studying the effect of parent-child interactions on children's recovery from serious illness. In retrospect, I am sure that given my misconceptions and limited training, in these early years I offered little help to the few children within the Autism spectrum I was called upon to evaluate.

But, from the onset of my career I had been driven to understand the essence of emotion-based relationships. As a young child, I spent many years emotionally detached and alone during my mother's cancer and following her death. During the hours I spent in my friend's houses, I developed a keen eye and just as great hunger for the easy warmth and understanding I observed in these typical families. I became the eternal guest, tolerated and even welcomed, but always excluded from deep emotional connections.

By the time I left academics to pursue private practice, I had developed a reputation as someone who enjoyed the "hard" cases—the children and adolescents who confused or even frightened others. I have devoted my career to providing my patients, whatever their age or problems, the experience of participating in emotional connections and the belief that they have the capacity to achieve emotional intimacy in their lives, no matter what obstacles they initially brought with them.

Given my penchant for challenges, it was inevitable that I would work with a number of children in the Autism spectrum. Looking back over my personal history, it was equally inevitable that I would experience a deep sense of kinship with these individuals, who for entirely different reasons were perpetual outsiders in the world of emotional encounters.

After working with dozens of children with Autism, conducting many social skills groups and using the latest behavior modification approaches, I was disappointed with the results I was obtaining. I consulted my colleagues to make sure I was approaching my work in the most effective manner. To my surprise, they informed me that, given the nature of these children, I was achieving excellent results. My patients made more eye contact. They possessed a greater repertoire of social scripts. They were better socialized—they took turns, stood on line and obeyed more rules. They were better tolerated by their peers. A number were functioning in regular classrooms where their typical peers were accepting them in a limited way.

Despite my colleagues' praise, I still believed that something was missing in my treatment approach. I was using all the accepted interventions. But, they all seemed geared to teaching the person with Autism the superficial trappings of social interactions, not the internal experience of being in a relationship.

My patients were working hard to make even limited progress. They learned to greet me in the waiting room with an emotionless "Hello Dr. Steve." They learned to smile at me and to say goodbye and to ask for things they needed. Several children developed a much more sophisticated repertoire. They knew appropriate language structures. They understood the rules of their classroom and always received excellent conduct grades. They made good eye contact. A few could even express and accurately "read" others' emotions. But, even for these highest functioning children, their abilities were not enough to have a real caring friendship with another child.

Not a single one of my patients had learned to be genuinely curious about my feelings. None could, on their own, maintain the topic of his conversation with a pal, or share a tender moment. Some key element was missing that kept them from learning the critical parts of friendship.

I recall one poignant example that became a turning-point in my determination to find another approach. At the request of Neil, a highly intelligent child with Aspergers Syndrome, I spent a good deal of time teaching him to master the timing of common "Knock Knock" jokes. He became quite proficient at a familiar variant:

"Knock knock."	"Who's there?"
"Banana."	"Banana who?"
"Knock knock"	"Who's there?"
"Banana."	"Banana who?"
"Knock knock."	"Who's there?"
"Orange."	"Orange who?"
"Orange you glad I didn't say banana?"	

After he had practiced on cooperative adults, it was time for a trial with children. The first child he tried the joke on was a pre-school aged boy, unfamiliar with the format. Neil began his scripted joke in the usual way, but was met by an unexpected response:

"Knock knock."	"Who's there?"
"Banana."	"Ha ha ha. That's funny!"

Neil responded to his partner's laughter and enjoyment—the real point of telling a joke—with anger and frustration. He spent several minutes, until I intervened, attempting to coerce the now frightened child into following the "correct" social script and saying, "Banana who." Rather than acting as a vehicle for mutual joy, the joke, a social "skill" I had so painstakingly taught Neil, had turned into a cruel obstacle.

I wasn't satisfied with the empty futures I saw awaiting these heroic children. I wanted my patients to experience the excitement and joy of relationships and not just enact social scripts, learned through reinforcement or rote practice. Using the social skills methods at hand seemed at best to create only the outside veneer of what a relationship might be. They could learn a behavior, but not the moment-to-moment emotional reactions the rest of us rely on and live for.

I knew each child could not make the same progress, or reach the same goals. But, regardless of their abilities or limits, there was something more I wanted to give each of them. I wanted my patients to smile when I walked into the waiting room because they were happy to see me, not because they received an M&M as a reward. I wanted them to feel excited in their groups because they were working together as a team. I wanted Neil to understand the real point of telling a joke and share in the laughter of the child who supplied the "wrong" answer. I wanted my patients to direct their curiosity towards the inner feelings of the people around them and the topics that interested and excited them and be genuinely curious about what was on other people's minds. For a special few, I dreamed that they might someday fall in love and have that love requited.

Before I could proceed, I needed to answer a few fundamental questions. Why do even the most able people with Autism remain cut off from this basic aspect of human existence? Why do even the people at the top of the continuum, with IQ's in the superior range, fail to develop the relationship competence we take for granted in a typical three-year-old? What essential elements do they fail to learn? When do they miss out on this learning?

It was with this goal in mind that eight years ago I began spending hundreds of hours in libraries, reading everything I could find about typical relationship development, as well as the development of people with Autism. I began consulting experts doing seminal work in the disorder. What I learned drastically changed my understanding of Autism, as well as my methods of treatment.

I was startled to learn that researchers had determined that many people with Autism develop interest and considerable ability in a limited part of their social worlds. Even without treatment, many seemed to understand the part of social behavior that does not require the sharing of emotions, ideas and perceptions. Some become highly proficient in what researchers term "instrumental" social actions, where the interaction serves as an instrument—a means to an end to obtain some desired object, or information or stimulation. Research indicated that when operating for instrumental purposes, people with Autism can display affection, make eye contact, point, take turns and engage in a number of social behaviors that many people believe are missing in people with this disorder.

Along with these instrumental interactions, which serve the purpose of helping us meet our basic needs, there is a critical second type of interaction, referred to as *Experience Sharing.* The sole purpose of this type of social behavior is to provide an opportunity to share some part of oneself with a partner.

From the beginning of life, these two forms of social behaviors are learned in very different ways. Instrumental actions, like standing on line, are learned as scripted routines, performed in a specific manner to achieve a specific endpoint. They can be learned like an actor learns his part for a play, with other performers responding in a highly predictable manner.

On the other hand, sharing our experiences requires a unique type of information processing, referred to as Emotional Coordination. When we act as a partner in an Experience Sharing interaction, we function as a coordinated part of a highly fluid, constantly changing system. To be successful, we must process a constant stream of information about ourselves "in relation" to information about another person, while making split-second judgments based upon this data. It is a way of perceiving interaction, more akin to the rhythm and timing of a teenage dance. You are successful only if you follow your partner's lead, making sure at the same time that she follows yours. Emotional Coordination involves learning to make constant subjective evaluations and re-evaluations of participants' degree of connection to each other. "Do I feel too far away from you? Do you really understand my meaning? Am I too rough?" Continually asking and answering such questions fosters the maintenance and repair actions needed to keep the interaction from degenerating into chaos.

When I thought about my patients, it became clear that while I had been successful in increasing their instrumental repertoire, I had failed to help them develop proficiency in the emotional coordination needed for Experience Sharing. They were developing socially in a highly unbalanced manner and missing out on the most important part of why we interact with others. When I returned to the Autism literature, I found that a number of researchers had come to similar conclusions. Many studies have found that Autism can actually be well defined as the inability to develop the capacity to use emotional coordination in Experience Sharing relationships.

The best minds in the field—theorists like R. Peter Hobson of the world famous Tavistock Institute in London—believe that people with Autism are born with a range of different neurological problems. These collectively interfere with their ability to do the type of information processing that makes Experience Sharing so simple for the rest of us. For example, they do not connect to the constant stream of emotional communication

> ...sharing our experiences requires a unique type of information processing, referred to as Emotional Coordination.

that surrounds them. Even when they perceive other people's emotions, they remain unable to link this data with their own feelings and personal experience. These deficits severely limit their ability to enjoy and fully participate in the most valuable parts of our lives.

I decided to find out whether a treatment program could be developed to teach people with Autism to desire, enjoy and participate as partners in a variety of Experience Sharing relationships. Surprisingly, while research clearly demonstrated the deficit in Experience Sharing as a core feature of Autism, there was a large gap between what was being learned in laboratories and the clinical interventions that were being used. No methods existed that provided even a glimpse of how to teach people the foundations of Experience Sharing in a systematic manner. The social skills training approaches were all geared to instruction in instrumental interaction, the very skills that people with Autism were already capable of learning.

My response was to once again return to the literature on normal development. If effective clinical intervention methods were to be developed, they would certainly have to parallel the manner in which typical children acquire their Experience Sharing proficiency. The result, after several years of grueling analysis and evaluation, is **Relational Development Intervention** (RDI), the intervention described in this book. RDI is modeled upon the means by which typical children become competent in the world of emotional relationships. It is an intervention approach quite different from the typical social skills programs found in the field.

As someone trained to marvel at the intricate progression of the stages of natural development, I was shocked to see how much intervention in the field of Autism appeared to occur in a haphazard manner. Skills were taught without considering the developmental needs of the person or whether they had the foundations necessary to adequately use the skill. Examining most methods of social intervention painfully reminded me of the time I attended a school meeting for a young man who was severely dyslexic. When it was time to discuss special remediation for his reading disorder, an assistant principal remarked that he believed the best treatment for dyslexia was simply to read more. I was determined that my model for intervention would begin with a careful assessment to pinpoint the specific stage of readiness—the appropriate developmental place to begin working. We developed the Relational Development Assessment (RDA), an assessment tool we have found to be indispensable.

Overview of the RDI Model

In RDI, the initial setting for intervention is purposefully artificial. It is the equivalent of a laboratory designed to eliminate distractions and help the child make relationship discoveries. We work in a pleasant room with covered windows and walls without decorations. We minimize visual and auditory "noise"—simple background for most people—but highly distractible to a person with Autism. Similarly we remove objects like toys or games that can detract from attending to social information. By removing the competition for attention, it is easier to spotlight critical social and emotional information for the child.

We carefully select highly structured and routine-based activities that are motivating for the child to experience positive emotion sharing and excitement. These simple activities allow for gradual variation and introduction of novelty.

When we first see children with Autism, most do not have the desire for the rigorous practice needed to master Experience Sharing relationships. We expend considerable time and effort helping children obtain a regular sample of the pleasure available in meaningful relationships.

Parents are intensively trained to take the lead in "Guided Participation," as they would in typical development. They learn to set clear limits, minimize distractions and develop an "emotionally attuned" relationship, before leading the child through the elements of social choreography. Gradually, as a child learns to assume more responsibility for maintaining the coordination of interactions, parents allow her to introduce variation and creativity into their encounters. Of course, this serious work of play cannot occur solely in our offices. Parents must spend many hours per week practicing activities at home and eventually in other settings.

We gradually prepare children to move beyond their sole reliance on parents, by introducing them to carefully matched and prepared peers— first in the form of a two-child dyad. Dyads eventually transform into groups, while the setting shifts from the initial therapy room to the more normal chaotic world in which these children must derive their future social discoveries.

Over the past eight years we have evaluated over 500 children and adolescents and treated over 200 of them. Treatment is long term and progress can be slow. Our average child will be with us for many years. But we are seeing results. Last year we sent five of our children off to college. All are still doing well. In fact, we've had three parents tell us their concerns are that their child is spending too much time socializing and is not putting enough effort into their studies. All three were quite aware of the irony of their complaints. Our older children have learned to hold their own in social interactions. They are not befriended by typical peers out of pity or compassion, but because they are genuinely fun to be with. Several of our teenagers are dating and have girlfriends and boyfriends.

Some of our results are harder to quantify, like the reactions we sometimes get from audiences who see videotapes of our patients and—noticing the spontaneity, the flexibility and readiness to compromise and the emotional spark, insist that they were not really autistic to begin with. Or the hilarity in our hallways when our dyads and groups laugh and run and do all of the things we expect typical children to do. Or the way that their eyes light up when their buddies come into the waiting room. Parents' depression lifts and joy fills them instead. They tell us things like "My child has become someone who desires to play with me and doesn't care that much which game I choose." "My child looks at me from across the room and gives me a smile to reassure me that all is well." "He notices my face and comes up to me wondering if I am sad." These are scenes that our parents had come to believe would never occur in their lifetimes.

What this book is about

This book is a bridge in understanding and treating the social deficits in people with Autism. It provides a framework to help people with Autism learn to participate more fully in relationships. By beginning intervention early in life, carefully staging the setting, choosing appropriate participants and gradually introducing activities that expose the child to new skills in the proper state of developmental readiness, we can significantly improve the quality of life for people with Autism.

Not every element of our approach is new. Parents and therapists will find many, if not most, of our activities and ideas to be familiar and intuitive. Nor does our approach negate or diminish the value of other forms of social intervention. This book is narrowly focused on the journey to develop more systematic ways to help people with Autism develop meaningful emotional relationships. This does not imply that we see no importance in working on the full range of social and non-social objectives. For example, no one doubts the value of teaching children with Autism to use the essential tools of language, follow instructions, or integrate their physical movements in more fluid ways. These abilities and a host of others are critical objectives in their own right. In our clinical practice, we spend considerable time and effort teaching children to pay attention to adults, accept instruction, follow basic social rules and behave appropriately in different settings. Fortunately, excellent methods for working on these aspects of development are readily available.

How the Book is Structured

Autism Aspergers: Solving the Relationship Puzzle guides you through an appreciation of how Experience Sharing develops in typical children, contrasts the deficits inherent in Autism, then outlines the essential components of the RDI model of treatment. In the first chapter, we introduce you to Isaac, and trace his relationship development through several years in our program. Throughout the book, we use actual case histories to illustrate relationship concepts and/or parts of our intervention activities. Following this are several sections outlining the nature of relationship development in Autism, as contrasted with typical development. These chapters will be crucial for readers interested in the theoretical underpinnings of our treatment approach.

If you are hungry to get to clinical methods, you may be tempted to skip over these sections. Resist that temptation! They provide a critical foundation of knowledge that has been neglected in most of the current social development intervention methods in Autism. You will come to appreciate the degree of time and effort infants spend mastering their social worlds. You will be able to recognize the relationship proficiency possessed by a normal twelve-month-old, still bereft of language and barely tottering around. After reading these initial chapters, you will more fully appreciate the components of relationships, stripped of the complex language and social scripts that we often erroneously view as the essential elements of our social world.

The remaining chapters summarize the RDI method, our goals and objectives, general principles of treatment, as well as our mode of evaluation and treatment planning. These chapters detail the treatment process as it moves from an early focus on the pleasure of shared excitement and the earliest structural games, through an emphasis on mutually coordinating actions, into more fluid play and eventually into the sharing of inner worlds and enduring friendships.

Let our journey together begin!

Isaac

$\mathcal{M}$y first impression of Isaac was of a sturdily built, three-year-old boy with light brown hair and an angelic face. Isaac's eyes ventured everywhere and anywhere, in a seemingly unfocused and random manner. Several minutes later, Isaac was walking around aimlessly in the hallway, shrieking in horrific high-pitched noises, with a lopsided smile on his face. He seemed to be going nowhere and looking at nothing. His mother, Susan, ran after him, caught him and under protest he was escorted back to the playroom to continue their work with my wife Rachelle.

Case Study

Something about Isaac struck my curiosity, so I entered our tiny observation room behind the one-way mirror. Isaac was banging his head against the wall, not so hard as to cause damage, but repetitively and without any intention to stop. Susan pulled him away from the wall and intently tried to engage him in a game where they took turns holding each other's faces and making funny noises. Each time she let go, Isaac tried to wander away, presumably back to the wall to continue his head-banging ritual. The session—his fourth as I later found out—continued in this manner for the next half hour, as Susan and Rachelle each vainly attempted to involve Isaac in some activity.

There were only two things Isaac enjoyed doing and would engage in for hours at a time: getting on a spring rocking horse and rocking frantically and rolling his toy train on the top of the sofa, watching the wheels go back and forth, over and over again. For no apparent reason he would frequently bang his head. Isaac had no language and made no attempts to communicate. He made no eye contact and appeared uninterested in sharing emotions with others. He didn't even seem to notice his parents once he was several feet away. When distressed Isaac wanted physical contact, but would back his way into his mother's arms, never even glancing at her.

Living with Isaac held its own set of challenges. He didn't have the massive, frequent temper outbursts of some of our patients. Nor was he aggressive. Aside from his head banging he was a passive child who, if left to his own devices, would seem fairly content. But Isaac rejected all attempts to teach him or play with him. He refused to participate in even simple first-year games like peek-a-boo. At three, he still had not played his first game of chase. He ignored all other children, even his brother John, who was one year older. Any attempt to show him how to play with toys sent him back to his horse to start rocking.

The doctor who initially diagnosed Isaac with autism at two years and nine months of age, told his parents not to expect that Isaac would ever attend a normal classroom, or live an independent life. During that meeting, Darryl, Isaac's father—a brilliant medical researcher—broke down and cried for the first time in his adult life. Susan later told us that it was months before she ever cried. She kept thinking that she had a lot of hard work ahead and had no time for tears or sadness. But, Susan—a deeply religious woman—also revealed that during that time she kept telling herself "I can't wait to go to heaven...there I'll finally be able to have a conversation with my child."

Fast-forward three years. We have been working with Isaac on a regular basis, using our Relational Development Intervention approach. I am sitting in the same observation room watching Susan and Isaac. Susan is sitting next to Isaac and side-by-side they are building a tower together. This is a game from the 50's called Bill Ding, where small wooden grooved men hang by their feet, head or hands from all the other men. Although Isaac started talking quite some time ago, they rarely use his full range of verbal expression during sessions together, as this would interfere with their mutual enjoyment.

> **Although Isaac started talking quite some time ago, they rarely use his full range of verbal expression during sessions together, as this would interfere with their mutual enjoyment.**

"Mommy, let's play Bill Ding" he says. "I hate Bill Ding" she replies, teasingly. Then she adds, "I hate turkeys." Isaac replies with, "No, I hate turkeys. I love Bill Ding. I love Bill Ding's turkey." The laughter reaches a crescendo as they build with Bill Ding. Isaac is at the stage where he is beginning to understand that Susan's body posture and tone of voice do not necessarily match her words. Isaac can enjoy these gentle, teasing exchanges and add his own variety to their interaction without disconnecting from her.

As Isaac and Susan build their tower of men, I think back over the tough road Susan, Darryl and Isaac traveled over the past three years. There were the times they squeezed him to stop the head banging. There were hundreds of times when Susan repetitively hid behind beanbags and required that Isaac find her, not emerging even when he burst into tears, so that he would learn he had to take the initiative, to reference her. There were the months of repetitively teaching him the simplest movement activities like falling and jumping together. And, there were constant attempts to hook him into the shared excitement of joint attention.

Isaac and Susan hold hands, facing each other from opposite sides of their people sculpture. They count to three and then try to knock the tower over by blowing it down. Their count is not a simple 1-2-3. There are pauses where they both abruptly stop in mid-count, laughing and gazing at their partner slyly. These moments of exaggerated hesitation, which would initially have led to a great degree of distress and discomfort for a child with Autism, now only heighten the excitement they experience. Just before they finally blow their little sculpture over, Isaac's gaze shifts between Susan's face and the sculpture. When their tower of little men finally explodes, it is Susan's face he watches. It is her excitement that makes this game fun for him—not the crashing play figures.

"Let's play Bill Ding soccer game"—another game Isaac loves. Susan tells him that they are going to play Battleship first. The tone of her voice and expression tell him she is firmly in charge as his guide and is not joking. "Then soccer with Bill Ding?" "Umm, no. Then Connect Four and I am going to beat you," she tells him in a mock serious tone. "I'm going to beat you!" he emphatically replies, with a smile on his face. They laugh again and he says "Then Bill Ding?" "OK." Susan gives in with a pseudo-reluctance that belies her real pleasure with Isaac's new sense of emphasis on their mutual enjoyment and his ability to flexibly adapt to her requests.

Finally, it is time to play Bill Ding Soccer, a game the two of them have invented. Isaac and Susan set Bill Ding up as the coach of their soccer team. A disc from Connect Four becomes the soccer ball. There is a five-point limit for the game and Susan wins by three points. "No, No, Mommy. I want to win," he cries. "Play another game?" She refuses, "Next week." Isaac cries a bit harder, for dramatic purposes. He hates to lose but sputters out an insincere "Congratulations!"

Fast-forward again to the present. Isaac is now eight years old. He attends regular classes in his neighborhood public school. Isaac speaks with fluid language that is exceptional for children with Autism, but typical of children who have been through RDI. It is highly emotion based and in context. He plays on a regular soccer team where he is the star. He also plays baseball on a team for typical children. He recently started receiving invitations to other boys' houses to play. Isaac now has a wonderful relationship with his brother John. They play as equals, with each expected to hold up their end of the interaction. John does not cut Isaac any slack. Watch Isaac with his two-year-old sister, Rachel, and you will be amazed at what a patient and loving teacher he has become.

Isaac's conversations are still limited. But his intent is excellent. He asks about feelings. He notices facial expressions—"Are you sad Rachelle?" He can stay coherent with a conversational topic. He teases gently and appropriately. When he and Rachelle play chess, unlike typical children with Autism, he knows the game is just a backdrop for their relationship. When Isaac realizes he's going to capture one of Rachelle's men, he starts laughing and says, "I'm ruining your strategy." Or, he will pretend he has a great move to make by saying, "I'm going to ruin your strategy." Rachelle responds with, "No way, my strategy is better." Both laugh uproariously at this easy banter.

When their tower of little men finally explodes, it is Susan's face he watches. It is her excitement that makes this game fun for him—not the crashing play figures.

Isaac has begun making his own social discoveries—a sign that he is generalizing Experience Sharing into his everyday life. He exhibits many social behaviors that he's never been taught to do. For example, when his mother and sister visited our special summer camp that he attends for two weeks each year, Isaac made sure they were introduced to all the other children. Isaac had a partner at camp-Phil. Phil was sick one day and couldn't come. All day Isaac went to the window saying, "Maybe he's stuck in traffic, Rachelle?"—what she used to tell him when Phil was late in the past for their sessions together. Rachelle tells him, "No. Phil has an ear infection and can't come today." The next day Phil came to the door and Isaac ran across the room and said, "Phil you had an ear infection. Is your ear OK now?" Then the boys took hands and ran off to play blocks together.

All on their own, Isaac and Phil have made up a new game they play with their blocks. This is another hallmark of our program. Children learn how to be co-creators with their partners and together share the joy of inventing new activities they jointly take pride in. They pretend that one of the blocks is a car. They drive over to one of their pretend houses for a pretend birthday party for one of them. When they arrive, they sing happy birthday together. One boy gives the other presents. And then it's the other child's turn for a birthday party and so they drive to his house for the celebration. They pretend to blow out candles, eat cake and sing happy birthday at the top of their lungs.

> Isaac now appreciates the joy and excitement inherent in social interactions. He understands why we human beings connect and actively seeks out situations that reinforce those feelings for him.

Isaac is also developing a true sense of compassion for others, a major milestone for children with Autism who find it difficult to understand and relate to the emotions and feelings of another person. One day at summer camp, a younger child attended for his first day and began crying as soon as his mother departed. Isaac noticed the child's distress and immediately went over, took the child's hand and said, "Don't cry, I'll take care of you." He put his arm around the child, held his hand and said "Don't be scared." Isaac kept talking to him in a soothing way "It will be OK; I will help you." Isaac carefully showed him how to play with the toys in the room. During baseball time, Isaac took the boy's hand and ran the bases with him, forgoing his own turn at bat. Within several hours, the boy had stopped crying and began to enjoy camp.

A once withdrawn, solitary little boy, unaware of and with little concern for the world around him, Isaac now appreciates the joy and excitement inherent in social interactions. He understands why we human beings connect and actively seeks out situations that reinforce those feelings for him. Does Isaac still have autism? Most definitely. He still has difficulty with too much sudden change. He still misses subtle social cues. He still can be overwhelmed in noisy groups.

It took years of coordinated intervention to arrive at the level of functioning that Isaac exhibits today. However, he has gone beyond learning 'social skills' to mastering 'social awareness', a pivotal understanding that helps him in all areas of his life. While there is still much work to be done, Isaac's life has already been enriched beyond measure. He is assured of a future that involves other people in meaningful ways. Who knows what possibilities lie ahead. One day, he too may be caught making weird and exaggerated faces at a baby he happens to see in a restaurant. But, no matter what his eventual course, we know that Isaac will always have friends. He will go to his high school prom. His peers will seek him out, not out of pity, but because he is so much fun to be with. Isaac's mom, Susan, did not have to go to Heaven to have the conversation she yearned for with her son. The dramatic change in her, the radiance and joy which emanate from her face, tell us that she has found her Heaven on earth.

2

Experience Sharing

*W*hile one of the hallmarks of Autism is impaired social relationships, Autism is not a social disorder per se. Many people diagnosed with the condition learn various forms of social behavior that permit them to function, albeit in a rote and scripted manner, with their world. They learn to make eye contact, point and request things, ask questions to get what they want and follow basic social rules; some in a highly developed manner, with others learning just barely enough to gain a small degree of independence. However proficient they may become, they remain locked in the realm of Instrumental competence, limited to acquiring these skills for the sole reason of getting their needs met.

The unifying characteristic that eludes even the highest functioning individuals with Autism or AS is an understanding and appreciation of Experience Sharing. Despite the many treatment options at our disposal, like intensive behavioral modification or social skills training, it is this deficit in Experience Sharing that ultimately robs people with Autism of true social connections.

Instrumental social behaviors are a means to achieving an end; they have little to do with the specific person with whom we interact. Experience Sharing on the other hand, has as its focal point, the pleasure derived from specific social encounters as a unique end in itself. At first glance, the differences appear simple and straightforward. However, upon closer inspection, distinguishing between these two forms of interaction is not as easy as expected.

Instrumental interactions and Experience Sharing are similar in five ways:

- The same behavior can be used for both purposes.

- The same activity can have both Instrumental and Experience Sharing goals.

- The purpose of children's play can be either Instrumental or Experience Sharing.

- Both types of behavior can produce emotional reactions.

- Conversational formats can be used for both types of interactions.

An identical activity may be used for either an Instrumental or Experience Sharing purpose. Pointing can be an attempt to request a desired object, or a means of sharing an interesting observation. Eye contact may be the result of training in appropriate social contact and a learned precursor to obtaining a desired reward. Alternately, it may be an indication that the child is interested in his partner's emotional reactions.

Typical children often engage in the same activity for Experience Sharing and Instrumental purposes simultaneously. For example, two boys can play catch to improve their skills (Instrumental purpose) while at the same time enjoying each other's company (Experience Sharing).

Furthermore, we cannot distinguish the two types of interaction by the emotional reactions of the participants, or by viewing one as "play" while the other is not. A frightened child with Autism, backing into his mother's arms to receive her comfort, is operating for Instrumental purposes. Similarly, children can smile and laugh while playing with peers and still be operating primarily in an instrumental way. When participants view their partner only as a means to achieving their desired end, even when emotion, eye contact and other social behaviors are present, the interaction is Instrumental. Even activities like riding on a seesaw, or playing monopoly may be Instrumental, if the participant only engages with a partner in order to derive the excitement and enjoyment he desires from the activity itself.

Conversation—an activity well-suited for Emotional Sharing, can also be confusing to judge. When an autistic child bombards a person he has just met with endless questions, or insists on reciting trivial facts that his partner shows no interest in, he is engaging in an Instrumental manner. His partner is inconsequential and interchangeable. In the previous chapter, when Neil practiced his "Knock Knock" joke on a younger child, he was more interested in both parties performing the routine correctly, than in sharing anything with the particular child. When a child with Autism goes through the appropriate verbal routines, like asking another child her name, where she lives and goes to school, without the slightest real curiosity about her partner's responses, she may still be involved in an Instrumental interaction.

After studying the similarities between these two forms of interaction, I began to understand why professionals are often confused about diagnosing Autism. Many clinicians observe instrumental social actions and conclude that these abilities rule out the diagnosis of Autism, even though research clearly demonstrates that people with Autism may not have a deficit in Instrumental interaction and communication. For example, they witness a child making eye contact, pointing, following social rules and talking in a conversational format and conclude that the child cannot have any form of Autism. Many parents unaware of the distinctions between Instrumental and Experience Sharing interactions do the same. Several parents have disputed my diagnosis of Aspergers Syndrome for their child, because they routinely see him/her playing with peers with real enthusiasm and constantly engaging in "conversations."

How, then, can we reliably distinguish Instrumental interactions from true Experience Sharing behavior? Through careful observation of my own patients, five critical markers became apparent.

1. The predictability of the end product

We engage in Instrumental interactions with a clear goal in mind. There is something very specific we expect to receive by taking certain actions with another person. Furthermore, we become quite disappointed if we

> **When participants view their partner only as a means to achieving their desired end, even when emotion, eye contact and other social behaviors are present, the interaction is Instrumental.**

take the requisite actions and do not receive the expected result. In contrast, Experience Sharing occurs for no particular reason. It is undertaken without any clear objective, except the enjoyment or positive feelings we derive from the interaction.

2. The relationship of the partner to the goal

In Instrumental encounters, we engage other people because there is something we wish to obtain from them—information, an object, or participation in an activity. Other people are agents, perceived as necessary only to deliver the product to us. If we can achieve our goal without interaction, we will do so. If a partner is not available, we may proceed anyway to reach our objective. In contrast, Experience Sharing, by its very nature, welcomes other people into our world. What transpires between our partners and us—the novel actions, perceptions, ideas and feelings—motivates us to interact. Through our actions with a partner, we hope to create a unique, shared experience that we can never obtain on our own.

3. The interchangeability of partners

Any partner who knows the right rules and possesses the necessary knowledge or skill will serve in an Instrumental encounter. In this respect, partners are fairly interchangeable. Furthermore, we may quickly—and in a decidedly detached manner—exchange a partner with whom we have shared experiences for a new inexperienced partner, if that new partner is more willing to provide us with what we seek out of the interaction. In contrast, memories of shared experience with a particular person greatly enhance the pleasure of Experience Sharing. Our relationships are strengthened by the perception of a shared past and potential common future. In addition, we learn that partners who are aware of each other's unique ways of relating have an easier time maintaining the relationship.

4. Reliance on scripts and rules

Instrumental interactions follow highly predictable scripts and roles enacted in a specified order. Once these scripts and roles are learned and can be performed on cue, participants believe that they should be successful most of the time in achieving their objectives. It's like playing the same videotape over and over. In contrast, Experience Sharing depends upon partners constantly evaluating the degree to which there is a "match" between their experience and that of their partner(s). Based on observing the degree of relationship between self and others—referred to as Social Referencing—we are expected to make constant adjustments to increase coordination with our partner(s).

5. The need for emotional communication

People may have emotional reactions while engaged in, or as a result of Instrumental interactions, but emotional communication is not necessary for success. Participants can largely ignore each other's emotional

> Experience Sharing depends upon partners constantly evaluating the degree to which there is a "match" between their experience and that of their partner(s).

Distinctions Between Instrumental and Experience Sharing Interactions

Attribute	Type of Interaction	
	Instrumental	Experience Sharing
Specificity and predictability of the end product	Expectation of a highly specific, predictable end product. Failure to reach expected end point leads to disappointment, and/or anger.	The excitement of unplanned results is a critical reason to engage in the interaction. We interact for novel experience.
Role of the interactional partner	Interaction is conducted to obtain something that is wanted or needed from another person. If he can obtain it without interacting, he will, with no loss.	Interaction is conducted solely to create a unique, shared experience with a partner that cannot be duplicated through individual actions.
Interchangeability of partners	Despite shared history, partners are interchangeable so long as they possess requisite skills and knowledge.	Prior history with partners makes future interactions more satisfying. Partners are highly valued for prior shared emotional experiences.
Reliance on predictable scripts, rules and structured role actions	Completely reliant on rigid scripts, rules and role actions. Expectation of a highly predictable sequence of actions taken by both partners.	Only partially reliant on rules and role actions. Mostly rely on both partners' ongoing observations and actions to maintain mutual understanding and coordination.
Emotional Communication	No desire or need to observe or experience any emotional linkage or connection with partners.	Need to constantly observe, evaluate and experience the extent of emotional linkage with partner(s).

reactions and still attain their desired objectives. In contrast, Experience Sharing is highly dependent upon emotional communication. Participants use their partner's emotional reactions as an ongoing "reference point" to evaluate the degree to which their experience is being shared by their partners and to determine the actions they should take next.

A vignette about Neil, the young man with Aspergers Syndrome who wanted to learn joke telling, poignantly illustrates these differences. Neil loved to play board games like Monopoly or Risk. When entering my room for his small group session, the first thing he would do was make eye contact as he had been taught, appropriately greet me and his group partner Albert, and then politely, but firmly request to play the specific game he had already chosen. At this point, nothing in Neil's actions clued us as to whether his intentions were Instrumental, or about Experience Sharing. However, the differences soon surfaced. It became apparent that playing the game he had chosen, in the manner that he believed it was supposed to be played, was more important to Neil than sharing the experience, or even the identity of the person he played with. Neil recited his opening social routine in an automatic, emotionless manner. But, if Albert agreed to play the game he had chosen, Neil's eyes would light up and he would show excitement for the first time. As long as Albert followed Neil's rigid interpretation of the rules, Neil would smile and enjoy playing the game. But, if Albert's actions varied in any manner from Neil's interpretation of the rules, Neil would be quick to scold him and demand that he play the game "correctly." If Albert committed the "sin" of deciding he didn't want to play Neil's game that day, Neil would instantly react as if Albert did not exist, turn and quickly ask me if I wanted to play. If Albert failed to show up one week, Neil might inquire as to his whereabouts, but then quickly get down to the "business" of requesting that we play the game he had chosen. At no point did Neil pay attention to the emotional reactions of his partners. Nor did he show the slightest curiosity about what we wanted to do, or what was going on in our minds. It did not matter whether or not we enjoyed playing the game with him—just that we did play it and follow his rules.

The Six Levels of Experience Sharing

Despite a large quantity of research on Experiencing Sharing, no systematic description of how it actually develops existed. By painstakingly organizing the research findings, it appeared that the different experiences we all share could be grouped into six levels. This model became the foundation for our RDI method. Each level represents a new kind of experience we share. Within each level are four distinct stages, representing the critical breakthroughs in methods of sharing made during the interval. While this model is clearly a gross simplification of the millions of situations we experience, it provides a useful framework for appreciating the foundation that each level provides for the subsequent developmental discovery.

The chart on pages 12–13 summarizes the six levels and stages of Experience Sharing, with the approximate age typical children begin working at each level.

Levels and Stages of Experience Sharing

Level 1: Tuning In (Birth)

- **Emotional Attunement: Face-to-face emotion sharing with adults is the center of the child's attention.** "When our faces meet, we feel like the same person."

- **Social Referencing: Observing adult facial reactions for approval, safety and security.** "Mom and dad's face help me figure out how to feel about things."

- **Excitement Sharing: Deriving primary excitement from parents' introduction of novel stimulation.** "Watching the new things that people do is the best show in town."

- **Simple Games: Understanding and enjoying the structure of simple social activities.** "I understand the game and I get excited, even before the good parts."

Level 2: Learning to Dance (Six Months)

- **Frameworks: Enjoys learning the rules, roles and structure of sequenced Experience Sharing activities.** "I am learning to understand the basic dances."

- **Variations add the Spice: Adults' introduction of variety becomes the highlight of social activities.** "When my parents add new steps to the dance, it makes it more exciting."

- **Dancing Lessons: Participating as a partner in synchronized actions.** "First you do your step and then I do mine."

- **Moving Together: Carefully observing and regulating actions to remain coordinated with a partner.** "We lead and follow at the same time."

Level 3: Improvising and Co-creating (Twelve Months)

- **Constant Co-variation: Enjoying the shared introduction of novelty while engaged in fluid, coordinated actions.** "The fun is in the new steps we add to the dance."

- **Fluid Transitions: Enjoying and participating as a partner in chaining activities into a fluid sequence.** "We go from one dance to another without a pause."

- **Improvisation: Enjoying activities where partners collaborate to continually modify rules and roles, while maintaining their coordination together.** "We can dance together without knowing the dance. We just mix steps from all the other dances."

- **Co-creation: Developing new activities, with each partner contributing to the rules and theme equally.** "Something new emerged from our improvisation. "

Level 1: Tuning In

During the first six months of life, infants and parents spend thousands of hours working one-on-one in a natural classroom. This repetitive and intensive state of interaction develops a critical foundation for all future Experience Sharing. They become highly aware of and sensitive to each other's facial expressions. The infant learns that he can judge the state of his world by the visual cues he sees on Mommy or Daddy's face. The parent learns just how much stimulation the child can accept without pushing her into a state of anxiety and discomfort. In this six-month period, parents act as the primary source for introducing novelty, excitement, and emotional soothing to the infant. By the end of Level 1, a baby is

Level 4: Sharing Outside Worlds (Eighteen Months)

- **Perception Sharing: Enjoying visual and verbal emotion sharing, following the joint perception of an external stimulus.** "Look at what I see!"

- **Perspective Taking: Actively seeking to compare and contrast perceptions.** "We may see different things. You can't see what I see unless you move over here."

- **Unique Reactions: Sharing unique reactions becomes a highlight of the joint attention experience.** "It looks huge to me. Does it look huge to you?"

- **Adding Imagination: Shared addition of imaginative elements to elaborate perceptual events becomes a highlight of the joint attention experience.** "That cloud looks like a castle to me. What does it look like to you?"

Level 5: Discovering Inside Worlds (Thirty Months)

- **Sharing Ideas: Enjoyment is obtained through the integration of ideas between social partners.** "We can make things together using just our minds."

- **Enjoying Differences: Excitement is enhanced by different ideas and themes brought into play and conversation by social partners.** "It's great to know that there is more than one way to think about it."

- **The Inside and Outside Worlds: Viewing internal reactions as different and more important than external reactions.** "You can say one thing but feel another."

- **The Primacy of Minds: Recognizing that thoughts, feelings and ideas are the critical elements of Experience Sharing.** "What's important is what's inside."

Level 6: Binding Selves to Others (Forty-Eight Months)

- **Unique Selves: Relating to other people for the purpose of better defining a unique sense of self.** "Some parts of me are like you and some are different."

- **Belonging to Groups: Membership in varied groups becomes a critical part of identity.** "Part of who I am comes from what I belong to."

- **Pals and Playmates: Appreciating pal-ships on the basis of shared interests, activities and history.** "What do I need to do so that you will play with me more? We like to do the same things."

- **Enduring Friendships: Valuing close friendships built upon mutual trust and caring.** "We have a special history and future that binds us together."

able to anticipate simple games and shared laughter is often observed. Children are able to signal for the initiation, continuation and termination of social activities.

Stages of Level 1—birth to 6 months of age

- Emotional Attunement

- Social Referencing

- Excitement Sharing

- Simple Games

Emotional Attunement

Daniel Stern refers to the first three months of a baby's life as the stage of **Emotional Attunement.** During this period, parent and child become extremely sensitive to the facial expressions, head movements and voice tones of the other. They react to the world as if they share one nervous system. Anxiety or joy in one instantly produces the same reaction in the other. Researchers have found that changes in parent heart rates become increasingly correlated with similar changes in their infant's during the first three months. The infant's facial expressions also become increasingly correlated with those of his parents. The attunement process sets the stage for parents to safely introduce a great deal of novelty into the infant's world without overwhelming the child.

Social Referencing

By the end of the fourth month, the typical infant has learned that the soothing voice tones and facial expressions of familiar adults can serve as a reference point, bringing instant emotional relief, even when not being held or physically comforted. Faced with confusing or ambiguous situations, it becomes second nature for babies to respond to their increased anxiety by gazing at a parent's face. If their facial expressions are calm and positive, this produces a rapid reduction in the child's distress. Alternatively, if the parent's facial expression appears anxious or it is blocked from view, the child's distress will rapidly escalate. This process, called **Social Referencing,** plays a crucial role in the further development of Experience Sharing. Through Social Referencing, the infant gains security and confidence in interacting with his world. Once it has been learned, parents can begin more actively introducing novelty and variety into the child's life. They know that, even as they make the inevitable errors in providing too much or too powerful stimulation, the infant will be able to easily recover, through gazing at Mom or Dad and using their calm and happy emotional reassurance as a reference point for his own emotional state.

Excitement Sharing

By the fifth month, infants are craving an ever-increasing amount of novel stimulation. They quickly learn that the best form of excitement can be obtained through interacting with a parent or familiar adult. Developmental researcher Alan Sroufe writes that infants learn to become "excitement addicts" under the careful tutelage of their parents. In order to study the effects of parent introduction of sudden, exciting and novel actions to their babies, Sroufe measured the heart-rate response of babies to different types of events. For example, a mother slowly approaches her baby with an amplified smile, which suddenly, without warning, changes to a momentary grimace before returning once again to a smile. The typical infant, reacting to this rapid emotional change exhibited on mother's face,

> **By the fifth month, infants... learn that the best form of excitement can be obtained through interacting with a parent or familiar adult.**

moves from the edge of distress to outright relief at her rapid change to a smile. Sroufe found that this type of encounter provides a physiologic surge of pleasure unmatched in the infant's world. In short, babies become addicted to paying rapt attention to the facial expressions of parents and other adults who make the unknown, known and the unfamiliar, familiar in a safe, but exciting manner.

Of course, infants would not continue to crave this type of parent inter-action if the result was fear and confusion, rather than positive excite-ment. As in all Experience Sharing encounters, a constant "referencing" and "regulating" process must be in place to ensure that novelty and euphoria does not turn into confusion, or anxiety. At this early stage of development, the onus is on the adult to keep the experience poised at the edge of the excitement/distress continuum. Parents rely on subtle changes in their child's facial expression and body tension, as well as their own feelings, as cues in determining their subsequent actions. Using their own Social Referencing, parents carefully observe the infant's reactions and routinely fine-tune their introduction of novelty by regulating their actions.

For example, Jim is playing with his four-month-old son Jonathan by looming his head close and making "boo" noises. Both partners are sharing in the excitement and pleasure of the game. Without realizing it, Jim's voice gets louder and becomes over-stimulating to his son. Jonathan's facial expression subtly changes and displays increased ten-sion. Jim immediately notices this reaction; he perceives that there is a poor "match" between his own positive excited actions and Jonathan's mildly distressed reactions. Jim takes immediate steps to regulate his actions so that his emotions are more coordinated with his son's. He instantly flashes a reassuring smile, which Jonathan quickly references. His voice softens and his actions become gentler, as he slightly decreases his own level of excitement. Jim notices that Jonathan's face is now more relaxed and has a happy, alert expression, so he continues the game, with both partners operating at a slightly less stimulating but more mutually comfortable state of excitement.

Simple Games

By the sixth month of life, Experience Sharing has moved to the arena of simple repetitive games with highly exciting climaxes. Babies quickly learn to reference their parent's actions during these games, to the point where they can enjoy a "preview" of the excitement that has not yet occurred. For example, a baby, anticipating his Mom's next action, begins to laugh during peek-a-boo, even before Mom uncovers her face to reveal herself to the child. Babies also become proficient at observing the state of parental attention and are able to determine the best time to initiate an invitation to play.

> ...babies become addicted to paying rapt attention to the facial expres-sions of parents and other adults who make the unknown, known and the unfamil-iar, familiar in a safe, but exciting manner.

The ability to anticipate the elements of an interaction allows for the introduction of even greater amounts of novelty and variation. The infant learns that it does not matter whether mother uses a scarf or her hands to cover her face—the game remains the same. Nor does it matter whether she says "boo" or "peek-a-boo" or even "beep" for that matter. The game has not really changed. It has just become more fun.

> **Bubba is five and a half months old. He lies on his back on a sofa with his mother above him. Mother gently sings "Ta, Ta, Tatatata," while clapping Bubba's hands in rhythm. She synchronizes the opening of his hands with a higher pitched "beep" and continues this sequence three times. On the fourth time, instead of the "beep," she puts Bubba's hands to her cheeks and blows out in an exaggerated way. This produces Bubba's first laugh. Suitably reinforced by Bubba's laugh, mother now repeats this new variation, getting a laugh each time. On the third round, mother moves her mouth to Bubba's belly and blows on it. This produces a new and even louder laugh.**

Infants quickly begin to offer information that parents can use to reference and regulate interaction more easily. With greater communication from the infant, parents have to do less guesswork of the infant's state. Therefore, they are able to safely add more novelty and excitement with less risk of overwhelming the child. By the end of the sixth month babies routinely provide signals that help parents determine when to initiate, prolong and terminate interactions.

Daniel Stern describes these emerging abilities of the typical six-month-old in the following manner:

> *"Infants ...can avert their gaze, shut their eyes, stare past, and become glassy-eyed. And through the decisive use of such gaze behaviors, they can be seen to reject, distance themselves from, or defend themselves against mother. They can also reinitiate engagement and contact when they desire, through gazing, smiling and vocalizing."*

This example illustrates the roots of a parent-child co-regulation system that will come to fruition by the end of Level 2. At this early stage, the infant is by no means an equal partner in regulating the experience. However, he is beginning to be an active participant in the regulatory process by offering more specific information about his emotional state. In the next level, he begins a serious apprenticeship in the ways of being a relational partner.

Level 2: Learning to Dance

Level 2 interactions typically occur between six and twelve months of life. They signal the onset of learning and using basic structural frameworks for coordinating actions with others. Adults and children participate in simple, engaging games that employ a high degree of amplification and repetition. The child learns to synchronize his actions with those of his partner, and to time his actions to engage in rudimentary co-regulatory activities. By the end of Level 2, children learn to use referencing and self-regulating actions to coordinate their actions with those of a partner on a moment-to-moment basis. Children are able to experience the enjoyment of moving together with a partner without relying on external rules or cues. At this point the child is ready to become a true partner in Experience Sharing.

Stages of Level 2—6 to 12 months of age

- Shared Frameworks

- Variations add the Spice

- Dancing Lessons

- Moving Together

Shared Frameworks

> Parents and babies spend thousands of hours in playful, but repetitive instruction. Parents act as the guides, exaggerating their timing, facial expressions, gestures and voice tones to spotlight and frame the actions they want the baby to know are most important.

At the beginning of Level 2, the parent's job is to teach the infant to understand the structures inherent in Experience Sharing. Intuitively, they go about it in a very careful manner, beginning with simple ritualized games like Pat-a-Cake and Ittsy Bittsy Spider that have a clear sequence and structure. Parents and babies spend thousands of hours in playful, but repetitive instruction. Parents act as the guides, exaggerating their timing, facial expressions, gestures and voice tones to spotlight and frame the actions they want the baby to know are most important. Initially, parents play all the "parts" and handle the rules and timing of the encounters. They are careful not to introduce too many actions or too long a sequence too quickly. Their goal is for the infant to learn how actions fit together and which actions are critical to the successful execution of the game.

Variations add the Spice

Following the sixth month, children's laughter is almost always initiated by a parent's introduction of new elements into familiar, ritualized play. If critical elements remain intact, babies realize that the same game is being played, even though specific elements may be altered, omitted or conducted out of order. The child learns to see the essential versus non-essential elements of the framework that hold the game together as a unit.

Bubba is now a month older. He and his dad John are playing one of their favorite games together. John is lying flat on the living room rug and Bubba is sitting on his stomach. John has hold of Bubba's hands. John sings the song, "The Wheels on the Bus." When he gets to the part of each verse that describes what the wheels do... "The wheels on the bus go..." John pauses for an instant and then moves Bubba's hands in a simple similar motion. For example, in relation to "the wheels go round and round" he moves Bubba's hands in a circular motion. Bubba is raptly attentive to his father's face and actions. They repeat the game identically for several rounds. Then John begins to introduce variations. Instead of the wheels going "round and round" he sings them as going "up and down" and moves Bubba's hands in the same manner. By his behavior, John can see that Bubba obviously thinks this is hilarious. So, he continues, "The children on the bus go round and round," while making circular motions with Bubba's hands and again Bubba indicates delight in the variation. Although he has no idea what the words mean, Bubba can appreciate the variation while still understanding that the basic structure remains the same.

Dancing Lessons

Now that the baby can anticipate the structure and sequence of interactive games and manage the adult's introduction of variation, she is ready to become a more active participant in Experience Sharing. Parents use **Guided Participation** to very gradually allow the child to take on more of a participant role, as the child demonstrates greater capability to do so.

By nine months of age, a child can observe her parent and use the end of her mother's turn as a reference for her to take her own turn. For the first time, the baby can act as what relationship theorist Alan Fogel refers to as a **Co-regulator** of the interaction. She is able to take responsibility for determining when and how to take her own turn and to communicate with her partner to take his turn.

Picture a mother and baby playing an early Experience Sharing game of pulling on a piece of string. First mother pulls the string from the baby's hand. The baby grasps the string and pulls it from mother's grasp and so on. Mother pulling the string away serves as a cue for the baby to reach over and grab the string from her. At this stage of development, a baby can co-regulate an experience, as long as there is a clear sequence of role-taking actions, such as my turn-your turn, giving-taking, pulling-pushing, as well as cues to indicate timing like ready-set-go, or in the previous case, the string leaving the partner's grasp.

Moving Together

By the start of the second year, typical children learn to regulate various types of interactions, even those that require partners to coordinate their actions in a fluid and simultaneous manner. Babies learn to reference their partner's actions on a moment-to-moment basis, using that information to make adjustments to their subsequent actions. It is at this point that the child possesses the skills needed to act as a true co-regulator of an experience.

Alan Fogel points out that by 12 months of age, the string pulling game has advanced to "tug-of-war." Instead of pulling the string away, the baby, still under mother's careful guidance, learns to pull on the string just hard enough to move mother's hand closer, but not so hard as to yank the string out of her hand. Initially the parent largely orchestrates the process and outcome, placing the string in the infant's hand and then tugging very gently while holding the infant's hand to make sure he doesn't let go. Gradually, parents diminish this direct orchestration and allow the child more autonomy, recognizing that he understands how to co-regulate the encounter and will not let go when mother pulls, or pull the string too hard and yank it away from her.

> ...as Experience Sharing becomes more fluid and less reliant on structured games, children learn to reference their partner's prior action on a relative rather than absolute basis and modify their own subsequent actions in subtle increments.

In earlier games, coordinating with a partner is very clear in its expression. Even the most advanced form of a sequenced turn taking game such as "Simon Says," operates in a digital "on-off" manner, only requiring partners to know whether their current action is correct or not correct, based upon the prior action of the other partner. There is no way to be more or less correct. Similarly, when playing a board game, it is either my turn or yours, not more my turn or less your turn. However, as Experience Sharing becomes more fluid and less reliant on structured games, children learn to reference their partner's prior action on a relative rather than absolute basis and modify their own subsequent actions in subtle increments.

A second major shift in the nature of activity occurs around 12 months: the movement from sequential to simultaneous synchronized activity. Billy at 12 months is playing his old game of Peek-a-boo that has recently evolved into Hide-and-seek. Anna, his mother, is hiding behind a wing chair. Anna peeks out from the chair's right side in full view, sings "hi" until she and Billy briefly laugh and then once again hides behind the chair. Billy is visibly more excited and "seeks" his mother by moving his head and body over to that side. Anna pops out on the left side and sings "hi," then returns to the right side and pops out again, this time saying "peek-a-boo" in an excited voice. Billy laughs, but he is a bit confused and unsure of what to do. Anna continues to slowly appear and disappear on alternate sides of the chair. After a few trials, Billy anticipates his mother's actions and moves his head to the predictable side, coinciding with her emergence. His laugh turns into an expression of true joy as he realizes he has figured out the game. They continue to play with the same rules over and over, as Billy moves in time with his mother, meeting her gaze as she moves back and forth. These more evolved games require a child to simultaneously coordinate his actions with his partner's, a much more difficult task of timing and synchronization.

Repair Actions

By the end of Level 2, children are taking much more responsibility for maintaining the coordination of shared encounters. They are also learning how to recognize that the coordination of the activity has been lost, and to perform a type of regulatory or repair activity. For example, Billy and his mother are playing their tug-of-war game with a piece of string. Billy accidentally yanks a bit too hard and pulls the string out of his mother's hand. He shifts his gaze for a moment between the string in his hand and his mother's face. He realizes that coordination has been lost and initiates a repair action—he holds the string out with an expectant expression, while glancing at his mother's face. When she doesn't immediately respond, he tries again by moving the string closer, so that it touches her hand.

As the child learns this new moment-to-moment referencing, as well as effective repair strategies, when coordination inevitably breaks down, the parent and child can slowly abandon their reliance on much of the structure and sequence of earlier games and add enormous amounts of variation and novelty into their interaction. This development sets the stage for the next level of relating.

Level 3: Improvising and Co-creating

By the beginning of the second year of life, children have become partners in introducing variation into their encounters with parents. They can move from one game to another without the required transitional cues and the games begin merging into one another. They can rapidly reference the relative state of coordination with a partner and make repair actions immediately when coordination breaks down. By 18 months of age, children start co-creating new games with their partners.

During the second year, adults and older children remain the exclusive interactional partners for the young child. Peer behavior is still perceived as too unpredictable. However, the types of improvisational actions the child is starting to understand lay the groundwork for peers becoming the most attractive partners.

Stages of Level 3—12 to 18 months of age

- Co-variation

- Fluid transitions

- Improvisation

- Co-creation

Co-variation

By fifteen months of age, the child is adding variation to games at the same rate as her adult partner. A daughter becomes aware that if Daddy introduces a variation, he must reference the response of his child to ensure that she has noticed the variation. If not, Daddy will engage in repair actions by repeating the variation, or drawing more attention to the change.

> **Fifteen-month-old Billy is playing a new type of hide-and-seek with Anna. Anna and Billy start the game in a familiar manner, by hiding from and finding each other on opposite sides of a wing chair. Suddenly Anna varies the game by crouching under the coffee table until Billy finds her. Next, Anna hands Billy a small blanket. Billy takes the blanket and immediately hides under it. Anna pauses for a moment; she doesn't immediately search for Billy. Billy lifts up the blanket, laughs, makes an inviting noise and hides again. Now he stays hidden until Anna crawls over and uncovers the blanket.**

We also witness emerging co-variation skills in early role-playing games. Mommy and daughter are having a tea party. While pouring the tea is a framework for the interaction, each time they have the party, they do it a little differently. Unlike the child at the early stages of Level 2, where exact repetition is needed for her to learn the basic framework of the game, the child at Level 3 has no desire to do it the same way again and again. The excitement and surprise inherent in adding novelty and variation to the interaction is now what makes it fun.

Fluid Transitions

Along with added variation, adults and children learn to make rapid transitions, where one game merges into the next, without any demarcation point or signals. Crawling back and forth together may merge into hide and seek, which then turns into slapping hands on the floor while making exciting noises.

Improvisation

Very rapidly, frameworks that are recognized by both parties—the rituals we call "baby" games—are no longer necessary for Experience Sharing. Parents and children take elements from a number of prior activities and combine them in novel ways. Once this on-the-fly coordination ability is in place, the excitement of improvisation, where neither partner knows exactly what will happen next, becomes a major function of Experience Sharing encounters.

> **Jordan at 14 months of age is beside me at a restaurant on a late Sunday afternoon. She no longer requires specific scripted games to maintain coordination. During the two hours we spend together, our interaction is completely improvised. There is no way that either of us can predict what the other will do next. This improvisational quality is fundamental to the enjoyment we share. Jordan gets two hunks of buttered bread, puts one in her mouth and hands the other to me. She carefully watches that I take the bread from her without dropping it. Jordan then observes my face to make sure that I put the bread in my mouth and that I enjoy eating my bread with her. Every action I take towards her is carefully referenced by her study of my facial expressions. We move from the bread and play with several strings of Mardi Gras beads in an improvised fashion. There is no clear sequence or signal to indicate when a "round" has begun or ended. Jordan no longer desires or needs this type of external structure.**

This type of improvised action will inevitably lead to a higher rate of misunderstandings and loss of coordination between partners. However, by this stage, the child has become more familiar with frequent, small breakdowns and has developed a sense of confidence in initiating a variety of repair actions that rapidly restore coordination.

Co-creations

The climax of Level 3 occurs when both partners recognize they can create their own unique games that emerge spontaneously from their shared improvisational actions. While these creations may be an odd amalgam of noises, words and actions akin to a tribal dance, they represent a critical discovery for the young child of the power of Experience Sharing interactions to create new meaning.

> **My wife Rachelle is observing young children at a local university lab school. Her eyes meet with an 18 month old child standing inside a small wooden bar structure.**

**Without a word, the toddler enlists Rachelle in a sophisti-
cated version of Peek-a-boo. The child alternates popping
out from one side of the house or the other and then suddenly changes the pattern. Rachelle utters the exciting
noises that correspond to the child's patterned movement.
A large part of their enjoyment is the knowledge that they
have created their own game, one that nobody else knows.**

Level 4: Sharing Outside Worlds

Level 4 brings into play the sharing of unique perceptions through Joint
Attention. By 18 months of age, the typical child is involved in sharing
his discoveries with those around him. Games tend to revolve less
around gross motor activity and contain more perception and attention
shifting. The child not only shares his own perceptions but also
becomes fascinated with learning about the unique perceptions of partners. Through perception sharing with others, the child learns that he
and his partners may not see the same things, or may see the same
things in different ways—the origin of perspective taking. The child
also begins sharing his unique emotional reactions that accompany his
perceptions—for example "Scary man", "Yucky bug" or "Nice doggy!"
Finally, children learn to add imaginative elements into their perceptions
for heightened enjoyment. This serves as a transition into sharing our
internal worlds.

> The term "Joint
> Attention" refers
> to two or more
> partners sharing
> common emotion-
> al reactions within
> a common external
> frame of reference.

Stages of Level 4—18 to 30 months of age

• Perception sharing

• Perspective Taking

• Unique Reactions

• Adding Imagination

Perception Sharing

Until now, the purpose inherent in a young child's relationships has
been to coordinate his actions with those of an adult. However, by 18
months of age a toddler learns that he can share with others his own
unique experience of the world. He and his partner can simultaneously
share their emotional reactions to an experience by coordinating their
perceptual gaze towards an object in their environment. The term **Joint
Attention** refers to two or more partners sharing common emotional
reactions within a common external frame of reference.

> **Fredrick is 20 months old. He is full of excitement
> derived from his encounters with an ever-enlarging
> world. His favorite new word is "look it" as he points**

out his discoveries to dad. Six months ago Fredrick shared his treasures by bringing them to his parents for inspection—a blue glass marble or a woodchip off the playground. But butterflies and flying airplanes elude the grasp of toddlers. Now Fredrick points excitedly, and when assured that his dad is enjoying his discovery, he returns his gaze to his discovery.

A closer look at this brief episode reveals that Fredrick is doing more than just pointing and babbling. It involves a more complex type of Social Referencing. Once Fredrick has engaged his father, he first makes sure that his father directs his attention to the spot that Fredrick intends it to go. He already recognizes that his father's visual perspective is not automatically the same as his own. He knows that for the experience to be shared, pointing and physical proximity are not enough. He must act to coordinate his father's focus of attention with that of his own. Fredrick observes his father's gaze and excitedly yells out "Look! Look!" until his father notices the discovery. As soon as Fredrick is assured that his dad is directing his attention correctly, his gaze immediately shifts to reference dad's face for emotion sharing. Fredrick basks in his ability to choreograph their shared enjoyment.

As children become more adept at Joint Attentional encounters, they learn not only to share discoveries with partners, but to enjoy their partner's unique discoveries as well. By 24 months of age, the child is experiencing his environment through both his own and his partner's eyes in a fluid manner. Both observers contribute equally to their shared experience. Joel at 21 months likes nothing more than to take walks with his dad in the park and point out and attend to the great discoveries that each of them makes as they stroll along.

> By 24 months of age, the child is experiencing his environment through both his own and his partner's eyes in a fluid manner.

Perspective Taking

By 18 months of age, typical children are beginning to demonstrate their understanding that two people in different locations may not be able to see something in the same way. By 24 months, children know that their partner may not be able to see an object if something is obstructing their view that is in plain sight to them. Twenty-five month old Bubba is seated on the floor, turning pages of a picture book. His mother sits on a chair in front of him. He comes to a picture he wishes to share with his mother and without hesitation, turns the book so that mother will be able to see the picture.

With the growth of perspective taking in the third year of life, children learn that other people perceive things differently than they do. Fredrick at 23 months sees a familiar shape in a tree and says, "Look, a squirrel!" His father gazes at the tree and then back at Fredrick and says, "It sure looks like a squirrel. But, it's a tree branch." Now Fredrick looks again and notices that his father is correct. It is a tree branch after all. It just resembled a squirrel. Fredrick is learning that sometimes his partner's view can provide a more helpful perspective than his own. He develops a desire to find out how his partners see the world as a critical complement to his own perceptions.

Unique Reactions

At the same time that children recognize they live in a world of multiple perspectives, they learn that each of us may have our own unique reaction to the same thing. Fredrick sees a jet plane in the sky and says to his father "Wow, Daddy. That's fast." Father, looking at the same plane responds with, "Yeah and it's big too. It's a Jumbo Jet." The plane, high in the sky, looks small to Fredrick. But, he knows that jets are big when you see them close. The next day Fredrick is playing in his pre-school sandbox and having a great time. A little girl walks over to him, looks at the sand and says, "Oh yucky sand." Fredrick is puzzled and replies with "It's not yucky. It's great sand! Why do you say yucky?" Vignettes like this, occurring more frequently in the latter half of the second year, represent early attempts at true conversation. For the first time, the youngster seeks to share some part of himself that is not apparent on the outside. He notices that people have different emotional reactions to the same experience. Or, that when gazing at the same object, they find some critical or striking characteristic that he didn't notice.

Adding Imagination

Early in Level 4, adult partners greatly enhance the excitement of a child's perception by adding imaginative elements to the encounter. A small doll is treated like a real baby. Parents say "meow" sounds when they point to a picture of a cat. Later in Level 4, parents introduce a true imaginative quality to perception sharing. Fredrick's father looks at a cloud and says, "Look Fredrick. There's a castle in the sky." At first Fredrick is puzzled and somewhat distressed. But after a while he begins to understand that Dad is pretending and that the cloud he is pointing at only looks like a castle. Fredrick is thrilled that he can look at the cloud and see the castle shape himself. In time he can look at a cloud and see different things. He and Dad take turns telling each other what they see when they gaze at the clouds.

Imaginative sharing is also learned as parents introduce multiple functions for objects. A hat can be turned upside down and used as a basket for Easter eggs. At a later stage, objects instantly become other objects. A broomstick becomes a horse to ride. A cat becomes a man-eating lion to run away from. The use of imagination permits a blending of the child's external and internal worlds. It helps him understand that the "real" world is made up of subjective impressions that can be altered and

> At the same time that children recognize they live in a world of multiple perspectives, they learn that each of us may have our own unique reaction to the same thing.

changed at will. This shift in perception propels the child to start sharing his internal world.

Level 5: Sharing Minds

Learning to coordinate unique perceptions, emotional reactions and imaginative embellishments into our experiences with others opens the door for the next major series of social developmental breakthroughs. As the child becomes more self-aware and his personal world becomes more complex, he develops the desire to share these new internal experiences with others around him.

Accompanying the move to Level 5 is an emerging interest in ideas and internal emotional states. The child can now differentiate between what is really felt as opposed to what may be overtly expressed. He becomes interested in deciphering people's intentions as well as observing their actions. The enduring preferences and opinions of those around him become important. At this level we observe a great interest in coordinated pretend play, using improvisational role-playing as well as symbolic figures. Peers become highly valued as collaborators in the world of imagination. Level 5 culminates with the child engaging in conversation aimed at sharing his unique internal experiences. This conversational proficiency typically develops over several years beginning in the preschool years.

Stages of Level 5—30 to 48 months

- Sharing Ideas
- Exciting Differences
- The Inside and Outside Worlds
- The Primacy of Minds

Sharing Ideas

By 24 months, with the discovery of pretense, role-playing takes on a new dimension. Children can pretend to be someone other than who they really are and coordinate their role actions with those of a partner. They no longer need external props or objects to carry on this pretense. By the close of the third year, children carry on fairly sophisticated imaginative dramas with an adult. For instance, both partners realize that an object, like a banana, can easily become a pretend telephone. Furthermore, the child is able to direct complex pretend play involving the thoughts and feelings of several characters that interact with each other in a related manner.

Also by the end of the third year of life, children turn to peers as a major social source of novelty and excitement. The different and unpredictable games and ideas that peers provide become a major attraction, especially when compared to the relative predictability of adult behavior.

Children's playground behavior and peer conversations take on a highly improvisational quality; they are constantly in flux. New roles are created in an instant: "Hey, I've got an idea. Let's play Alien Invasion. I'll be the evil alien invaders and you can be the Air Force." There are sudden role reversals: "Now you be the bad guy and I'll be the good guy." There are on-the-spot negotiations: "O.K I'll play the policeman, but I get to be the bad guy next, right?" These examples remind us how different are typical children's play encounters from the scripted social interactions we often think of as "social skills."

Also by the 36th month, children combine their imaginings with those of their friends and form creative co-creations. Mark and Jonathan invent a new animal called an Ele-Zebra—an elephant with stripes that can run very fast. Through the mingling of their minds, children gain an opportunity to experience the world in new and exciting ways, not possible alone.

Through the mingling of their minds, children gain an opportunity to experience the world in new and exciting ways, not possible alone.

Exciting Differences

Once children enter the world of ideas, they inevitably learn that their views do not always coincide with those of their partners. Children start searching for commonality in ideas, to confirm the validity of their own viewpoints. However, they are equally fascinated by partners who introduce novel ideas. Differences become a way of differentiating people, but are not seen as a barrier between them. Michael takes his mom on a tour of his pre-school class and tells her, "That's Billy. He likes LEGGO's. That's Annie. She likes dolls." Joe shows Michael a new way to play superheroes and within minutes, it becomes Michael's favorite game. Children recognize that differences can also lead to conflicts and simple compromise skills begin to emerge. During Level 5, children come to appreciate that the world they live in contains a preponderance of differences, but that the differences add a spice to life, rather than pose a threat.

The Inside and Outside Worlds

After 30 months of age, children start to notice that people have unique internal worlds that may not be revealed by their outside appearances. By the end of the third year, they recognize that a facial expression may not accurately represent a person's true emotional state. They know that people pretend and that what is seen on the surface is not always what lies beneath. The 30-month-old can excitedly feign fear as I pretend to chew up and swallow his fingers, knowing that his fear and my aggressiveness are equally fictitious. Children learn the difference between good-hearted teasing and cruel name-calling, using the voice tone and facial expressions of the teaser as their reference point. The older three-year-old discovers that he can sometimes cover up his real reactions and engage in deception. The desire to decipher what is really going on behind the surface increases, setting the stage for Experience Sharing to move more into the realm of our inner world.

The Primacy of Minds

The real essence of interactions with people is exploring what goes on in their inner worlds. Once a child realizes that people have their own minds—containing unique thoughts, impressions and viewpoints—he understands that sharing physical proximity is not the same as sharing his experiences with them. As children distinguish that emotions occur in themselves and others on an internal plane, a natural desire develops to share experiences with others on this more internal level. By age four, children are able to talk about other people's feelings apart from their direct observations. Determining how another person really thinks and feels becomes more important than deciphering what his actions or facial expressions mean. Conversation becomes the primarily tool for delving into our inner selves and will remain so throughout life.

At this point, typically after the age of four, there is not surprisingly a surge in acquisition of Theory of Mind skills. This term, popularized in the Autism field by Dr. Simon Baron-Cohen and his colleagues in London, refers to our ability to understand that other people have perceptions, perspectives, feelings and ideas—internal states—that are different from our own. Children ascribe desires and intentions to the actions of others and use this information to coordinate their own actions. For example, a five-year-old will assume that you intended to hand her an object when you reach out to give it to her and it accidentally falls from your hand. We see the roots of empathy developing as children begin to relate other people's experiences to similar events in their own lives and share emotions in a new way. Children start distinguishing between someone doing something to hurt them "on purpose" or "by accident" and react to the same action in drastically different ways depending upon the attribution.

> Once a child realizes that people have their own minds—containing unique thoughts, impressions and viewpoints—he understands that sharing physical proximity is not the same as sharing his experiences with them.

Level 6: Binding Ourselves to Others

Once a child reaches Level 6, she has acquired the basic skills needed to interact with people in her environment, coordinate her actions with those of a partner, create novelty and use imagination to keep excitement alive in her interactions. Level 6 represents the child's drive to form relationships from which she will derive her own unique identity and sense of place in the environment. This stage marks the emergence of the child's real interest in "pal-ships" and curiosity about the groups to which she belongs. The child becomes increasingly aware of and interested in the way her shared past experiences and potential future plans intersect with others. Eventually, she starts developing true friendships and enduring links with others. This desire and the accompanying skills involve us in one degree or another for the remainder of our lives.

Stages of Level 6—48 months and older

- Unique Selves
- Belonging to Groups
- Pals and Playmates
- Enduring Friendships

> Children alternate between contrasting their differences with their continuing search to find ways to link themselves to their peers.

Unique Selves

As children discover that they have their own unique ideas and viewpoints, that may or may not be shared by others, they begin to develop a sense of personal identity. Other people, especially peers, become crucial reference points for discovering their unique preferences, interests and abilities. Experience Sharing becomes a search for attributes in peers the child can compare and contrast with his own. Psychologist Zick Rubin points out that at this stage, interacting with peers provides a context in which children can meaningfully carry on these comparisons. Children alternate between contrasting their differences with their continuing search to find ways to link themselves to their peers. Rubin illustrates an encounter between two pre-schoolers:

> (Steven and Claudia stand near the sandbox and hug each other affectionately)
>
> **Steven:** *"You're bigger than me-right Claudia?"*
>
> (They turn and stand back to back, measuring themselves. Claudia is in fact taller than Steven.)
>
> **Claudia:** *"We're growing up."*
>
> **Steven:** *"Yeah. I'm almost as big as you, right? I'm gonna grow this big, right?"* (He stretches his arms far apart.)
>
> **Claudia:** *"Me too."*
>
> **Steven:** *"I'm going to grow up to the sky! I'm going to grow that high!"* (He jumps into the air.)
>
> **Claudia:** *"Me too."*

Belonging to Groups

From the time we recognize our separate identity as unique individuals, we develop a desire to become a member of larger, more powerful entities, from which to derive greater influence over our worlds.

Enduring group memberships become our anchors in an increasingly confusing, chaotic world. These emotional bonds provide a stability that contrasts with our outer world, where we are required to frequently change roles and where so many of our expectations turn out to be unfulfilled. Children come to value their place as a member of a nuclear and extended family. We witness how children take pride in being part of Ms. Jones' Third Grade Class and not a little First Grader. Children swear absolute loyalty to their clubs and gangs and teams.

Developmental Scientist Bob Emde refers to this final class of co-ordination functions as "We-go"—a group ego providing more safety, power and significance than can be experienced alone. Human beings are ingenious in finding groups to belong to. People join organizations based upon IQ scores, shared last names or favorite dog breed. As this desire to belong to a group grows in a child, so too does his understanding that he must coordinate himself in specific ways to maintain his status and membership. The child learns that, unlike in his family, membership in other groups is not guaranteed. The idea of needing to "work" to maintain a relationship emerges.

The longing for group acceptance initiates a more conscious social process psychologists refer to as Impression Formation. Children being to deliberately act in ways that will bring them acceptance and admiration by desirable group members.

> As Impression Formation increases, children begin to notice that their current actions impact the future of their relationships. They start exhibiting behaviors that bond them to others.

Playmates and Pals

To the four-year old child, a friend is whomever she is playing with at a particular time. Children at this stage do not yet have an understanding of a lasting relationship that exists over time. What makes a friend centers on common physical attributes like hair color and size. Two friends at this developmental stage might say, "We're both big, right?" Common activities also link friends together: "We both like LEGGOS."

As children move into Kindergarten age, they develop Pal-ships, which require a more conceptual understanding of common interests and activities. Children begin to seek out peers who share common interests and with whom encounters are predominantly successful and enjoyable.

As Impression Formation increases, children begin to notice that their current actions impact the future of their relationships. They start exhibiting behaviors that bond them to others. A child desires a particular pal to visit his house. Being a good host, by making sure his pal is having fun, is viewed as important to secure a return visit. Pals maintain shared memories of their previous fun times together. Conversations about these enjoyable experiences and plans for future activities solidify the mutual connection children feel. Children begin to experience the loneliness of not having a pal to play with, or spending a Saturday alone when nobody wants to come over to play. These feelings of loneliness serve as a powerful lifelong motivation to secure stronger connections with peers.

Enduring Friendships

By the age of 11 or 12, children view friendships as enduring entities that take shape over time, with strong foundations that last into the future. They also recognize that there are different levels of friendship, from superficial pals to good friends to highly intimate best friends. Children may experience grief and mourning over the loss of a close friendship. However, these feelings reinforce the relative fragility of close relationships and the need to work hard to preserve and strengthen existing bonds.

The basis for considering someone a friend has evolved from common interests and physical attributes to more psychological factors, like mutual trust and shared traits. "We share all of our secrets with each other." or "We're both more quiet." Pre-teens also base friendship selection on more abstract interests such as, "We both feel strongly about the environment."

As children develop into young adults, close friends are defined as someone who knows your true inner self and wants to share and affirm it. During moments of success, a good friend feels as excited for you as you do for yourself. During moments of despair, a good friend feels it too and is there to help. The teen learns that sharing emotions opens the door to increased love, excitement and joy, as well as the negative experiences of anxiety, sadness and anger. They experience the comfort that comes from another person understanding their emotional state. The lifelong search for intimate partners begins.

Autism: Life Without Experience Sharing

*W*hy do people with Autism share a deficit in Experience Sharing? What is the essential missing element? Does the answer lie within the brain? Many professionals feel we will never find a single neurological origin to Autism. Scientists like Pete Hobson, at the world famous Tavistock Institute of London, point out that the many different ways Autism presents itself argues against a single neurological cause of the disability.

We commonly hear "No two people with Autism are alike." In my practice, I can affirm that sentiment. Some of my patients have excellent language and a vocabulary that would shame a professor of literature. Others do not now, and may never, engage in conversation. Some of our patients demonstrate what are considered classic signs of Autism like hand flapping, poor eye contact, and the need for intensive sameness in routine and environment. Others do not show any odd behavioral mannerisms, have good eye contact and seem to tolerate changes at least as well as some non-autistic people I know.

Regardless of the initial source of the disorder, Hobson believes these various etiologies all converge swiftly and silently at one point of social development where individuals with Autism learn to engage in Instrumental interactions, but miss the road markers for Experience Sharing. What happens at this crossroad? Why isn't the ability to engage in one lost without the other?

Hobson hypothesizes that the different social awareness in children with Autism versus their typically developing peers lies within the information processing ability, Emotional Coordination. Described in the last chapter, Emotional Coordination requires children to observe the degree of relationship between their partner's emotional reactions and their own. It acts as a gauge to regulate their interactions with others. *Am I walking too far ahead of my partner? Is my partner interested in what I'm saying?* Hobson provides convincing research documentation to demonstrate that Emotional Coordination does not develop in children with Autism.

While typical children carry out Emotional Coordination effortlessly, Hobson points out that it is actually a highly complex process, requiring the integration of a number of different brain centers. Success requires rapid attention shifting, careful observation and evaluation of subtle emotional states, an awareness of personal space and internal reactions to a number of other elements. If at any point even *one* of the many components does not function, the entire process of Emotional Coordination breaks down. Hobson's theory sheds light on how children with various forms of neurological dysfunction could all present with the same Autism diagnosis.

But why would a breakdown in Emotional Coordination result in the loss of Experience Sharing abilities but not the loss of Instrumental interaction? The answer is found within Systems Theory. Every time people interact, their collective actions form a type of temporary system. The nature of the created system limits the type of interaction that can occur. Two fundamentally different types of systems exist, each setting the stage for a very different type of interaction.

Fluid Systems are constructed to manage a great deal of novel information produced through the interaction of the participants. By their very nature, Fluid Systems cannot be overly restrictive. Therefore, the system is regulated and maintained only partially through its structural elements. Rules provide a bare framework for determining what will occur between the participants. Furthermore, there is no specific end product to guide behavior. Participants cannot count on a specific chain of actions to provide predictability. What then keeps the system from degenerating into chaos?

Members of Fluid systems work very hard to balance novelty and variety with the maintenance of organization and structure. Ongoing co-regulatory actions are employed in place of specific structural elements. Participants reference the emotional reactions of their partner(s) on a moment-to-moment basis and use this information to determine whether they should increase, or decrease, the level of variation—in other words, they exhibit Emotional Coordination.

In contrast, Static Systems are created to **limit** the flow of new information into the system. System members are assured of highly predictable outcomes. Static systems are critical for many of our society's social functions. We think of waiting in a supermarket checkout line or at the bank as events that should progress in a highly predictable manner. Similarly, we hope that most surgical procedures occur in relatively static systems.

Static systems rely on specific rules, a repeatable sequence of actions and a clear outcome to maintain their structural integrity. As a result, they are relatively simple to teach in a scripted manner. At any bank throughout the world, the rules for waiting on line will be very similar and easy to teach in a step-by-step manner. Because the rules make the structure so inflexible, Static systems require little ongoing maintenance actions by system members. Furthermore, people are interchangeable in a Static System as long as they follow the prescribed rules and scripts. A bank teller can leave to go to lunch. As long as a replacement immediately takes her place and efficiently processes transactions, no one standing in line will object.

As opposed to Fluid Systems, adding novel information or attempting to vary the structure in a Static System is viewed as disruptive. System members typically try to sanction or exclude people who persist in such actions. For example, students who suddenly get out of their seat in a classroom and stroll around the room are often punished. While the student's action is highly meaningful to system members, it is viewed as a rule violation to be stopped immediately, rather than a novel twist within the interaction to create more excitement.

> Members of Fluid systems work very hard to balance novelty and variety with the maintenance of organization and structure. On-going co-regulatory actions are employed in place of specific structural elements.

The fundamental purpose of Experience Sharing is a collaborative effort to create new meaning among partners. It requires a system that is highly tolerant of a rapid influx of novel information, and responsive enough to maintain structure, even when participants may feel overwhelmed or confused. Only Fluid Systems can meet these requirements. On the other hand, Instrumental interactions exist to obtain a predictable result without variation, if possible. Obviously, Instrumental interactions occur in Static Systems.

Viewed in conjunction with Systems Theory, Hobson's conclusion about people with Autism makes more sense. Because of their neurological deficits, people with Autism are unable to function in Fluid Systems. Their brain wiring prevents them from learning to reference other people's emotions, actions and perceptions, as ways of regulating their interactions. Without Emotional Coordination, Experience Sharing abilities never develop. As a result, people with Autism perceive normal Fluid Systems not as potential sources of joy and excitement, but as overwhelming foreign environments.

> ...people with Autism perceive normal Fluid Systems not as potential sources of joy and excitement, but as overwhelming foreign environments.

Mike is an intelligent and gentle nine-year-old boy with Aspergers Syndrome attending The Monarch School, a program based on our RDI model. It is joke-inventing time in Mike's class. His classmates, several of whom do not have Autism, and their teachers are improvising jokes in a hilarious manner. Without any overt agreement, their interaction has evolved to the point where anyone can start a joke with a question and anyone else can answer it—hopefully with an unexpected response. One child blurts out, "What is the state bird of Texas?" Another answers, "A Bush Bird!" Mike is patiently sitting at the table waiting for his turn. Unfortunately, the others are not engaged in turn taking. Their interactions are spontaneous and fluid. Finally, he blurts out "Is it my turn yet?" Because everyone in the class wants Mike to join in, they reply "Sure." Mike smiles and begins his joke: "What is the state food of Texas?" Ted immediately replies "French Fries!" Everyone else laughs hilariously, not because of any logic in Ted's reply, but because they have all been enjoying unexpected, incongruous answers.

Mike is not amused. He yells out "France is not a state. France is a country! That's wrong!" The others politely ignore his outburst. Then Bryan, who believes he is helping Mike by providing a compromise, blurts out "Texas French Toast." Mike bursts into tears. He jumps up from the table and runs from the room yelling, "I hate jokes. I'm no good. I'll never tell a joke again!" A teacher runs after Mike to calm him down. Meanwhile, the other students continue with their improvised jokes.

Five minutes later Mike returns. He has heroically composed himself and is ready to give it another try. He sits at the table, again waiting his turn. By now the jokes have moved far beyond states and countries to a host of new areas, but Mike is oblivious. Again, he asks if he can have a turn and waits for everyone to agree, which they happily do. He begins by lecturing the group, "I figured it out. I get to ask you a question. You take turns saying your answers and then I will tell you the right answer." The other students are confused but know better than to directly challenge him. Mike begins his joke again: "What is the state food of Texas?" The participants throw out a number of illogical answers. Once again, Mike is devastated. "You're not taking turns. You're not listening to the right answer! I hate myself. I'm never telling jokes to children again, only to adults. They do it the right way." One of the teachers tries to reason with Mike. "We're not trying to hurt you Mike, we're just having fun." Mike's reply is poignant. "What's fun for you is punishment for me!"

> One of the teachers tries to reason with Mike. "We're not trying to hurt you Mike, we're just having fun." Mike's reply is poignant. "What's fun for you is punishment for me!"

High functioning individuals with Autism like Mike try valiantly to figure out how to participate in their social worlds. They study social interactions, seeking the clues that will unlock the mystery for them. Unfortunately, they mistake the static frameworks that assure success in Instrumental interactions as the main purpose of all their interactions. In the prior example, the other participants didn't care that someone answered with a state or a country; what mattered was the shared joy and excitement. They were happily willing to sacrifice specific rules and alter the framework in order to share moments of mutual creation and zany joy. But Mike was oblivious to the intent of his classmates. He believed that what mattered in the social interaction was getting the structure correct to produce his intended result. He wanted the other children to laugh, but only at the conclusion of the joke, after he had delivered the correct answer.

Even when their efforts to be part of a social situation are unsuccessful, many high functioning individuals with Autism do not get mad at their peers. Rather, they are devastated and view it as a personal failure. However, without Emotional Coordination, try as they do again and again to understand social situations, their efforts are doomed right from the start. Unless all the participants are willing to act in an artificial manner to "humor" the person with Autism, their interactions become repeated sources of distress.

Because of their limited understanding, the social discoveries of even the most able child with Autism are inevitably confined to a very few areas:

- The child accumulates "procedures" for interacting with his social world to obtain esired results, objects, participation and information.

- He develops methods to avoid negative consequences and fit in appropriately in social settings, and

- He finds an audience to provide social attention when he desires to perform and who participate in the scripted manner that he alone determines as correct.

The Social Science of Typical versus High Functioning Children with Autism

Both groups are scientists, driven to discover and test theories about their social worlds. But their neurological differences lead to completely different fields of study.

Social Science of the Typically-developing Child

The typical child specializes in studying a universe whose elements are constantly breaking apart and coming back together in different, but exciting and meaningful ways. His science is one of seeing relationships amidst a backdrop of continual variation and novelty. His brain permits him to search for states of connection between himself and others, although like a radioactive isotope, these connections may exist for only brief moments. Because of his unique tools and ability, Experience Sharing encounters in Fluid Systems are the most interesting and challenging phenomena to study. He spends an amazing amount of time during the first years of life involved in such study. He is an obsessed scientist, driven to determine how he and the people around him can share more aspects of their world with one another. Each time his interactions create unexpected new ways of perceiving, feeling and thinking is a victory for his science.

Social Science of the Child with High Functioning Autism or Aspergers Syndrome

The High Functioning child with Autism specializes in studying social relationships in a universe where the sheer amount of noise invading his brain constantly threatens to overwhelm him. He learns to specialize in avoiding chaos, by shutting out and avoiding most elements of variability and novelty. Instead, he focuses on the non-changing aspects of his environment. Elements that remain the same provide him with the greatest experience of meaning and relation. He is obsessed by his search for stable patterns and unchanging relationships in his social universe, like the immutable laws of mathematics, the unvarying progression of video games and other predictable sequences that occur the same way over and over. He focuses on an interaction style that, for him, is a matter of survival. The only means he has for enjoying social encounters is to discover ways to predict and/or control social events. Each time he participates in an interaction that progresses in a predictable manner is a victory for his science.

The Social Development of People with Autism

Sometime during the first year of life all children with Autism embark on a different social developmental pathway. This road does not include the typical child's thousands of hours spent referencing his parents or discovering the joys of joint attention. Neither does it include experimenting and practicing more sophisticated forms of co-regulation, from which more powerful and varied emotional payoffs are experienced. A research study conducted at the University of Washington by Julie Osterling and Geraldine Dawson provided a poignant illustration of this early deviation. Armed with only brief segments from various First Birthday Party videotapes, they were able to identify children with Autism from their normally developing counterparts with over 90% accuracy. The distinguishing characteristics were social referencing and communication actions related to Level 1 Experience Sharing.

By the end of the first year of life, exploring the world of objects begins to compete for the attention of children. The typical child enters the object world as an enhancement to, rather than departure from, the world of Experience Sharing. He has already learned that adults are the best reference points for continued safety, obtaining meaning, introducing excitement and resolving confusion and ambiguity. That's why you'll notice infants constantly dividing their attention between a new object and a familiar adult. They reference adults for their emotional reaction to the object—*Is it safe?* for the enhancement of meaning—*Is it important?* and how to interact and get the most out of their discovery—*What do I do with it?* They also shift gaze to amplify their excited feelings of discovery, by referencing their parent's equally excited facial expressions and exclamations when they encounter something new.

As typical babies continue to explore their new world and begin to move around on their own, they are careful not to become so focused on their destination that they lose their connection with adult reference points. They operate much like early sailing ships, which needed to keep land in sight to navigate safely. Soon toddlers feel the courage to go off on expeditions where they are briefly out of sight of parents. These excursions are short and always end with the child returning with some object to share with an adult. This process leads, by the middle of the second year, to Joint Attention, where the child realizes that he can share his new experience of the object world with adults. He can actively direct their attention to his discovery; others can share his perspective, along with his excitement.

> The typical child enters the object world as an enhancement to, rather than departure from, the world of Experience Sharing.

In contrast, children with Autism never develop an emotionally attuned relationship; they do not experience the context of security from which they can carefully explore their world. Without the feedback an attuned relationship provides, they are overwhelmed by the intense stimulation that typically developing children find so attractive. Mommy's smile or reassuring gaze holds little meaning in helping them feel safe.

Furthermore, children with Autism never learn to view their parents as primary sources of meaning in their world. Marta keeps trying to seat her four-year-old autistic son Sean in her lap to show him different exciting toys. As soon as Marta pulls him down, Sean is immediately back up, preferring to roam aimlessly around the room. He moves wherever his eyes happen to land on anything that attracts his attention, never giving Marta a chance to entertain him. Sean is not aware of Marta's ability to show him how to obtain meaning from his environment. He appears more interested in creating his own meaning through seemingly random encounters.

> In contrast, the child with Autism has had limited and mixed memories of sharing experiences as any form of excitement. ...It is easy to see how the world of objects, TV's and computers can so quickly dominate his interests and energy.

For the typical child, encountering the world of objects enables him to enhance the level of experiences he can share with those around him. But for children with Autism, the discovery of the object world becomes a critical obstacle to Experience Sharing. Since they do not typically reference parents for meaning or enhancement, gaze shifting from object to adult hardly occurs. Without this shared feedback, they see no reason to bring their discoveries back to their partner, nor does it propel them to develop joint attention. Researcher Peter Mundy and his colleagues have found that the failure to initiate joint attention alone discriminates 80-90% of young children with Autism from children with other developmental delays.

By the time the typical child ventures off to explore their object world, they have had months of exciting participation in Experience Sharing. Countless memories of unmatched pleasure and joy have been obtained safely through social excitement. They are also well on their way to being active participants in the process of co-creating that excitement. They have developed a sense of their own competence in managing Experience Sharing interactions as active partners, not passive victims. In fact, by the end of the first year, managing Experience Sharing is their area of greatest competence, especially when compared to newly developing motor abilities and instrumental language. Because these feelings of proficiency are based in Experience Sharing, typical children are not likely to give up this interaction style to develop competence in interacting with objects. Rather, they are highly motivated to integrate these two worlds for the enhancement of both.

In contrast, the child with Autism has had limited and mixed memories of sharing experiences as any form of excitement. He has not experienced competence in being an active co-regulator in Experience Sharing interactions. Therefore, he is starving to derive a sense of competence elsewhere. It is easy to see how the world of objects, TV's and computers can so quickly dominate his interests and energy.

When he was diagnosed with Autism shortly after his second birthday, Mark displayed many classic symptoms of the disorder. He became upset with any change in routine. He engaged in long stretches of ritualized, stereotypic behavior—hours playing with a piece of string, watching the same videotape over and over, vocalizing repetitive, rote phrases captured from TV or tape.

Although Mark was very attached to his parents, he was completely lacking in social referencing. Like so many children with Autism, he developed his own idiosyncratic, limiting ways of organizing even pleasurable social interaction. During his first year of treatment, I often faced the paradoxical decision of whether or not to force Mark to participate in simple interactional routines—ones that seemed to give him so much pleasure. For example, Mark loved a ritual he had developed with his parents. He would lie on a beanbag chair, his parents would say "Ready, set, go" then lift him in the air, count to three, and end the activity with Mark being tossed onto another mound of beanbags. After a number of continuous rounds of this activity, we stopped interacting with Mark for several minutes to observe his reaction. We hoped he would signal us on his own in some manner to initiate a round of the game. Without a glance in our direction, Mark dragged a beanbag to the assigned place and started flopping into it. We wondered whether this behavior was, in fact, his signal. However when we approached him, Mark quickly got up and moved away, finding another beanbag as far from us as possible to repeat the process. He continued to flop on the beanbag for a while, but quickly lost interest. Each time we approached, Mark moved away. It was obvious that Mark did not derive pleasure from his version of the game. But, he was unable to discern what elements of the interaction were critical to his enjoyment. He did not understand that his pleasure had little to do with his interaction with a beanbag, but was derived from his interaction with his parents. In Mark's idiosyncratic way of understanding the world, eliminating the actions of other people made the game more understandable. Unfortunately, removing the people also removed the joy.

Thwarted in the laboratory of Experience Sharing, many High Functioning children with Autism soon encounter feelings of competence within their non-social environment. In contrast to their low motivation for doing the work needed to coordinate relationships, these children often have a great desire to relate to and master the world of objects and information. Objects don't move around and change from moment to moment. Facts remain facts. Coordinating with things and data becomes easier and more understandable than interacting with people.

Our patients often initially struggle to add objects, like board games, that require partner interaction into their sessions with us. Most of the children devote so much of their attention to ceiling fans, miniature trains, books, videos, and computer games, that not even the most proficient person would be able to maintain Experience Sharing. They are

> In Mark's idiosyncratic way of understanding the world, eliminating the actions of other people made the game more understandable. Unfortunately, removing the people also removed the joy.

not relating to objects and information to irritate, or shut people out, although for some children this may be the case. More frequently, they are motivated to relate to objects with other people acting as a captive audience. They want mom to sit nearby as they watch their favorite videotape. They want little brother to play a board game, so they can win. They may want a stranger to spend considerable time answering repeated questions about the dimensions of hotel rooms, or listening to their recitation of every species of dinosaur, never considering his desire to disengage from these activities. Since the child with Autism is not receiving the payoffs the rest of us derive from Experience Sharing, even if he wants social involvement, he will often choose to supplement it with something more interesting—and satisfying—to him.

Unfortunately, the objects, activities and topics children with Autism select use up the child's already limited attentional capacity and make it impossible for the child to notice aspects of his relatedness to others. This, in turn, produces motivational problems that interfere with our efforts to teach these children Experience Sharing. Our initial attempts to limit object involvement, so the child can sufficiently attend to this new type of relating, usually involves a major struggle, especially with older children. It is ironic that some of our most intellectually competent patients, because of their mastery of the non-relational world, have less interest and motivation in working with us than some of our less capable patients. Unfortunately, these Instrumental proficiencies are often over-valued by well-meaning adults, creating an even bigger obstacle to teaching Experience Sharing.

> **Unfortunately, the objects, activities and topics children with Autism select use up the child's already limited attentional capacity and make it impossible for the child to notice aspects of his relatedness to others.**

The failure to develop true joint attention leads to its own share of disastrous consequences. I am no longer surprised when one of my verbally fluent patients continues talking to me as she walks out my door into the hallway, unaware that I can no longer hear a word she is saying. I am sitting across from Joseph as he scans a book of interesting photographs. He is very excited by one of the pictures and begins to tell me about its features: "Over here is the silly hair and there's the funny nose." Joseph completely fails to recognize that by not turning the album around to show me the picture, I cannot appreciate or even understand what he is trying to convey.

People with Autism fail to develop their own unique reactions to perceptions, or any interest in our subjective impressions. The world is a concrete, literal place without personal embellishment. In typical children, the growth of language is greatly spurred by the desire to share their perceptions of the world with people around them. Language develops naturally in this fluid, Experience Sharing context. But for many children with Autism, as language develops it interferes with, rather than enhances, Experience Sharing. Instead of referencing his partner's excitement and jointly enhancing their perceptions with each other's unique impressions and reactions, the autistic child may recite all the facts you never wanted to know about what he is seeing, completely missing the point of the experience.

After several years of treatment, Michael could describe to us what he saw, but he could not comprehend my request that he tell me more about his perceptions. One day we were looking out the window together. I mentioned that the cloud we were both gazing at reminded me of a castle. Michael became upset. He proceeded to scold me and reminded me of the correct composition and location of castles. He lectured me about the scientific name of the various clouds and their detailed properties. He even told me about a time he flew through clouds on the way to Europe. Throughout our encounter he showed absolutely no interest in creating, or listening to, my imaginative interpretation of the clouds. Clouds were objects defined by their properties and classifications. Describing them in any other way was wrong and disturbing.

Lacking the experience of seeing the world from multiple perspectives, people with Autism become trapped in an absolute universe. Once an object is labeled or categorized or viewed in a certain way, it will always be seen that way. It can never become anything else. Each week, when I opened the door for his group session, Neil would be inevitably adrift in a book. The other three members of his group sat close by him in the waiting room. Once he entered the playroom, Neil immediately engaged his pals in many games. However, not even once in two years did Neil play, talk or even acknowledge their presence while in the waiting room. I asked Neil why he read in the waiting room instead of playing with his friends. He explained in the literal manner of children with this disorder, "This is a waiting room. That means you're supposed to wait. When we get to the playroom, **that's** the place to play."

For typical children, language becomes a critical vehicle during the third year of life for sharing their experiences. Children play with made-up words, silly phrases and songs. They communicate to better coordinate their actions. Language becomes an important means of enhancing the enjoyment derived from perception sharing. When children begin Level 5, it is the vehicle they use for sharing their internal worlds. Conversation becomes a natural medium for Experience Sharing.

While a difficult idea to accept, some people with Autism experience language as a major obstacle to Experience Sharing. Rather than a means for co-regulation, language becomes a vehicle for chaos, or a means to control others. There is no more powerful example of this seemingly paradoxical statement than trying to converse with a highly verbal child with Aspergers Syndrome, who incessantly bombards you with seemingly random information questions, oblivious to your growing discomfort or boredom despite the subtle and direct cues you provide.

Without an interest in coordinating actions and perceptions with a partner, or learning about his internal experience, conversation becomes a highly deviant process. The child with Autism perceives having a conversation as announcing, informing and questioning; with no idea of the Experience Sharing purpose it serves the rest of us. He tells you things

> The child with Autism perceives having a conversation as announcing, informing and questioning; with no idea of the Experience Sharing purpose it serves the rest of us.

with no real curiosity about what you think or what is in your mind. He pays no attention to your emotional state of boredom or discomfort and just continues to talk. Without the desire for sharing or the use of emotional coordination, conversation becomes shallow, uninteresting and decidedly one-sided.

Conversation provides us with a means to truly explore the way we think about our world and compare and contrast it to others. Conversation gives us the opportunity to learn that other people can conceive of things in vastly different ways than we do, without either of us being right or wrong. However, rather than feeling excited about engaging in conversation with another person, about having a chance to expand their understanding or learn a new viewpoint on a subject, people with Autism usually become upset and angry. Their idiosyncratic and static perspective keeps them locked into attitudes and beliefs that narrow and restrict their world.

Jim, one of my wife's Aspergers patients—a highly intelligent 16 year old—became enraged when he noticed that our office had purchased a color laser printer to produce our Connections newsletter. "What right does an office like yours have to buy an expensive $5,000 machine like that? Those are only for large corporate offices, not places like this!" He became increasingly agitated until my wife explained that we had purchased the machine for half his estimated price. At that point, he immediately calmed down and resumed a pleasant interchange.

One of the more tragic consequences this 'mind-blindness' produces is the absence of true empathy in people with Autism. Temple Grandin is probably the most well known example of a person with Autism who appears to have developed competence in conducting social interaction for instrumental purposes, without developing Experience Sharing. Dr. Grandin, author of several autobiographical volumes, an accomplished scientist and speaker, has painstakingly developed a repertoire of social skills to successfully maintain her academic and consulting positions. However, she has no close friends, has never been on a date and has no idea of what falling in love would feel like. The noted neurologist and author Oliver Sacks, wrote about Temple in his book, *An Anthropologist on Mars*. In it, he provides an excellent example of interacting with someone who does not possess Emotional Coordination. He recounts a brief moment several hours into his initial interview with Dr. Grandin:

> *"I was feeling somewhat exhausted, hungry and thirsty—I had been traveling all day and had missed lunch—and I kept hoping Temple would notice and offer me some coffee. She did not; so after an hour, almost fainting under the barrage of her over-explicit and relentless sentences ...I finally asked for some coffee. There was no 'I'm sorry, I should have offered you some before,' no intermediacy, no social junction. Instead she immediately took me to a coffeepot that was kept brewing in the secretaries'*

office upstairs. She introduced me to the secretaries in a some-
what brusque manner, giving me the feeling, once again, of
someone who had learned, roughly, "how to behave" in such sit-
uations without having much personal perception of how other
people felt ..."

By the end of the third year peers have become important partners for
the typical child. They are perceived as exciting new sources of novelty
and variation. Their tendency to improvise and their very unpredictability becomes a major source of excitement, making them more attractive
for some things than adults. Children view peer encounters as providing
new ways to perceive, imagine and conceive of things. Each day brings
new discoveries.

Children searching for their unique identity recognize that comparison
and contrasts are more likely with people who are more like them—children their age. By the beginning of primary school, children are also
eager to form groupings with their mates. They provide a sense of 'we-
go'—a collaborative union. Unlike adults in the child's world, peers don't
dominate their interactions. Peer collaboration provides a sense of partnership without losing one's own competence and efficacy. Two boys lifting a box together feel better than doing it with an adult. "No Mrs.
Johnson, it's O.K. Billy and I can lift the box. We don't need any help."

Conversely, children with Autism do not desire additional perspectives
from their peers. Different viewpoints and novel ways of doing things are
threatening. Peers become a means to an end and social interactions the
vehicle to control children to get them to act in scripted ways. Initiations
with peers are more about greeting and giving out information, while the
initiations of typical children are more about sharing personal information. No desire develops to negotiate, compromise or reconcile conflicts.
The child with Autism develops no interest in impression formation or in
determining how to make a pal happy so he will want to come back and
visit again. At its worst, children with Autism develop the idea that peers
are to be avoided, as they create too much chaos.

People with Autism never gain the awareness that they have a unique and
emerging identity to compare and contrast with others. As Donna
Williams, probably the most poignant narrator of the autistic condition,
recounts in her autobiography: "By my teenage years, I began to be too
aware of the feeling of being alien. Unable to have even consistently
shared true self-expression or real felt emotions with anyone, I grasped the
absolute emptiness of what the world held for me. My answer to this was
to follow and mimic anybody who would take me along for the ride..."

It is no surprise, then, that friendships hold little meaning for the child
with Autism. Because they have no interest in shared memories, common beliefs or attributes, or the potential for shared futures, their
response to the question, "Who are your friends?" is a list of children
who agree to perform certain actions in a prescribed manner, as the child

> **People with
> Autism never
> gain the aware-
> ness that they
> have a unique
> and emerging
> identity to com-
> pare and contrast
> with others.**

believes they should be done. A person with Autism never experiences the instant emotional uplift from the silly smile of a best friend who is determined to cheer up his buddy and get him out of the dumps. He never fantasizes about finding a mate to share his dreams and desires. He has no awareness of how powerful it feels to have an ally who stands close by, ready to chase off a bigger bully.

As children with Autism get older the problem often gets more serious. The gap between payoffs for object and idea interaction and payoffs for social interaction widens. The social world becomes more confusing and rejecting, or boring. The requirements for even minimal social success seem totally out of reach. At the same time, the world of objects, facts and procedures stays predictable and satisfying and the potential for competence and mastery remains.

Roger is a sophomore at a top university. He receives A's in advanced courses. He is an excellent musician and fair actor, and plays a decent game of basketball. Roger is a good-looking young man, with a wry sense of humor. His language and non-verbal communication skills are excellent. His voice tone is normal and carries emotion. My non-specialist clinical colleagues would clearly miss his diagnosis of Aspergers Syndrome.

When he was younger, Roger never had friends. He would invite a boy over to play and then ignore him once he found something more interesting to do—which never took very long. When I first met Roger, almost ten years ago, he was an unemotional young man whose most important relationship was with his Nintendo machine. Roger cried all night following one family meeting where I told him he had to choose between his Nintendo and his parents—either one or the other had to go. His father later related that he and his wife spent an equally sleepless night, fully expecting to finish in second place.

> **Roger cried all night following one family meeting where I told him he had to choose between his Nintendo and his parents—either one or the other had to go.**

Five years later Roger came to see me on his own initiative. He was obsessed with the lyrics from a music CD written by Kurt Cobain—a rock star who committed suicide at the height of success. Many nights he lay awake, unable to get the lyrics out of his mind. We spent several hours reviewing them, deciphering the cryptic phrases. The song was about a person so emotionally cut off from others that even though they tried to care for him, the caring never got through. Understanding the song's personal meaning to Roger in light of his Aspergers condition seemed to provide him some relief. I encouraged Roger—a talented musician—to write his own lyrics to express his feelings and to get ready to join a band.

Two years passed before Roger contacted me, again in a state of crisis. He sounded so desperate that I stayed late that night to visit with him. I was amazed at the continued progress Roger had made towards "normalcy." His social graces were impeccable. His eye contact was perfect. His voice tone was normal. During our conversation he waited for my reply, listened carefully and responded in a highly related manner.

Roger came to talk about his emptiness. He was seriously thinking of killing himself. He felt he had become an expert at faking normalcy, but to what end? Roger's formula for social encounters was to constantly analyze what he believed were others' expectations and then deliver as close an approximation as he could. He had learned to read facial expressions and body language with an incredible degree of accuracy. He had succeeded in "fitting in"; no one thought he was weird. No one teased him cruelly as in the past. However, it was a hollow triumph with no emotional payoff. Despite his success at conforming to social norms, Roger was aware that something was missing...not in his methods, but in his reasons for relating to others.

The effort to blend in had taken an enormous toll on him. Roger believed he had to always be on guard. If not, he would be "found out" and become the subject of ridicule as he had during his pre-teen years. As a result, he viewed his social encounters as pointless, tortuous ordeals to survive. He told me that he was retreating more and more from his peers into the safety of his own world. And yet, with each retreat he worried that the door he had worked so hard to open, for so many years, was closing.

Like other more capable people with Autism, Roger had become, as the renowned neurologist Oliver Sacks observed, an anthropologist living within an alien culture. He tried desperately to blend in. Like a tolerated observer, Roger had learned to avoid attention but held little hope of ever becoming an accepted member of the tribe. Given his disorder, he saw no way to bridge the ever-deepening emotional gap between himself and others. Despite progress that most observers of Aspergers would see as a triumph, Roger knew enough to realize he had failed. His despondency was caused by his recognition of an insurmountable gap between himself and others that no manner of socially appropriate behavior could narrow. Bereft of the feelings he was wise enough to know accompany our relationships, Roger—facing a life of empty social pretense—surmised that suicide might be a rational option.

For Roger, going back to a world without Experience Sharing is inconceivable. He has come too far beyond his prior autistic "mind-blindness" and can no longer accept the confines of his former life, which he describes as "totally without color." Ironically, in Roger's despair lie the seeds of hope and eventual triumph. Because Roger can discern what he is missing, because he deeply yearns to share his feelings and ideas with others, to have intimate companionship in his life, he is much farther along in reaching his dream than he realizes.

Social development is like a treasure hunt. Each new discovery fills us with awe and a renewed sense of our place in the world. While the RDI program gave Roger his own road map, the missing piece he needed, it's up to him to find the courage to follow the path.

Relational Development Intervention

Henry ran into the playroom with a big smile on his face, flopped onto the beanbags and began rolling around. Rita, his mother, walked over and tried to lift him up. Henry went limp like a sack of potatoes, still smiling. She finally succeeded in getting him into an upright position. Immediately Henry ran off and tried to yank open a cabinet door. Rita followed Henry to the door and asked, "Do you want to see what's inside?" Henry ignored her words and kept yanking at the door. Rita opened the door for Henry. He looked at the objects inside for a moment, found a number puzzle and became immediately engrossed in counting the numbers out loud in an excited voice, while running back and forth.

Henry, who was diagnosed with Autism at age three, is a handsome five-year-old boy with a pixyish smile. His parents, Rita and Jim, admitted that he absolutely ruled their home; they allowed him to do pretty much as he pleased. Henry had just completed a year in a school designed primarily for children with Autism. However, progress was minimal. He largely ignored other children in his small class. He had spent the time doing nothing but sitting by himself doing math worksheets. Henry loved math, and while he was not a "savant", he was somewhat obsessed with numbers.

During our evaluation, we observed Henry while he was alone in our playroom. Henry sat in the middle of the room doing nothing for over 30 minutes. He showed no apparent signs of distress. Rita, a vivacious and passionate woman, confessed to me in tears that this scene of Henry alone in a room, seemingly oblivious to the vast potential of the world around him, was a terrifying glimpse of her greatest nightmare for her son.

The Goals of RDI

Many parents, like Rita and Jim, fear the possibility that their beloved child may spend his or her entire life alone, without knowing the companionship of family and friends. Even for higher functioning children, like Henry, without some way of teaching them the Experience Sharing part of life, their lives become little more than learning to act in life, but not to enjoy Life itself. Without some new form of treatment, Henry would never grasp what it feels like to have a best friend. He would never know the special strength and closeness of belonging to a team. He would never laugh at a new version of an old joke. It was a future where Henry would expect the world to fit into his black-and-white style of thinking, never understanding how to go with the flow and adapt to changing circumstances. It was not a future that led to what any of us would consider even a minimally satisfying quality of life.

However, when children succeed in Relational Development Intervention (RDI), they become true participants in their world. They feel the sense of connection and meaning that the rest of us take for granted in our lives. They develop an eagerness to be part of a shared experience and willingly do their share of the "work" of maintaining coordination with a partner. As they progress through the different stages of treatment, they no longer see coordinating with their partners as work, but rather as a demonstration of competence in their social world and as an intrinsic part of the enjoyment derived from interactions.

The children we work with develop a desire for Experience Sharing on as many levels as possible. Each new discovery increases their motivation to find and practice new skills that enable them to relate with others on a still deeper level. They discover increasingly more complex reasons for sharing what they find meaningful with others, and they learn to share their emotions, actions, perceptions and ideas. Some even find emotionally intimate and enduring relationships.

Their relationship success goes beyond the clinical setting. They are able to internalize their motivation and skills and apply the relational discoveries they make in treatment to new settings and new people. They develop the flexibility to "go with the flow"; to continue enjoying their social encounters, even when expected scripts suddenly change.

We can easily spot a child who has been through a more scripted skills program when he joins one of our groups. The child tries to use his scripts and becomes upset when they inevitably do not work (as will happen in any normal peer encounter). Unlike the children who are trained through RDI, he is more concerned about whether the other group members have followed the script than his partner's happiness and enjoyment. He has no backup "Plan B" if the script doesn't work.

Our clients learn to understand and appreciate a world of multiple perspectives, where there is no one right or wrong answer. They come to understand that these gray areas—encounters where we do not know exactly what will happen next—hold the most enjoyment and potential for learning about their own unique identity.

> **Their relationship success goes beyond the clinical setting. They are able to internalize their motivation and skills and apply the relational discoveries they make in treatment to new settings and new people.**

The Goals of RDI

Through Relational Development Intervention, we help children:

- Understand and appreciate the many levels of Experience Sharing.

- Become an equal partner in co-regulating Experience Sharing interactions.

- Understand and value the uniqueness of other people—their perspectives, ideas and feelings.

- Value and work to maintain enduring relationships.

- Become adaptable and flexible in both social and non-social problem solving.

- Recognize their own unique identity that can continue to grow and develop.

The Uniqueness of RDI

RDI shares many features with other treatment approaches. Readers familiar with Autism intervention will recognize contributions from Structured Teaching, Behavior Modification, the work of Arnold and Eileen Miller and Barry Prizant, among others. Many of the activities we use are not our creation, but adapted from these programs as well as other effective social and communication intervention methods. But there are several unique aspects to our work.

The hallmark of RDI is our emphasis on the development of Experience Sharing. Social Skills training approaches, whether they realize it or not, mainly work within the realm of instrumental behaviors. That is, they seek to develop discrete skills, or scripts to be followed, based upon "if/then" reasoning. The child is taught specific behavioral responses that are appropriate in specific situations: What to say when another child says hello; How to make eye contact when you wish to speak; How to take your turn when you play a board game. Make no mistake about it. These are essential life skills that need to be taught; we work on them as well in our program. They are designed for functioning in those static systems where most instrumental transactions occur, like sitting at your desk in class, or waiting on line for the bus. Unfortunately, this type of conditional behavior will fail miserably during a typical school recess. Even worse, these "skills" may themselves become impediments to success.

Program Tip
Remember, the goal of Experience Sharing interactions is to sense the joy and stimulation intrinsic in our social encounters. Each partner brings unique thoughts, feelings and actions to the interaction for the purpose of jointly understanding and sharing their emotional reactions. Conversely, the goal of instrumental interaction is to follow a script to reach a specific endpoint.

The Three Cardinal Principles of RDI

Learning to be proficient in even the simplest forms of Experience Sharing requires totally different abilities and it is here that RDI moves beyond most social skills programs. Continued change and unpredictability are two inherent aspects of Experience Sharing encounters. Scripted or discrete learning simply cannot work in these situations. There is no way to teach a script or formula to address every partner's next movement that inevitably and unpredictably changes from second-to-second. Three major principles lie at the foundation of RDI: Social Referencing, Co-regulation and Functions before Means.

Social Referencing

Experience Sharing is based upon Social Referencing, a highly specialized form of perception and information processing we refer to as "you-me" thinking. Proficiency in Social Referencing allows the child to constantly read and interpret his relationship with his social partners to determine his degree of coordination with them. The desire and capacity for Social Referencing is the foundation of Experience Sharing development.

Instead of watching for a specific cue, Social Referencing involves the ability to make rapid comparisons between oneself and others. The child learns to evaluate the degree of similarity and/or coordination between something he is doing, feeling, perceiving or thinking and that same aspect in his partner. For example, at any moment in time we may reference our respective facial expressions, our movement across a room, what we are paying attention to and our ideas and preferences. We may, in fact, reference all of these variables within seconds. What makes referencing even more complex is that these evaluations are conducted while we are both constantly moving and changing, reacting to new things and having new thoughts and feelings. There is rarely an "instant replay" if information is missed. An encounter just keeps moving along, without "time outs." Most often, referencing must also be conducted while we are engaged in doing something else, like running together towards a pile of beanbags, or gazing together at an interesting bird in the sky.

The importance of Social Referencing—constantly evaluating the state of relationship, prior to and following any action or performance—changes the entire nature of social intervention. No longer is the child dependent upon a series of rote responses that may or may not be applicable to the situation. When we teach him to understand how to operate in a fluid system, where the important information occurs in an ongoing feedback loop, we are opening up a whole new world to him. When Henry and I are walking together and I begin to lag behind, I want him to notice the distance between us, see that distance as important information and act to close the distance, without my telling him to do so.

> The importance of Social Referencing— constantly evaluating the state of relationship, prior to and following any action or performance— changes the entire nature of social intervention.

Functions Precede Means

Henry needs to learn both to perceive the increasing gap between our bodies and to care about it. Why should he care? At each Level of Experience Sharing development we introduce to the child new reasons to care, new aspects of experience that can be shared. At Henry's level of development he might care because if he walks ahead of me he doesn't get to see all of the silly faces I make, which he finds so funny. When Henry progresses to a higher level of development he might care because he wants me close enough to read my non-verbal reactions to his statements, to see how I am feeling.

Although some Social Skills programs teach skills that could conceivably be used for Experience Sharing, they do so without any formal evaluation of the child's developmental readiness to understand the Function—the reasons or payoffs—of using the skill. The children don't understand the greater emotional connection the skill can provide. Therefore, the skills are rarely used, or are used inappropriately. A powerful example of the futility of teaching social skills, even those that could potentially be used for Experience Sharing, without first evaluating the child's readiness to understand their value, follows.

Over the past fifteen years, Dr. Simon Baron-Cohen and his research team in London have carried out a series of studies on Theory of Mind skills. They have demonstrated that people with Autism are deficient in understanding that other people possess minds that think about things differently from their own (what we refer to as Level 4 and 5 skills). This work is so convincing that a Theory of Mind deficit is now accepted as a defining characteristic of Autism.

In one recent study, Dr. Baron-Cohen's group decided to provide instruction in Theory of Mind skills. Their multiple week course taught a group of intelligent children with Autism methods of understanding how other people think and perceive things. All the children completed the course and passed the "final exam." In theory, they now possessed the skills to go into the world and become involved in understanding the unique minds of the people around them—literally opening up a whole new universe to these children. Yet, in their follow-up of the children's real world behavior, the investigators were dismayed to find that the children did not act any differently in conversations. They were no more curious about other people's minds than prior to the course. The researchers had not stopped to first evaluate whether any of the children were developmentally ready to understand the importance of these new skills. If the children had been interviewed, they may have responded with a single sentiment—"Why should I bother?"

Typically developing children learn new ways of interacting in their relationships—the Means of Experience Sharing—only after they perceive the desire to share a new and deeper type of experience with their social

> Typically developing children learn new ways of interacting in their relationships—only after they perceive the desire to share a new and deeper type of experience with their social partners...

partners—the Functions of relationships. Their desire for a greater Experience Sharing payoff leads them to pursue and spend many hours mastering difficult new skills. In RDI, we teach skills only after we have carefully determined that the child is developmentally ready for them. Readiness has nothing to do with the age of the child. It is based on his ability to understand, use and value the particular skill.

By carefully evaluating the stage of readiness prior to intervention, we create potential for the child to understand the meaning of what is being taught. The child feels the enjoyment inherent in the interaction with his partner. He comes to understand that the actions he and his partner perform together lead to the pleasurable result. He begins to feel competent in understanding the relationship of actions and results, so that he can reproduce it in other settings.

In the RDI program our children practice their new skills without prompts or external rewards; our goal is that they feel rewarded by the joy intrinsic in the interaction. They do not do their work for M&M's or to get us to play the game they want to play, or to give them their favorite video. Our clients, like Henry, learn to interact for the sole purpose of sharing their world with others. They become eager to try out what they have learned, both in and out of treatment settings and to apply even limited skill repertoires wherever and with whomever possible. I have witnessed a number of occasions in which our patients, even those who possess impaired language and a small social repertoire, were able to achieve great social success with peers, because they cared enough to observe their degree of emotional coordination with a play-mate. A simple smile, nod, gesture or a few enthusiastic words at just the right moment can maintain a playfully coordinated interlude for a long period of time.

> **Co-regulation refers to the spontaneous action on the part of one partner, to alter his actions in order to maintain the shared meaning of the interaction.**

Co-Regulation

Once children have mastered Social Referencing, and begun to understand the Function and Means of interactions, we introduce co-regulation in various stages. Co-regulation refers to the spontaneous action on the part of one partner, to alter his actions in order to maintain the shared meaning of the interaction. For instance, Henry will develop to the point that not only does he notice that I am lagging behind, but he cares about the increasing distance between us, enough to do something about it. In most interactions with children with Autism, adults take all of the actions necessary to maintain coordination. The adult follows the child around the house, moves away when he unknowingly invades personal space and changes his position to maintain face-to-face interaction. However, in RDI, children learn to be responsible for their part of keeping an interaction intact; they become co-regulators. They learn a special form of communication that serves to increase coordination. And, they learn to self-regulate—to take actions that alter their own behavior so that it coordinates with that of their partner.

Co-regulation requires constant referencing of a partner: Do I need to speed up or slow down? Is my partner interested in my conversation? His referencing may indicate the need for a special type of action, called a repair or maintenance action, on his part. Children with Autism, like Henry, learn not only to bring new information into interactions, but also how to limit that novelty when it becomes too chaotic. This give-and-take interaction produces curiosity about the other person—What will he do next? As co-regulation becomes more proficient, it provides the foundation for moving into exploring another person's mind: What is he thinking? How is he feeling?

It may not be obvious, but the most crucial part of co-regulation is learning to observe when coordination has been lost, or is in jeopardy. Unfortunately, children with Autism do not perceive such moments. When we begin work on co-regulation, we amplify moments of non-coordination. For example, we teach parents to playfully, but deliberately, use gaze aversion, or dramatically stop talking mid sentence and delay an expected action, or perform their roles in a comically incorrect manner, as ways of framing for their child that a regulatory action is needed. We practice games where, if the child takes his eyes off of a parent even for a moment, the parent may run away. At other times, a parent's changing facial expressions provide the key information about what will happen next in the activity. Parents learn to wait longer when coordination has broken down, to allow the child time to recognize the need for repair actions. They will also require that a child repeat an interaction or start over again, if he acts in a non-coordinated manner. For example, if the child runs to the playroom ahead, without a word, a parent will escort the child back to the waiting room and start over again, until he can walk side-by-side with the parent.

Typical children spend thousands of hours and many years, beginning shortly after birth, accumulating the layers of social referencing and co-regulation necessary to be proficient in Experience Sharing. Development proceeds in a fixed manner through a series of progressive steps. While infants and toddlers are learning Social Referencing and Co-regulation, parents intuitively act slowly and work on one step at a time. For example, Mom may turn her son's body to show him an exciting object in the environment. She makes sure the child sees it and then turns his head to her, or moves around in front of her son, so they can share their joyful reactions with each other. Driven by the excitement felt from this discovery, the child will engage in this same interaction again and again and again, each time with a little less "scaffolding" provided by the more capable partner. Once the child has mastered this skill, he is ready and eager to experience the next discovery. The process continues on; discoveries followed by practice and mastery and more discoveries. But, without starting at the beginning and mastering the fundamental elements of Experience Sharing, children with Autism are unable to jump in at mid-level and grasp the intrinsic payoff of interaction. Despite their perceived high-functioning abilities in other areas of their life, not a single stage can be skipped without the entire process turning into a house of cards.

> Co-regulation requires constant referencing of a partner: Do I need to speed up or slow down? Is my partner interested in my conversation?

In RDI, we have learned this critical lesson from experience. Prior to working on any new skill, we always begin by making sure the child understands its functions and value. As in typical development, each step we take is built upon a prior stage of accomplishment. We work on improvisational activity only after the child has learned many ways of coordinating his actions with others and has sufficient reasons to take these actions. Sharing ideas and feelings becomes a treatment objective only after the child is adept at and excited by Joint Attention and sharing perspectives.

Preparing for Treatment

To help children with Autism learn to perceive, care about and react to their worlds in this new way, we provide them with a special setting that facilitates Social Referencing. The setting amplifies the critical information needed for this new type of information processing while minimizing any distracting information. We slow down the pace of interaction required in normal peer social encounters. Trained guides are integral to the process; they carefully and gradually introduce the child to Social Referencing and just as gradually require him to take on more responsibility for Co-regulation. Activities are chosen that focus the child on the enjoyment of Experience Sharing as well as provide opportunities for the child to successfully practice communication and self-regulation for coordination in slow and gradual ways. We take into account the unique ways that Autism impacts the learning style of each child and modify our methods accordingly.

Evaluation

Careful preparation is the cornerstone of successful treatment. Preparation is based upon thorough, precise evaluation and treatment planning, educating parents and preparing the proper time and space for successful work. When we evaluated Henry, we began with a thorough medical and neurological workup. We confirmed his diagnosis using the Autism Diagnostic Observation Scales (ADOS) and the Autism Diagnostic Interview Revised (ADIR), two new instruments developed by Catherine Lord and Michael Rutter, that have shown to be highly valid in diagnosing forms of Autism. Next we evaluated language, cognitive, perceptual and motor functioning, as well as Henry's capacity for attention and emotional regulation. The final step was an evaluation of Henry's Experience Sharing capability, as well as obstacles that might hinder further development and temptations that might facilitate it. Our evaluation process is designed so that by its end, we have a comprehensive treatment plan already outlined, prioritizing specific objectives appropriate to the different stages of the child's development.

Following this assessment, we determined Henry's precise level of Experience Sharing development using the RDA—Relational

Sample Items from the RDA

Level I:	Typical	Sometimes	Starting	Not yet
01 Sharing happiness and joy with social partners provides more pleasure than solo play.				
02 Shares the "contagion" of other people's excitement and joy. Easily "infected" by the emotions of others.				
03 Comforted by a glance and/or soothing words from adults.				
04 Pays attention to the facial expressions of social partners and reacts as if they are important.				
05 Checks to determine the reactions of adults to his/her behavior.				
06 When in a social setting, conducts frequent "scans" to observe what other people are doing.				
07 Clearly lets you know in a positive, inviting way, when s/he wants to continue an enjoyable activity.				
08 Invites people to play, without concern for the specific activity.				
09 Participates with enthusiasm when social partners introduce a new activity.				
10 Deliberately takes actions intended to please social partners.				
Level II:				
11 Shares greetings and goodbyes without being told to do so.				
12 Enjoys learning the rules and roles for new games and activities that other people introduce.				
13 Observes carefully to learn the proper rules and roles of an activity.				
14 Makes sure that his/her understanding of how to play a game is shared with partners.				
15 Stays "tuned in" to a playmate. Doesn't ignore social partners, even when there is some other interesting activity to do.				
16 Spends a significant amount of time observing other children to determine how to better interact with them.				
17 Appropriately carries out structured roles in activities, with the proper actions and timing: for example, playing catch or playing Simon Says.				
18 Obtains enjoyment from coordinating his/her actions with those of a partner.				
19 Observes partners to make sure they are enjoying shared activities.				
20 Enjoys variations to activities introduced by social partners.				
Level III:				
21 Makes sure that s/he doesn't walk ahead or behind you. Adjusts his/her pace to remain side-by-side with you.				
22 Communicates appropriately for clarification, when confused about his/her role in an activity, for example, "Should I go faster?"				
23 Enjoys playing games where both partners collaborate equally to modify some of the rules as they go along.				
24 Careful to check with social partners before changing the rules of a game.				
25 Quick to stop, or modify any action that confuses or bothers a social partner.				
26 Makes sure that social partners are agreeable before changing activities.				
27 Listens carefully to make sure s/he correctly understands what you are trying to communicate.				
28 Tries to compromise when his/her desires are different from others. Takes actions to prevent and reconcile conflicts.				
29 Works as an equal partner to make up new games that everyone contributes to and enjoys.				
30 Careful to make sure his/her actions are coordinated and stays synchronized with social partners.				

Program Tip
Using the RDA in schools

The RDA is a wonderful tool for formulating social development goals and objectives on a child's IEP (Individualized Education Program). School staff like it because it minimizes confusion and potential conflict and breaks objectives into small, manageable steps. Parents and advocates love the RDA because finally, social development goals for a child with Autism or Aspergers Syndrome can be as specific, appropriate and measurable as reading goals would be for a Dyslexic child. The RDA creates accountability for progress in social development.

Development Assessment—we created for our program. Henry's parents were asked to fill out a comprehensive questionnaire and interview based upon the six-stage model of Experience Sharing development. Additionally, we asked them to supply us with a videotape of Henry interacting in a natural social setting.

While we find observations in natural settings, as well as questionnaires and interviews with parents and professionals to be helpful in assessment, we are careful to supplement them with our own carefully controlled observational methods. We have found that even well trained professionals may sometimes underestimate a child's potential by observing him in natural settings, because of their noise and chaos. On the other hand, family members and well meaning professionals may inadvertently over-estimate their child's Experience Sharing development on questionnaires and in interviews. Often they are doing so much unconscious compensation that they perceive the child possessing abilities for co-regulation that are really the result of their own reactive efforts.

Henry and his mother participated in a structured observational format with father observing behind our one-way mirror. During this segment of our evaluation, Henry and his mother were videotaped while interacting in a series of structured activities designed to engage them in Experience Sharing interactions at different levels. The videotapes were carefully analyzed and rated to determine Henry's precise level of development within the six stage model described in Chapter Two.

An integral part of our observation is noticing what the child is doing to maintain or interfere with Emotional Coordination. We are not looking for discrete behaviors like "asking a question" but rather the degree to which the child references and regulates the interaction so that

Experience Sharing can take place. While the results will fall somewhere within our six level system, we have never had to proceed past Level 4 in the initial evaluation of a child with Autism.

The results of our evaluation indicated that Henry's development was mid-way through Level 1. This was confirmed by his parents' questionnaire and by other observational information. He was an emotionally attuned child. It was clear that sharing smiles with his mother provided more pleasure than solo play. Henry also engaged in some degree of Social Referencing for emotion sharing. When he appeared somewhat distressed, he would immediately turn to his mother for a comforting glance or soothing words. However, Henry did not reference on a frequent enough basis to track people's actions and reactions to his behavior.

When we looked at the third stage of Level 1, Excitement Sharing, we again found a mixed picture. Like many of the children we evaluate, Henry did not view either of his parents as the primary source of exciting, meaningful new information. Rather, his parents were too often in the position of following behind Henry, reacting and responding to whatever he chaotically became involved with in his environment. Because of this, Henry did not yet know any of the early games like Peek-a-boo, that children find so enjoyable and that teach them to understand the structure of interaction. Even when Henry briefly participated in one of Rita's games and showed pleasure, he did not communicate to let her know that he wanted to continue the enjoyable activity.

Henry's RDA enabled us to immediately zero in on ten specific, developmentally appropriate objectives for treatment, as outlined on the next page.

Obstacles and Temptations

Along with pinpointing developmental progress, we also catalogue the child's areas of interest, the activities that might serve as, what Barry Prizant refers to as "temptations" for the child, as well as any factors that may present obstacles to treatment progress. It is critical to assess those aspects of the child and his environment that—unless addressed—will ultimately prevent progress. Among the major obstacles we assess are the child's deficits in self development, his resistance in allowing adults to guide his participation in activities and place limits on his actions and most importantly, the beliefs and actions of important members of the child's social environment.

Giving up Control

RDI requires that parents initially take control of their child's physical environment, materials, activities and interactive rules. When we begin treatment, most children with Autism have too much control over their social fields. They play with objects that use up the bulk of their attention

> **RDI requires that parents initially take control of their child's physical environment, materials, activities and interactive rules.**

Henry's Initial Treatment Objectives at Level 1

Stage 02: Social Referencing

- Conducting frequent visual scans of adult actions and reactions to maintain a "fix" on the adult (referencing for security).

- Visually orienting to people entering proximity to make sure they are familiar and safe prior to shifting attention away (referencing for wariness).

- Actively referencing adults prior to, or just after engaging in behavior, in order to obtain approval or determine the reaction of the adult (referencing for approval).

- Actively referencing adults when uncertain or anxious (for clarification and "refueling").

Stage 03: Adults as primary providers of excitement

- Responding easily to adult cues to shift attention to an exciting action.

- Communicating positively, to obtain more novelty and excitement.

Stage 04: Learning simple games

- Paying rapt attention, as adults model, or demonstrate simple interesting activities.

- Sharing anticipation of enjoyable outcomes, through face-to-face shared smiles and laughter at appropriate times (e.g. laughing prior to adult revealing in peek-a-boo).

- Enacting simple role actions at designated times under adult guidance (e.g. fetching the balloon after parent releases it. Pouring marbles in adult's cup in Marbles Please game.)

- Communicating in an inviting manner for adults to initiate and continue enjoyable activities.

or they have idiosyncratic interactive rules with which they are reluctant to part. Some children become obsessed with whether or not their partner follows an anticipated "script." If a child has not learned to orient and comply with parents and accept parental structure without a struggle, Behavior Modification, to regain control of the environment and develop compliance, can be a critical initial component of treatment.

Attentional Problems

It goes without saying that any type of learning requires that the child be able to attend to specific aspects of the environment without distraction. Joint Attention and even fluid play require sophisticated, rapid attention shifting skills. Unfortunately having a diagnosis of Autism does not spare a child from having other conditions like Attention Deficit Hyperactivity Disorder. Children with Attention deficits may benefit from medication to increase their attention.

Emotional Regulation

There is a world of difference in working with a child who has a relatively even temperament, from a child with emotional regulation difficulties.

Some of the children we see are so easily triggered into upset and anger that it is impossible initially to provide them the experience of joy and positive excitement. Mood regulating medications can sometimes make a critical difference in working with these "explosive" children.

Organizational Problems

The movement from Level 1 to Level 2 requires that the child internalize sequences of actions that end in a pleasurable outcome. Many children with Autism don't understand the sequential way that actions are linked together—first do this, then do that. They live in a highly chaotic world, where things seem to happen on a momentary random basis. These highly disorganized children require training in learning and retaining sequential information, prior to practicing with a partner. Methods of behavioral intervention and techniques developed by Project TEACCH are extremely valuable interventions at this point in teaching children to retain and operate on the basis of sequential information.

Even the most basic Experience Sharing interactions require a participant to reference some aspect of his own functioning such as position in space, movement or perception. Some of our children are so organizationally impaired that they possess no position from which to take a "course reading" of themselves in relation to their partner. To cite an extreme example, Arnold and Eileen Miller point out that some children with Autism appear to be unaware that their arms and legs are attached to their bodies.

Co-regulation requires the ability for self-regulation —modifying your own actions based on their perceived consequences in the system. The Millers use the term "zone of intention" to point out that some children with Autism have difficulty understanding they can influence someone or something, that is not directly adjacent to them. For example, if I have no way of knowing that I can use my hand and arm to regulate the destination of a ball, there is no way I can coordinate my actions with a partner for a game of catch. I may have to walk over to you and hand you the ball. These children may have to be carefully taught that they can let go of a ball and still influence its movement in the direction of another person. Occupational Therapy is a critical intervention for these children, as it is for those with severe gross motor difficulties that prevent them from coordinating their movements with others.

Motivational Deficits

In contrast to their low motivation for doing the work needed to coordinate relationships, our patients often have a great desire to relate to objects and information. Coordinating with things and data is much simpler and understandable than with people. Objects don't move around and change from moment to moment. Facts remain facts.

> Many children with Autism don't understand the sequential way that actions are linked together— first do this, then do that. They live in a highly chaotic world, where things seem to happen on a momentary random basis.

Our patients often initially insist on involving themselves with objects as part of interactions with people. As in the case of Roger—the Nintendo addict of my earlier chapter—limiting the amount of object involvement may entail a major struggle, especially for older children. It is not always necessary that they choose objects over people, although for some children this may be the case. More frequently they are motivated to relate to objects while in the presence of people. They want mom to sit nearby as they watch their favorite video, or they want little brother to play a board game, so they can win. These objects or activities, even those that are age appropriate, like computer games, create attentional competition that use up the child's already limited capacity for relational functioning. The increased motivation to engage in these activities makes it impossible for the child to notice aspects of his/her relatedness to others.

As children with Autism get older the problem often gets more serious. The gap between payoffs for object and idea interaction and payoffs for social interaction typically widens. The social world becomes more confusing and rejecting, or boring. The requirements for even minimal social success seem totally out of reach. However, the world of objects, facts and procedures stays more predictable and satisfying; the potential for competence and mastery remains.

> **As children with Autism get older the problem often gets more serious. The gap between payoffs for object and idea interaction and payoffs for social interaction typically widens.**

Michael has severe language processing problems, gross motor difficulties and an IQ measured in the Borderline range. His dyad partner Andrew has an Above Average IQ, excellent language and good gross motor skills. Andrew is in regular education, and receives excellent grades with no outside support. Michael attends mostly regular classes, but requires a great deal of resource help and modification. Andrew is an excellent athlete, but Michael is too clumsy to play sports. Andrew obviously possesses many important abilities that Michael lacks. However, when we examine their relationship development, we might question which of these children should be given the label "high functioning." When Michael and Andrew were together in their dyad, Michael was the one who would tell Andrew it didn't matter what game they played, or who went first. Andrew entered the room with pre-determined ideas of how he wanted to spend our hour, including what specific subjects were to be discussed. Michael did not consider winning important, while it seemed to be all Andrew thought about. Michael never developed pre-ordained topics of conversation. He was more interested in finding out what was new and sharing his observations of what he noticed outside of the window. Michael was the one invited over to friend's houses, not Andrew. Andrew always sat alone at lunch, while Michael always seemed to be seated with two or three other boys.

Parent and Professional Misconceptions

Parents typically have to be trained to simplify the social field, before engaging in treatment. Often they have been told by well-meaning professionals to add greater complexity, like more language, stimulating toys, games and more peers. They may be operating from the principle that more stimulation is better, or that they should follow their child's lead, even though this goes completely against everything we know about the specific deficits of children with Autism. In this regard, parents may have unwittingly fostered an initial obstacle. There may be few or no limits on the child's interaction and they may allow him too much control. They may bombard the child with language, or have him in overwhelming social contexts. They may have over-emphasized instrumental learning and sacrificed Emotional Coordination.

When parents first come for evaluation, they often over-estimate their child's relationship development. They do not realize how much of the regulation they are doing to maintain Emotional Coordination. The child may turn away and the parent will unconsciously move to see the child's face. The child will walk away while talking and the parent will run to catch what the child is saying. The child randomly throws a ball and the parent runs to fetch it. If the child has older siblings or is in an inclusive educational environment, other children and adults may also be over-compensating in a similar, artificial manner. Convincing these well-meaning individuals to work less, so that we can teach the child to take on more responsibility in the relationship, can be a difficult task. Some of the typical obstacles we evaluate are outlined below.

Obstacles to Experience Sharing

- Giving up Control
- Attention Deficit Disorder
- Emotional Regulation Problems
- Organizational Problems
- Motivational Deficits
- Parental Misconceptions
- Language

Language as a Potential Obstacle?

Most readers are probably surprised by the addition of language as a potential obstacle to Experience Sharing. All of us appreciate the critical role that language plays in Experience Sharing, especially at higher levels of relationship development. Once we move to Level 6, we spend considerable time teaching children to recognize and verbalize their own unique perceptions, ideas and emotional reactions. Even at lower levels, language can play a critical role in enhancing enjoyment and communicating for better regulation. However, we use language strategically from the very beginning of treatment.

A much more difficult idea for people to accept is that language developed out of the context of Experience Sharing, can be a major obstacle and create disastrous consequences for the child. Psychological research demonstrates that human beings derive about 70% of the meaning of their communications from non-verbal information. Many, if not most children with Autism have language impairments. However, as bad as these language difficulties are, they are nowhere near as incapacitating as the severe non-verbal deficits that are universal in Autism. Language, cut off from non-verbal communication, will become an inadequate replacement for social referencing and prevent the child from ever learning to observe the emotions and reactions of others. Moreover, if children learn to use language without the proper emotional voice tone and emphasis, it guarantees that the child will be perceived as odd or that people will be unable to understand the feelings and needs of the child. When we reinforce language use that is isolated from non-verbal feedback, we are rewarding children for developing a highly limited and bizarre notion of communication.

Rather than a critical tool for enhancing shared enjoyment and co-regulation, language can become a force for chaos, or a means to control others. One of our new, nine-year-old patients, Mark, recently ran into his group, ten minutes late, but full of excitement. He remembered to look at the two boys already there and to say hello to them. Then he said—to no one in particular—"This is a great day. Today we're going to bake brownies. I brought all the stuff." He then started to unpack the shopping bag he was carrying, oblivious to the surprised reactions of the therapist and other group members who had never been consulted on Mark's decision. You can probably predict the mess that ensued when his fellow group members informed Mark of their lack of interest in cooking anything. In fact, they had been in the midst of an enjoyable game when he arrived, which Mark had failed to even notice.

There is no more powerful example of the potential off-putting effects of language developed without the desire for Experience Sharing, than enduring a highly verbal child with Aspergers Syndrome, bombarding you with endless questions or requests for information. Aaron, one of our new patients, is currently obsessed with Elvis. I cringed as I watched him approach another hapless "victim" in our waiting room recently and for the twentieth time ask, "Do you know the date of Elvis's final concert? Do you know which suit he was wearing?" On and on Aaron went, providing the answers to these and many more questions, oblivious to the growing discomfort and irritation of his listener.

When language has already developed in this abnormal fashion, as is often the case with our hyper-verbal Aspergers patients, we have to work hard to convince the child, parents, teachers and professionals that this "gift" may also be a curse; that language must be limited and non-contextual language actively discouraged, if we are to make any progress together. Because children with autism are not looking at our

A much more difficult idea for people to accept is that language developed out of the context of Experience Sharing, can be a major obstacle and create disastrous consequences for the child.

faces, well-meaning adults unwittingly communicate primarily through language and wind up talking more to these children than they would to typical children who they assume are getting a big part of the message from faces, voice tone and gesture.

A child with a highly limited language repertoire will make faster progress and has a better prognosis for eventual success, than the children described above, if he has learned to use what language he has in the service of Experience Sharing. Consider the example of Jeffrey, one of our young patients. Two years ago, when Jeffrey was three, he had acquired only six words after four months of treatment. But we were not concerned. At that time I observed Jeffrey playing with his dad in our playroom. Jeffrey pointed, made sure he had his dad's full attention, then pointed to the sky and said, with a dramatic emotional emphasis, "Up." Dad knew this meant that Jeffrey wanted to be tossed in the air. While in the air, Jeffrey shared laughter with his father and together they made "whew!!" noises. When he came down, Jeffrey again made sure he had dad's attention and then smiled at him and in an inviting tone of voice said, "More!" This went on for three more times. Then, Jeffrey pointed across the room to the bed, while catching dad's eyes and smiling. Dad knew that Jeffrey was asking to be tossed onto the bed. Even though Jeffrey had only six words in his entire repertoire, he was able to use them to maximize Experience Sharing.

We do not take language development for granted. In fact, we worked intensively on language with Jeffrey, as we do with many other children. But work on speech and language development is conducted in an integrated manner, within the context of genuine emotion sharing and social referencing. Within a year of the above example, Jeffrey was fluently talking in short sentences. He used emphasis, proper voice tone and a full range of emotions. He was also aware of the reactions of his listener; he was just as interested in what they had to say and the way they "punctuated" their words, as what was in his own head. Jeffrey may never possess the verbal repertoire of Aaron or Mark. But his language will always be a precious gift he can use to enhance his joy and success, rather than a cruel reminder of his differentness.

...work on speech and language development is conducted in an integrated manner, within the context of genuine emotion sharing and social referencing.

Henry's Obstacles

While in Henry's case the obstacles were clear and not particularly severe, they had to be addressed before we could proceed with treatment. Henry's attention span was good. He had a mild emotional temperament. There were no particularly aversive behaviors that had to be dealt with and he did not use language as an obstacle. Paper and pencils, or pens, in the immediate vicinity were a temptation for Henry to do math problems; these materials had to be initially eliminated, which was no great problem.

The greatest obstacle was Henry's parents' admitted tendency to allow him control of their interaction—they followed him around, reacting as best they could to whatever Henry did. It was difficult for them to set clear limits. However, to their credit, they recognized their behavior pattern from the start, and were willing to change it.

Like most of the children we work with, Henry's chaotic behavior added too much variability to the social field. It prevented him from noticing the enjoyment of more predictable social encounters. Furthermore, when his parents attempted to impose limits on his behavior, Henry often thought they were playing a game. Even though he did not exhibit any dangerous behaviors, Henry had to learn that adults were in charge of establishing the social framework, including the boundaries for his actions.

As a final step in evaluation, we determine temptations—those activities and elements that serve to enhance the interest and excitement of a particular child, without becoming an obstacle to Experience Sharing.

Temptations

As a final step in evaluation, we determine temptations—those activities and elements that serve to enhance the interest and excitement of a particular child, without becoming an obstacle to Experience Sharing. For example, we knew that Henry loved numbers and mathematical problems. While we had to be extremely careful that numbers did not become the primary focus of our interactions, we believed that we might be able to use Henry's arithmetical interest as a temptation to enhance his desire for Experience Sharing.

We also noticed that Henry loved movement related activities. We believed that simple activities involving repetitive running, falling, banging and similar kinds of gross motor activity would be extremely

Program Tip

There is a danger of introducing toys and object oriented games too quickly as a means of enjoyment. They may take the place of attending to people. Remember, the same object can have a different effect on different children. While we don't want to interfere with the child's development of solo play with objects, we do want to clearly distinguish between periods of self-play and social interaction. Therefore, during the first three levels of intervention, we purposefully keep social and solo play activities and objects separate and distinct.

attractive to him. Although not highly impaired, Henry had some motor insecurity. We were careful to construct activities that did not require too great a gross motor challenge. Given his early developmental level, activities needed to be simple, involving only a few steps or variations.

There are no 'absolute temptations' in our work—activities or objects that all children with Autism will relate to in the same way. Each object or activity can have a vastly different impact on different children. For one child, a ball is a temptation for emotional coordination; it has meaning only if the child finds someone with whom to play catch. For another child, it directly competes with his ability to attend to his partners. He might enjoy mouthing it, or throwing it against the wall and catching it himself. For most children, we are able to find objects that have a relationship "binding" function, ones that enhance their Experience Sharing rather than competing with it. In the beginning, we rely on large bean-bag chairs for many purposes, because of their amoeba-like shape. String, rope, balls, tunnels and drums have similar binding functions when used in carefully structured relational activities.

Parent Participation

As part of our preparation for treatment, parents are taught the basic principles and goals of our program. They attend several education sessions with a program therapist. We make sure parents understand the nature of their child's disorder and appreciate the profound implications of their impairment in Experience Sharing.

Henry's parents—Jim and Rita—watched videotaped vignettes and learned to distinguish between Instrumental and Experience Sharing interactions. They were taught to recognize the difference between a true coordinated encounter, where both parties share in co-regulating their actions to remain coordinated and what we refer to as "pseudo-coordination", where the adult or more proficient child does all of the work of maintaining coordination. Through reviewing videotapes of their own interactions with Henry, they observed the degree to which their actions created a brief illusion that they were involved in a reciprocal interaction. In reality, they were doing all the work of Emotional Coordination by constantly reacting to Henry's actions.

After their initial training, parents are asked to select an appropriate setting in their home —free of distractions and competition for attention— to be used as the primary location for therapy. Together, we develop a daily schedule of at-home work. Initially, we ask parents to spend about 2 hours per day with their child. We were fortunate in that Henry attended a therapeutic school that was willing to provide an hour per day of additional work, so we developed a plan for the school as well. With these steps accomplished, we were ready to move to the treatment stage of RDI.

Preparing for Treatment

- Comprehensive evaluation of the "whole" child.
- Pinpoint level of Experience Sharing development.
- Set specific short-term objectives.
- Analyze potential obstacles and temptations.
- Educate parents and other adult partners.
- Prepare the setting.
- Set up a schedule for practice.

Program Tip

One of the hardest parts of training parents and professionals in our program is helping them distinguish between "interaction" and Experience Sharing. Many high functioning children with Autism and Aspergers Syndrome are socially interactive even before we see them. They play board games and even follow polite rules like greeting people and shaking hands. Unfortunately this "rule following" ability may actually become an impediment for Experience Sharing. Be sure to spend enough time learning to understand and see the difference!

Principles of Treatment

$\mathcal{T}$he first treatment step for Jim and Rita was practicing how to remain firmly in charge, while acting in a manner that would heighten Henry's excitement and fun. They were taught to take control of Henry's social environment. They learned to set specific physical limits for Henry that entailed restricting his movements and keeping objects out of his immediate grasp.

Limiting Language

The most psychologically difficult change for Rita and Jim was limiting their use of language. Henry needed to learn that their faces were his primary information center—that responses to his needs, questions and requests were to be found in the non-verbal smiles, frowns, head nods and shrugs found on his parents' faces. Even when we used pictures and symbols to communicate, we made sure that parents held them up next to their faces. Rita and Jim used their language sparingly, as an enhancement to their non-verbal communication, or when no non-verbal means was possible. However, they only did this after they made sure that Henry had first visually referenced them. Similarly, Henry learned that he had to use facial gazing to get parental attention, before any of his communications were acted upon. When Henry verbalized, but did not first gaze at his parents, they were taught to respond by repeating a simple phrase "I can't see your words." That phrase became a cue to Henry that he needed to actively reference his partner first.

Because of Henry's limited language repertoire to begin with, Rita and Jim's willingness to create what seemed like an additional barrier to their son's language development took considerable courage and faith in their therapist, as it does for many parents first starting treatment with us. It helps parents to know that not once in the last 10 years, with over 300 children, has a child lost any language after beginning treatment with us. Still, it is frightening when these parents feel like they may be discouraging their child's attempts at communication, especially those who have been taught to reinforce any verbalization on their child's part, no matter how out of context or deviant the language may be.

The Freeze Game

A second means of teaching frequent Social Referencing, which we commonly use in combination with 'faces as information centers' is called the Freeze Game. The purpose of this game is to increase a child's desire to keep track of people's whereabouts. All through the day, Rita and Jim would sneak up on Henry when he was engaged in some activity or when he was just ignoring them. If they got close to Henry without his looking at them and reading their expression, they would take an action like tickle him, or put the baseball cap he liked to wear over his eyes, or even grab him and turn him upside down for a moment. We carefully chose activities that were neither too enjoyable as to reinforce ignoring his parents, nor so aversive that he would not immediately recover. At this beginning stage of treatment, our goal is increased wariness on Henry's part, not punishment or distress. If at any time during their approach, Henry fixed his eyes on the "sneaking" parent, he had to "freeze" in place and make a ridiculous facial expression and noise that always made Henry laugh. Then they retreated a certain distance, from where they might start to sneak up on him again. As Henry became more proficient at tracking his parents' whereabouts, we taught them to be sneakier. They hid behind objects like beanbags to heighten the excitement. They purposefully gave Henry very interesting solo activities and then attempted to sneak up on him while he was fully engaged.

Within two weeks of daily application of these methods, Henry was noticeably more compliant and was referencing his parents—as well as any other adult he came in contact with—on an almost continual basis. With these foundations in place, we were ready to begin working on specific Experience Sharing activities. We designed an initial series of Level 1 activities we believed would be exciting and understandable for Henry. Rita, Jim and Henry were asked to come to therapy once a week for one hour. They were also given specific homework activities that were to be practiced for at least 10 hours during the week.

Program Tip

Try the following to increase Social Referencing:

- Eliminate language responses whenever possible and require that the child reference facial expressions for information
- Develop wariness through using the Freeze Game.
- Amplify your facial expressions.
- Use verbalization to enhance your non-verbal communication, rather than replace it.

Typical children gain Level 1 skills as babies, before six months of age, at a time when they have limited motor and perceptual abilities. Children like Henry are often already fairly proficient at organized fine and gross motor movement and typically crave active interactions. In one of Henry's first activities, his parent or an adult would help him up onto one end of a sturdy table. Being on top of the table had the effect, as it does with many children with Autism, of increasing Henry's wariness, so he focused more on his parents' faces. Henry would carefully stand himself up on the table and walk over to the other end, into the waiting arms of one of his parents. Later we added a variation where Henry would jump onto a pile of beanbags, at his parent's signal. As Henry progressed, we developed a second activity, which was quickly chained to the first. Henry and an adult partner held hands, counted to a certain number (in each trial we would increase their counting exponentially e.g. 1,2,4, followed by 2, 4, 16, followed by 3, 9, 27 etc.), jumped off a low platform, then got ready to jump again. The complex counting increased the fun for Henry and actually increased his joyful referencing of his partner's face. Otherwise it would have been eliminated from the sequence. Gradually, over several weeks time, we developed a core group of six activities that became the basis for our work over the next several months. Henry and his parents practiced these activities at home for two hours each day, at four different 30-minute intervals, spaced out over the afternoon and evening on weekdays and throughout the day on weekends.

Within four weeks of initiating treatment, Henry was coming to the table by himself and communicating when he wanted to initiate the climbing activity. His social referencing was no longer a problem. While he was still trying to exert too much control in activities both by active insertion of numbers and through his passivity, he was truly excited to be with us. He was referencing and communicating, not because he had been taught to, but because he wanted to see what exciting things people might introduce to him. He was inviting others, not only with words but with his eyes and his actions, to participate in activities he had learned. Variations were accepted with pleasure. Henry was well on his way to completing Level 1 and learning the basic framework for being more of a true partner.

> **Within four weeks of initiating treatment, Henry was coming to the table by himself and communicating when he wanted to initiate the climbing activity.**

Program Tip
Use Language to Enhance Experience Sharing

We often use language embedded in singing, declaring, counting, chanting and self-narration ("We're falling!"), as binding elements. We make sure that language enhances but does not substitute for visually based Social Referencing.

An Overview of the Treatment Process

We typically begin regular weekly or twice weekly sessions with at least one parent and the child. (Out of town families work on a different schedule.) Parents are expected to set up a minimal stimulation environment in their homes and to spend between 10 and 15 hours per week practicing activities that are developed in the treatment room. College student assistants are often employed for part of the training. When we initially meet parents, we warn them that treatment should be viewed as having elements of a sprint and a marathon. Early intensive intervention is crucial. However, parents also have to pace their financial and emotional resources and conserve their energy for the long haul. Given our ambitious goals, the duration of treatment using RDI is measured in years. We've worked with a number of children from early childhood, through their teens and into adult years. To provide some perspective on the pace of treatment, recall the description in Chapter 2 of the 24 separate stages of Experience Sharing Development prior to teenage years. It is not uncommon for us to spend many months working on just one stage of a particular level.

Treatment progresses in a careful, step-by-step fashion, introducing skills as the child is ready for them. At a pre-determined point, the child begins to work in a small group with similarly trained peer partner(s), who are functioning at the same level of relationship development. Following this, we move to larger, more fluid groups, introducing more peers and more natural conditions.

Stages of Relational Development Intervention

- Conduct a Careful Assessment.

- Outline developmentally appropriate objectives.

- Educate parents and other adults.

- Prepare the treatment setting.

- Allocate sufficient time.

- Minimize obstacles to Experience Sharing.

- Construct simple, appropriate activities.

- Gradually shift the guidance function from therapist to parent.

- Gradually shift responsibility for regulation from adults to equal partnership with the child.

- Introduce carefully matched peers.

- Gradually add more levels of complexity to approximate "real world" settings and demands.

The Treatment Setting

People who conduct Social Skills training generally do so in natural settings, such as a classroom or shopping mall, believing that the skills will more likely be used if they are learned in the setting in which they are needed. If the goal is to teach instrumental behaviors and social scripts, such as waiting on line at a booth in a mall food court, or sitting quietly during circle time in the classroom, natural settings are clearly preferable.

However, natural social systems are far too complex and noisy to learn Social Referencing for people with Autism. We begin treatment in a highly controlled setting with minimal competition and distraction for a child's attention. Windows are well covered. There are no wall decorations. Objects are behind locked cabinets when not specifically needed for an activity. There is no permanent furniture, except for strongly reinforced beanbags. We ask parents to configure similar settings in their homes.

Program Tip
Creating a Simple Environment in Your Home

- Learning Social Referencing requires a highly controlled setting with minimal competition for attention.
- Begin working in a room where there are no wall decorations and windows are well covered.
- Keep objects hidden or better yet, out of the room, when not specifically needed for an activity.
- No permanent furniture except for strongly reinforced beanbags and a counter.
- Limit people in the room to only the child and one adult at a time.

Selecting Social Partners

A common belief among many therapists and doctors is that children with Autism will develop socially appropriate skills if they just get enough exposure to normal peers in regular settings. The problem with this theory is that it presupposes that the child with Autism can understand the nuances of the social system around him, that he can detect the verbal and nonverbal social communication that is occurring, and learn from it. Unfortunately, we know this is not the case.

Although children we work with often interact over the course of their day with typically developing peers, we choose not to use these peers as their practice partners. Normal peers are excellent role models, especially once the child has learned to be more sophisticated in co-regulation. However, at the beginning of treatment, when the child is still unskilled in Experience Sharing, normal peers take over too much of the responsibility for Emotional Coordination.

In our program, we use peers at similar levels of social relating, because we want our children to see themselves as capable of and responsible for co-regulation. Co-regulation will not emerge if one peer is far superior to the other. The more advanced child will wind up doing all of the regulation for coordination. Harvard Psychologist and friendship expert, Zick Rubin, makes this point cogently when talking about typical development when he says, "Unlike learning to play tennis, when one can usually do best by practicing with a more skilled and experienced player, when it comes to learning to interact with others the best method seems to be to practice with those who are as inexperienced as one-self. By practicing with peers who share one's own lack of social skill, toddlers are best able to learn to coordinate behaviors and to pull their own weight in social interactions."

We set up our groups from children who have been carefully matched for interest and tempo and who are functioning at similar stages of Experience Sharing development. Typically, by the end of Level 2 or the beginning of Level 3, we set up a small group of two (a dyad) or three (a triad) children who work together on a once or twice weekly basis. More intensive group work occurs with children who attend our therapeutic school during the year, or our summer day-camp experience.

Teaching Parents to be Guides

The famous Russian Psychologist Lev Vygotsky, described a parent's most important job as one of "Guided Participation", spotlighting what is meaningful and what is not for a child and then organizing the child's experience into meaningful patterns and relationships. In RDI we train parents in Guided Participation, with the objective that, through their careful tutelage, children will soon begin to socially reference on their own and gradually become co-creators of shared experience.

Parents are trained to take the lead in initiating and structuring encounters, while remaining sensitive to their child's responses. They are taught to guide the interaction and teach the child to be an observant apprentice. They learn to take control of the attention spotlight by removing any objects or stimuli that would compete with them and by amplifying their own emotional reactions and gestures. We teach them to adopt exaggerated facial expressions and voice tones that obtain the maximum attention and response from the child. Initially, language is

Six Phases of Guided Participation in RDI

1. **Education:** We explain the purpose and structure of the activity to the parent.

2. **Demonstration:** We model with the child how to conduct the activity successfully. Often parents will observe behind a one-way mirror, so the child is not distracted and the parent is not anxious. The therapist will often talk aloud, so the adult understands what the therapist is thinking while s/he acts. We also videotape the activity for later review.

3. **Coaching:** After explicitly modeling, the therapist gradually gives the parent more responsibility to manage the child and the activity. The therapist and parent work together with the child. The therapist provides a "scaffold" for the parents' work. After the activity, the therapist and parent discuss their perceptions and may review videotapes of home sessions.

4. **Independence:** When parents are ready they enact the activity independently, with the therapist behind the one-way mirror. At that point they are given their first homework assignment.

5. **Generation:** Parent and child begin to develop their own variations of the initial activity. Parents begin to feel pride in their ability to be creative and develop their own games. This is a critical step for parents in internalizing the process.

6. **Co-regulation:** Parents gradually teach the child to take on more of the co-regulation of the activity.

used sparingly as a means to enhance facial referencing. This simple interaction structure provides an opportunity for the child to focus on the relationship information her parents are highlighting for her.

Parents are taught to control activities and access to materials and to set up the structural framework for activities. They set clear limits regarding competing stimulation in the environment, as well as the amount of variation the child is permitted to introduce. Some parts of this shift in parent participation are more difficult for parents to adapt to than are others. For example, consider the jumping together exercise we often use. The parent and child count 1,2,3 together and then jump. Children new to the program initially count at their own rate, oblivious to coordinating their counting tempo with that of their partner. Parents almost always unconsciously change their own counting tempo so that it matches the rate of their child. It is a critical step in treatment when parents begin to require that the child match his counting to theirs.

Many children with Autism do not depend on parents and other adults to introduce excitement and novelty and to decrease their distress. Some children use interaction to enhance their excitement, but often without emotion sharing. A child might love to play board games, but would be just as happy playing with anyone, or even with a robot, as long as it follows the rules as he understands them.

Because some of our parents may not have received the emotional feedback that parents of typically developing children obtain, they may not have established an attuned relationship. In some cases these parents need to take control of the environment away from the child and actually increase the child's distress on a temporary basis, to create an opportunity to act as an agent of stress reduction for the child. As we teach parents to be guides in their child's development, we share with them the following information.

Getting Ready to Guide Experience Sharing

Set up a minimal stimulation environment in your home. Initially spend 15–20 hours per week practicing simple, structured activities based upon the evaluation. The ideal setting is a room large enough for gross motor movement, with no outside view, or wall decorations. Minimize visual and auditory noise. Remove objects like toys or games that can detract from attending to social information.

Structure the setting to provide safety and predictability. Gradually increase variety and novelty as the child learns to understand the framework. Don't rush! Reduce complexity when the child is confused.

Stay in charge of the activity and the setting. Guided participation is the key until the child is at the higher stages of Level 3. Gradually allow the child to add variability and novelty, as he demonstrates the ability for co-regulation and repair.

Spotlight important, relevant information, and especially moments of Emotional Coordination, so they stand out for the child. Use amplified and exaggerated non-verbal communication.

Keep it interesting. Make activities meaningful, but don't overly react to the child's immediate emotional response. Find activities that fit the child's tempo, attention span and that create excitement.

Teach the child to use faces as information centers. Make sure the child has enough reason to keep monitoring your emotional reactions. Make facial expressions key information for activities.

Gradually require more relational responsibility. Increase the demand for coordination and repair so the child learns to be a partner.

Gradually add more variables. Add complexity to the field, one element at a time, as the child becomes more competent.

Activities

The one factor that unites all RDI activities is their goal of producing exciting, enjoyable emotion. Because we are building motivation for Experience Sharing and not just teaching skills, all activities are strongly connected to a powerful, positive emotion. Autism is only partly a skills deficit; it is also a motivational deficit. Our children with Autism do not yet understand the payoff for doing the work involved in emotional coordination.

Alan Fogel points out that in typical development, Experience Sharing activities begin as highly ritualized interactions with simple, clear structures. Even so, they require many hours of frequent repetition until the young child internalizes the structure and sequence. Activities that begin with simple frameworks, which can be expanded and varied as the child is ready, make it easier for the child to process relationship information gradually, and allow parents to systematically vary one element at a time.

RDI activities also begin with simple rituals, where single elements of Experience Sharing can be clearly framed for the child. We work hard to create experiences with high degrees of emotional payoff for a particular child. Activities are selected so that excitement is directly linked to actions that occur in a coordinated manner. The pleasure and novelty the child experiences can only be duplicated through coordinating his actions and emotions with his partner.

> **Initial activities have clear physical boundaries, a simple sequence of events, differentiated roles, a clear beginning and an emotionally meaningful end point that culminates in Experience Sharing.**

Initial activities have clear physical boundaries, a simple sequence of events, differentiated roles, a clear beginning and an emotionally meaningful end point that culminates in Experience Sharing. For example, an activity often used during Level 1 begins with a child crawling through a long fabric tunnel. When the child is almost to the end of the tunnel, his parent's highly expressive face suddenly appears, with an excited voice shouting "You did it!" The parent may lift the child up and swing him for greater excitement. We add more or less to the activity depending upon the child's initial response. Since our goal is to gradually remove our prompts and scaffolding, we make the activity simple enough for the child to take over his/her role in a coordinated manner, without our help, fairly quickly.

Variety is systematically added to activities following the initial introduction of the play sequence. This helps children learn to function in fluid, constantly changing social systems, and prevents children from getting 'stuck' in routines and a fixed way of perceiving a sequence of events. If activities are rigidly performed for more than a brief period, the child with Autism often views them as parts of an unchanging, static system and will then resist attempts at variation. Because of this common trait among AS kids, we often begin treatment by developing new, unfamiliar activities, rather than relying on those the child already knows—especially activities the child already enjoys.

As previously mentioned, we prefer to use activities that begin as simple frameworks that can be gradually expanded by systematically adding small amounts of complexity. Children with Autism learn best from a "bottoms up" approach, whereby a complex task, like Social Referencing while acting, is learned in a stepwise manner. We choose activities that are expandable, and use them over several levels of intervention. Peek-a-boo evolves into Hide-and-Seek. Falling Together becomes Running and Jumping in a synchronized manner. You Bang, then I Bang turns into Banging Fast then Banging Slow and eventually into more improvised coordinated sequences integrating fluid changes of timing and rhythm. Our focus is constantly on relationship competence and not on learning new roles and rules. We purposely keep activities simple, so there is no question within the child that the excitement and novelty he feels is derived from the shared actions with his partner, and not on a new toy or game.

Each stage of treatment introduces activities that are appropriate to the work at hand. At Level 1 we focus on Emotional Attunement and begin with the therapist teaching the parent and child to enact activities with very simple rules and high emotional payoff, requiring the child to do little, if any, co-regulation. Activities focus the child's attention on facial expressions. Parents are taught to frame their actions for emotion sharing and soothing. They learn to control and manage the interactional field, carefully regulating novelty and variety.

As we move into Level 2, many of the simple Level 1 interactions are combined into complex chains. For example, a child may emerge from the tunnel, greet his parent with a big smile and hug and then move with the parent to sit side-by-side at a table and stack three blocks. As treatment progresses at Level 2, activities that frame different aspects of

Program Tip

It is essential that the activity chosen lie within the child and parent's physical capacity to perform and practice together at home. For example, throwing a ball back and forth may be too difficult for a child with very poor motor coordination, but he may be able to master the skill with a balloon. Running and jumping may be great for a child but impossible for his eight-month pregnant mother. Similarly, rules should be simple enough for a child that, following an initial introductory period, his focus is not directed on learning to play, but on referencing the actions and expressions of his partner.

Guidelines for Constructing Experience Sharing Activities

- Decide upon the purpose of the activity.

- Decide whether you really need a new activity. Try to get the most out of very few activities to keep the focus on relationship development.

- Keep the activity as simple as possible. Make sure the different elements of emotional coordination and Experience Sharing can be clearly framed for the child; don't get lost in too much action and objects.

- Develop an enjoyable "climax" that is reached through emotional coordination.

- Carefully evaluate objects you plan to use, to ensure they do not take too much attention away from emotion sharing with the social partner.

- Find objects that have a relationship "binding" function, where the object serves to enhance Experience Sharing, rather than competing with it and becoming the object of attention. We use large beanbag chairs for many purposes. String, rope, balls, tunnels and drums are also good.

- Use visual elements like masking tape, carpet squares and beanbag chairs to delineate physical boundaries, perimeters, the sequence of an activity, role positions and starting and finishing points.

- Use language as a relationship-binding element in an activity—singing, declaring, counting, chanting and self-narration ("We're running!").

- Limit language when it distracts from focusing on facial expressions, or where incessant talking interferes with focusing on the partner's emotional state.

- Evaluate the activity to make sure there is sufficient temptation for the child—that he will want to do it.

- Modify elements based upon the child's response—complexity, motor ability, interest, etc.

- Determine the degree of co-regulation activities to be built into the activity.

- Develop options for adding complexity, variety, and fluidity (normalizing the task) in a gradual, systematic manner.

emotional coordination are used: appearing-disappearing, moving closer-farther, or slower-faster. We also add ready-set-go or 1-2-3-go to start activities. Gross motor, movement related activities are commonly found in Level 2, activities like holding hands while running together, pushing and pulling, falling and jumping together. Simple games are introduced that require a pairing of role actions for coordination. Some involve parallel efforts: lifting and carrying an object together, while others involve complementary roles, one child choosing a block—the Giver—and handing it to another child who places it where he wants—the Builder. We introduce many activities that require facial referencing for timing and proper role actions, with language used to enhance and spotlight social referencing, "Watch my face—pull!"

After Level 3, sharing perceptions, internal experiences, imagination and ideas becomes the focal point of our activities. Role-playing, imaginative games, and conversations eventually become a crucial part of the treatment process. Activities involving identity, teamwork, family and group membership and aspects of friendship as enduring constructs are introduced.

Respecting the Uniqueness of Autism

Children with Autism learn Experience Sharing at a much later age, without the limited motor and visual limitations of the typical infant, but with their own set of handicaps and obstacles. Most importantly, they lack the motivation that typical young children possess. The children we begin treating—especially at a relatively older age—have no interest whatsoever in the games that captivate infants for hours. They also present with their own unique obstacles to coordinated encounters—obstacles that may have been reinforced over several years. Therefore, treatment must deviate in some respects from the typical course of development and address these differences and obstacles. Most children with Autism require a high degree of stimulation, active participation and some motor involvement.

Gary Mesibov and his co-workers at Project TEACCH have written extensively about the benefit of amplifying visual stucture when teaching people with Autism. Clear visual structure allows people with Autism to function independently; it alleviates constant prompting and cueing. In RDI, we use various visual means such as masking tape, carpet squares and beanbag chairs to delineate physical boundaries, perimeters, the sequence of an activity, role positions and starting and finishing points. For example masking tape is placed along a line indicating where the two partners are to return for their next round of running and jumping. Similarly two lines of tape running down the room aid children who are learning to run together to stay on course while they practice attention shifting and Social Referencing. Carpet squares indicate where two partners should be seated to start a game of "crashing cars." Beanbag chairs are used as a barrier for a mother to hide behind, to pop up at unexpected intervals in order to maintain, or increase the wariness of her child. Or, the barrier may be used to help the child use visual observation of his mother's face for comfort, rather than running over and clinging to her when distressed.

Taking it out of the Lab

Generalization, the desire and ability to use relational skills outside of treatment settings, is a critical step, akin to taking a product from the lab and "field testing" it. In our model, it involves gradually expanding the complexity of the relational field, by having the child work with different partners, increasing numbers of people, adding peers, increasing flexibility and teaching the child to be a co-creator of new activities. We gradually add more objects as competition for attention and remove the artificial boundaries and structures. We decrease the external structural elements, such as physical boundaries and auditory and visual cues that were needed to maintain coordination at earlier stages.

Skills are taught in a gradually more complex social field. We start teaching the child under the guidance of one parent. Then the child may work with a second parent, or adult family member, or older sibling. Similarly, we expand the non-social environment in which coordinated interactions take place. We begin in a highly controlled setting with few objects to distract the child from his partner. Gradually, as Functions and Means develop and especially as the focus of interaction shifts to a more perceptual and internal basis, activities move to more natural settings with more potential distracters as we seek to simulate the real-world environments in which these children must function.

Program Tip
How to Work on Generalization
- Increase the complexity of the activity.

- Have the child work with more and different partners.

- Increase the need for the child's co-regulation for coordination by reducing external structural scaffolding, like physical boundaries, auditory and visual cues.

- Practice breakdown and repair of coordination as a natural, frequent occurrence.

- Gradually minimize and eventually eliminate adult mediation of any kind.

- Gradually add more competition for attention, like favorite objects that involve solo play.

- Move activities to many different settings.

- Replace adults and more competent children with carefully matched peers.

Laying the Foundation for Relational Development

Level One

$\mathscr{D}$espite their differing ages and abilities, the vast majority of children with Autism, Aspergers and PDD-NOS whom we evaluate are missing some critical Level 1 abilities. It is tempting to skip this stage, especially with an older child who has language, intellectual ability and enough social knowledge to play games and take turns. However, we have found this to be a grave error. Level 1 is the foundation upon which all further work depends. It establishes the primacy of parents as the emotion and information reference center of the child's world and introduces social referencing—an ability that is critical to a child's further relationship development. Regardless of age, every child must become a

---

Level 1 Stages and Treatment Objectives

Stage 01: Emotional Attunement

- Face-to face emotion sharing with adults is the center of the child's attention.

- The child is comforted by a glance or soothing words from adults.

- The child is easily affected by adult facial expressions and voice tone.

Stage 02: Social Referencing

- The child observes adults, for approval, safety and security (refueling).

- The child orients to people entering his proximity and makes sure they are familiar or safe prior to shifting attention away (e.g. demonstrating wariness).

Stage 03: Excitement Sharing

- The child derives his primary excitement from parent's introduction of novel stimulation.

- The child responds easily and happily to adult cues to shift attention to an exciting action. She communicates positively for adults to provide more novelty and excitement.

Stage 04: Simple Games

- The child understands and enjoys the structure of simple games.

- The child shares the anticipation of enjoyable outcomes, through face-to-face smiles and laughter at appropriate times prior to the activity climax.

- The child enacts simple role actions at designated times under adult guidance.

---

novice to the patient guidance of his or her parents and learn to reference them and other people for information, assurance and guidance.

Case Study

> While only the first in a series of tasks, this initial unstructured 10-minute period almost always reveals whether or not a child possesses Level 1 skills.

Patrick was diagnosed with Autism at 42 months of age. He seemed to develop appropriately for the first year and a half, when significant behavioral differences appeared. At his special needs pre-school Patrick spent his time fervently sifting sand, vehemently refusing anyone trying to interrupt him. He did not interact with other children. Patrick had frequent tantrums when he did not get what he wanted. At four years old, he was not toilet trained and periodically smeared feces.

Our first Relational Development Observation (RDO) was conducted about 12 months after his diagnosis. Prior to beginning the RDO, we told his mother, Marybeth, that for the first segment, she should do whatever she thought would help Patrick relax and have as much fun as possible. While only the first in a series of tasks, this initial unstructured 10-minute period almost always reveals whether or not a child possesses Level 1 skills.

During our discussion, Patrick walked around the waiting room, oblivious to everyone. He looked up briefly when the examiner greeted him, but showed little interest. He appeared to have no anxiety about being in a strange setting and calmly allowed Marybeth to take his hand as they walked toward the open door of the playroom.

The walls of our evaluation room are bare and no toys are visible in the 12X14, monochromatic area. The room contains eight large beanbag chairs, a small plastic table, two small chairs and two carpet-squares set several feet apart on the floor. A large one-way mirror dominates one wall. Another wall has white cabinets, with a four-foot-high Formica countertop set in the middle. We videotape the RDO from behind the one-way mirror.

Once inside the room, without a glance at Marybeth, Patrick immediately disengaged his hand and wandered around aimlessly, randomly touching cabinets and walls while softly chanting to himself. He face was emotionless as he explored. For the first several minutes, he did not look at Marybeth at all.

Marybeth tried to engage him in a simple game. Despite his mild protest, she firmly took him in her lap, turned him around to face her, took his hands and started a game of moving back-and-forth while singing "Row, Row, Row your Boat." Marybeth wisely ignored Patrick's meaningless words spoken to the air, as she started the game. Patrick seemed to get little, if any, enjoyment from his mother's attempt to start the game. As soon as she finished the first round, with no warning or signal, he abruptly left her grasp, crawled away and chaotically flopped around on the beanbags, appearing more satisfied. Again, he did not observe Marybeth as he got up from the beanbags and continued to wander around. She tried to engage him in another game—playfully covering him with the beanbags. Patrick laughed for a brief moment, but then walked away screeching. When Patrick got close enough, Marybeth grabbed him and covered him again. Patrick smiled for a split second, but then just as abruptly walked away making noises to himself, without a single signal or glance at his mother's face.

Marybeth, with amazing perseverance and patience, made yet another effort to engage Patrick. She repeatedly called his name, with little response. Finally, she got his attention and visually indicated that he should sit on one of the carpet squares. When he finally complied, she took his hands and began rocking his legs back and forth. Patrick laughed initially, but then immediately wrestled free of her grasp. She grabbed him again playfully, rocked him and continued singing "Row Row, Row." Patrick did not focus attention on the game or on Marybeth's excited smile. When she finished the round he again returned to wandering, without a single glance at her.

When the examiner entered the playroom to instruct Marybeth on the second task, Patrick made brief physical contact with his mom, ostensibly for comfort, but then promptly walked away. Marybeth was given a box of toys, as well as a clipboard with forms to fill out. She was instructed to set several behavioral limits: to not allow Patrick to handle the pen and papers, to keep him from opening drawers or cabinets, and to prevent him from leaving the room. Additionally, she was told that Patrick was not yet allowed to handle the toy box, which is transparent, but closed with a plastic lid. Marybeth was instructed to work on the forms and ignore Patrick, unless he initiated any communication. If this occurred, she was to respond positively but briefly and then return to her work. During this period we observe how children respond to limits placed on them, the extent of their social referencing and how much responsibility they take for initiating and maintaining Emotional Coordination with their partner.

> It was interesting to see that when Marybeth was no longer gazing at him, Patrick looked over in her direction a bit more while he wandered. But, he still made no attempts to communicate.

Marybeth sat quietly on the floor in one corner of the room, working on her form. The toy box was next to her, in full sight. Patrick glanced over briefly and then ignored his mother and the box. After a minute, he came over, played with Marybeth's hair for a second or two and then walked away. It was interesting to see that when Marybeth was no longer gazing at him, Patrick looked over in her direction a bit more while he wandered. But, he still made no attempts to communicate.

The examiner entered and explained the third Level 1 segment to Marybeth. In this activity the child sits across from the parent, who uses the toy box to elicit as much excitement and interest as possible from the child. For young children the props include hats, masks, a stacking game, bubbles, balloons, wind up toys and objects we know hold special interest for the child we are testing—like the toy dinosaurs we placed there for Patrick. Marybeth was instructed to show Patrick the toys, but maintain control over their use.

Marybeth took out the bubbles and tried to get Patrick's attention by calling his name as she blew bubbles. After several seconds he came over briefly but then walked away, apparently not interested. Marybeth tried a second appeal with the bubbles, with the same result. We could clearly see that Patrick was not accepting his mother's attempts to guide and frame their interaction. Instead, he preferred to create and control his own disorganized activity.

Patrick went over to the small plastic table, dragged it to the counter and used it as a ladder to climb on to the counter-top—a good sign of intelligence. Marybeth got Patrick down from the counter and in a caring, but physical manner took him over to show him the bubbles. When she blew bubbles in his face he laughed, but then immediately went back to climb on the counter again. Once there he laughed again, without glancing at Marybeth. She preempted him and put the table away so he could not use it for climbing. She tickled him and tried to engage him with a toy dinosaur saying, "Who's that? He's going to bite you." Patrick again ran away as soon as he could. Marybeth kept trying to entice him to no avail. With infinite patience, she took out a wind up toy and started it. Patrick came over, looked at the toy sideways for several seconds, but never once glanced at this mother.

Marybeth's next task was to try to engage Patrick in a variation of peek-a-boo. The parent is given a small sheet or blanket and asked to play 10 rounds of hiding and revealing. Following this, they are instructed to make a barrier of the beanbags, hide behind them and then attempt to get the child to play peek-a-boo by leaning back and forth and enticing the child to approach and play.

Marybeth got a blanket and tried to engage Patrick in the task. She got him to sit in the chair and he complied. She covered her face and repeated, "Where's mommy?" Patrick pulled the blanket off her face, but did not share her smile and showed no recognition of the game. Marybeth put the blanket on Patrick's head and when she uncovered it, he laughed with her for the first time. Encouraged, she covered him again, pulled off the blanket and he laughed again. Now she covered him, moved a few feet away and hid herself under beanbags. Patrick remained covered by the blanket. She cued him with "Where's mommy?" Patrick, hearing his mother's voice, removed the blanket and turned his head in her direction, but made no attempt to find her. Instead, initiating his own activity, he picked up the blanket and covered his head. He kept his head covered for a while, apparently not realizing why his version of the game was less enjoyable than when Marybeth was guiding it. Finally, he took the blanket from his head and sat puzzled. Marybeth cued Patrick to

> We could clearly see that Patrick was not accepting his mother's attempts to guide and frame their interaction. Instead, he preferred to create and control his own disorganized activity.

find her again, but with no result. He did not perceive the similarity between her hiding behind the beanbags and the peek-a-boo game with a cloth that he and Marybeth had just finished playing. Marybeth came out from behind the beanbags and tried to teach him the game by hiding in full sight, but Patrick ignored her, despite repeated attempts to get his attention.

For the final task of Level 1, Marybeth was instructed to follow Patrick and act like his shadow, imitating everything he did. If physical shadowing seems to disturb a child, the parent can remain seated and enact a "play-by-play" narration of his actions using very simple language. Patrick was allowed access to the materials in the prop box. Patrick said, "Chitty Chitty Bang Bang." Marybeth imitated him and Patrick laughed briefly, without glancing in her direction. He ignored her other efforts at imitation and continued to wander aimlessly around the room, with no organization or notable structure to his actions. He seemed oblivious to his mother's shadowing and did not turn once to acknowledge her.

Patrick returned once again to the table Marybeth had put away and glanced to her, signaling that he wanted her to give him the table—a clearly instrumental communication. Even though she indicated "no", he tried to take the table down anyway. When she stopped him, Patrick, for the first time, appeared somewhat distressed and began saying, "Go bye bye" in an increasingly more vehement tone. Marybeth picked him up and tried to comfort him. Patrick tolerated this for a short time, but never seemed soothed by her touch, and never referenced her face. He quickly left her grasp, walked off and ignored her attempts to communicate with him.

Formulation and Treatment Plan

Patrick did not demonstrate any basic Level 1 skills on a reliable basis. As part of our evaluation, we confirmed with Marybeth that the behaviors we observed in our playroom were representative of Patrick's typical functioning. Patrick showed a basic attachment and affection for his parents. However, he did little emotion sharing or social referencing. Furthermore, he did not utilize his parents as primary providers of meaning, excitement and soothing, nor did he accept parental attempts to direct his attention. Instead he focused on whatever struck him as meaningful at the moment. Because Patrick did not easily attend to his mother, it was difficult for her to create frames to teach him in a slow, careful manner. Patrick's use of language—repeating unrelated phrases—was clearly an obstacle to their interaction, as was his disorganized activity. Patrick clearly insisted upon creating chaotic systems, with little structure other than what his momentary impulses suggested. He passively, and sometimes actively, resisted his mother's attempts to guide his participation in new activities.

We designed a treatment program for Patrick and began working with him and his parents on a regular basis. The following section summarizes the first six months of our work.

Emotional Attunement and Social Referencing

The initial phase of Patrick's intervention plan involved establishing core relational foundations, by cementing the role of adults in his development. Patrick had to learn to accept his parents as emotional soothers, through physical contact and across space. Along with soothing, we needed to teach him to utilize adults as reference points for excitement and to understand how to organize his perceptions in the environment. We wanted him to frequently orient to his parents without being cued. Their facial expressions, voice tones and gestures would become the central source of information for Patrick to learn about his world. Patrick's objectives for this initial work are listed in the following table.

Patrick's Level 1 Treatment Plan—Part A

- Patrick and his mother will form an emotionally connected system.
- They will learn to become highly aware of and sensitive to each other's emotional expressions.
- Face-to face emotion sharing with adults will become the center of Patrick's attention.
- Patrick will reference adult facial expressions to obtain soothing when he is distressed.
- Patrick will conduct ongoing, frequent observation of adults in his environment for approval, safety and security (refueling).
- Patrick will conduct frequent visual scans of adult actions and reactions, to maintain a "fix" on important adults.
- Patrick will visually orient to new people in his social field and make sure they are familiar and safe prior to shifting attention away (e.g. demonstrating wariness).
- Patrick will actively reference adults prior to or just after engaging in behavior, in order to obtain approval or determine the reaction of the adult.
- Patrick will actively reference adults when uncertain or anxious (for clarification).

Our work with Patrick and his parents began in much the same way as with Henry and his parents. They were trained to make their faces into Patrick's primary information center and taught how to play The Freeze Game with him. Our first playroom task with Patrick and Marybeth was to further strengthen his emotional attunement and social referencing. In Level 1, it is critical to establish visual emotion sharing as the primary channel of communication. Afterward, we can supplement this with the auditory channel. Joyful noises can be very potent, but the visual component is critical to further development.

As soon as Patrick entered the playroom he was directed to crawl through a 6-foot fabric tunnel. Marybeth moved to the far side of the tunnel and called to him. Initially, when Patrick saw his mother's face at the far side he settled in and remained in the tunnel—trying to control the interaction by creating his own pace. However, when Marybeth was no longer visible at the end of the tunnel, Patrick immediately crawled through to find her. Marybeth was Patrick's secure base of attachment. However, Patrick assumed that she was always available and that he did not have to orient to her to ensure her presence. Once she was out of sight, and he found himself in a strange location, his need to reference her increased dramatically.

When Patrick emerged from the tunnel, Marybeth quickly led him to a sturdy table. He was placed on the table and Marybeth, at the far end, held out her hands to him. Arnold and Eileen Miller have observed that movement on elevated structures can help children with Autism sharpen their focus because they become more wary of their environment. In fact, the first time we observed Patrick actively fix his gaze on Marybeth with both apprehension and anticipation, was when he approached her on the table. When Patrick reached Marybeth, she joyfully took him in her arms and placed him, facing her, on her lap.

> ... movement on elevated structures can help children with Autism sharpen their focus because they become more wary of their environment.

With Patrick feeling some heightened arousal, this was a perfect time for Marybeth to help him learn the value of her as a stress reducer or "soother." Often children with Autism obtain soothing through touch and physical contact, rather than facial emotion-sharing. Our parents and children often spend many hours during the beginning stages of treatment developing this emotionally soothing relationship. If the child actively resists soothing, we sometimes heighten his anxiety by playing a game called "Save Me," in which a therapist suddenly snatches the child from a parent's grasp and pretends to hide him. The parent then quickly pulls the child away and "rescues" him. As the game progresses, the child learns to prevent being snatched by clinging tightly to the parent and eventually by holding on and gazing at his parent. By the close of Level 1, the child should be able to use emotion sharing to obtain comfort from his parent, even when several feet away. To help Patrick learn to use and accept soothing from his mother, Marybeth hugged Patrick very tightly and sang "Ma Ma Ma Ma Ma" to the tune of Row Your Boat. Patrick felt the soothing vibrations as Marybeth sang and appeared visibly relaxed.

Excitement and Simple Games

Once parents have taken control of framing the shared environment and are perceived as having a soothing function, the focus shifts to increasing their value as the primary providers of excitement and novelty. We choose simple, yet exciting movement activities. Children are tossed into the air and onto a pile of beanbags, or they may jump and fall in unison with a parent.

The second part of Level 1 treatment begins with the introduction of adult frameworks for activities. This includes the child's accepting physical and behavioral limits, proper body orientation and the sequence of actions within specific activities. The major objectives for Patrick's work on Stages 3 and 4 are listed in the following table.

Patrick's Level 1 Treatment Plan—Part B

- Patrick will derive his primary excitement from adult introduction of novelty.

- Patrick will attend to adults for introduction of novelty, excitement and new learning.

- Patrick will respond easily to adult cues to shift attention to an exciting action.

- Patrick will communicate positively for adults to provide more novelty and excitement.

- Patrick will demonstrate understanding and enjoyment of simple games.

- Patrick will learn to take several simple roles, in a short activity sequence culminating in shared excitement and laughter.

- Patrick will learn to anticipate the exciting climax of games.

- Patrick will frequently communicate for the initiation and continuation of simple games.

- Patrick will pay attention as adults model, or demonstrate simple interesting activities.

- Patrick will enact simple role actions at designated times under adult guidance.

Patrick, like many of our patients, was a child who enjoyed and seemed to need to be physically active. He had a relatively short attention span and quickly moved from thing to thing. He participated in an interaction for only brief periods and before he could learn the structure of the activity, he would withdraw and set up a static framework—one that excluded other people, except possibly as an audience. He resisted attempts by Marybeth to create organization for him.

Over several sessions, we developed a ritualized sequence of activities for Patrick and Marybeth that involved a good deal of organized movement and varied levels of excitement. We helped Marybeth understand that rather than holding Patrick to teach him, it would be more effective to work with his preference for gross motor activity. Marybeth was taught to direct him from place to place and require a brief action of her choosing at each location, before moving to the next activity "center."

In planning these later Level 1 activities, we keep in mind the following principles and sequencing:

- The activity is a simple exciting social interaction.

- The activity is ritualized and occurs in a specific sequence that is repeated many times.

- The activity does not require the child to take any active role or remember any specific sequence.

- Gradually, parental actions become predictable to the child and the child can anticipate the sequence of adult action and obtain pleasure through anticipation, even prior to the most exciting moments of the interaction.

- Success does not require observation of the parent once the interaction has begun.

- Gradually observation occurs to learn and anticipate the sequence of parental actions.

- The adult takes all responsibility for regulation of actions.

- The adult acts to coordinate emotional states; to maintain the child's excitement and minimize discomfort.

Marybeth—under the therapist's direction—was in charge of Patrick's movement. She took his hand and led him from location to location at a very rapid and exciting pace. The fast pace was chosen partly to provide enough stimulation for Patrick to practice the ritual over and over, but also so that he would have no time to protest or develop a static framework around any one activity. An initial series of tasks was repeated rapidly, in the same manner a number of times, until Patrick could participate in the entire ritual without hesitation. We were then able to gradually add small amounts of variation, so that he would learn to be excited by novelty, but also to prevent his forming a Static system around the entire ritual and demand that it progress in a highly specific manner.

As Level 1 progresses, the child should be able to communicate in a simple manner for initiation and continuation of the activity, even attempt to repair the interaction when the adult hesitates, or does not initially respond to the child's signal. The child also learns simple self-regulation like seating himself on the beanbag or carpet square at the right time.

As rapidly as possible, parents frame the importance of their faces and voices in every activity they introduce. This cues the child to reference the parent's face to anticipate what will happen next: a surprise, a good thing, a scary thing? Patrick quickly learned that the timing of events could be predicted by watching Maybeth's facial expressions and noticing when her frown turned into a smile.

After two weeks of practicing their ritual, Patrick entered the playroom and began the first activity without any prompts. Not only had he started to visually reference for timing, smiles and shared laughter, he also began to communicate in simple ways for initiation and maintenance. Over the next several weeks we added new elements and varied others. The table on the following page describes the modified ritual Patrick was doing after six weeks of therapy.

> **As rapidly as possible, parents frame the importance of their faces and voices in every activity they introduce. This cues the child to reference the parent's face to anticipate what will happen next: a surprise, a good thing, a scary thing?**

- Patrick crawls through the tunnel to Marybeth's waiting arms; she gives him a big hug.

- He walks across the table and falls into Marybeth's arms.

- She holds him and sings "Ma Ma."

- Patrick sits on a carpet square and erases a whiteboard after Marybeth draws lines. He also gets to draw a line or two that she erases.

- The therapist and Marybeth swing Patrick on the beanbag, changing the timing of the count each time.

- They play Kaboom (adapted from the TEACCH manual) and add the new game of Motor Boat.

- Patrick and his mother begin a game of "1,2,3, fall". Marybeth changes this after a few times and holds Patrick and they fall together. Once they fall, she lies there with Patrick for a few moments, tickling him.

- They move to the table and use a five-foot cardboard tunnel and toy cars. Marybeth pulls Patrick's hand to her face and say "Vroom Vroom Beep Beep". Then she teaches him to put the car in the tube and watch it shoot out the other side.

- Marybeth shows Patrick the car, says "blue jeep" and rolls it to him. He takes the car and puts it in the tube.

- Patrick leaves the table and goes through the tunnel to start the ritual again.

After eight more weeks of practice, Patrick looked for his mother across the room, without any prompting and oriented his body to play with her. We asked Marybeth to hide behind the beanbags while Patrick went through the tunnel and when he emerged he actively searched and found her. Patrick and Marybeth had developed a repertoire of pleasurable interactions that culminated in mutual laughter. He was learning that there was a type of choreography to the interactional activities that he and his mother enjoyed together. He was able to remember these activities as chains of "me-you" actions in which his mother's actions fit with his, helping them complete the activity together. Patrick began to anticipate what should happen next in a sequence and enjoy the excitement of this anticipation. Because of his new capacity for organized memory, we could begin adding small variations to the sequence and increase his enjoyment.

At this point, we began a more intensive program with Patrick. Work with his parents was supplemented by an additional 15 hours per week of intervention in our offices, using trained college students as aides, supervised by program therapists. Within three weeks of beginning the program, Patrick had completed three of the four stages of Level 1 and was well on his way to mastering stage 4. He had generalized his excitement for emotion sharing to all of the adults in his environment, and acted as if he could not get enough of the social enjoyment that was provided. He worked for no reinforcers whatsoever, except emotion sharing. He had become a completely different child than the detached Patrick that had walked into our offices four months before.

About six months after starting treatment, Marybeth sat in our office reviewing the videotapes of his initial evaluation. Her eyes welled up with tears and she began sobbing and laughing at the same time as she related her feelings:

> *"It's the way he holds me now; I don't have to keep him from pulling away. I can feel, for the first time, that he doesn't want to let me go. It's the way he looks at me. He really looks at me now. For the first time it really feels like love."*

Sample Level 1 Activities

Me-You: Some children start with little or no referencing of self or others, even when in close proximity. With these children we start by positioning ourselves at the child's eye level, taking his hands in our hands, and repetitively moving his hands from our face back to his face, while saying something like "Dr. Steve, Austin, Dr. Steve, Austin." While we are placing his hands on his face, we turn the child's face towards ours with his own hands, giving him the feel of orienting himself to our face. As we progress we will take an object like a hat and place it back and forth from the child's head to the adult's head saying "Hat on Bobby's head. Hat on Dr. Steve's head."

Faces as Information Centers: Permission and other critical information is provided only via the parent's face. Children learn to reference parent facial expressions to determine what will happen next in an activity. "I can't see your words" may be a helpful verbal cue to the child when he is not referencing.

The Freeze Game: Sneak up on the child while he is not referencing you, and grab him if he doesn't fix his eyes on you. If his eyes fix on your face before you reach him, they can "freeze" you in place and you have to go back beyond a certain perimeter (which you can demarcate with masking tape). Have the child perform an interesting activity and then slowly sneak up on him (can use beanbags as camouflage to heighten excitement.) Roles can be reversed if the child understands and can abide by the framework.

The Tunnel: The child is placed at one end of a six-foot long cloth tunnel and instructed to crawl through. The parent is waiting at the end of the tunnel and either puts his/her face inside the tunnel, so that the child is totally focused on the parent's face, or plays a form of peek-a-boo, hiding and emerging just when the child reaches the end of the tunnel.

Marbles Please: The child and adult each have a 20 ounce plastic cup. The child's cup is half-filled with small marbles. The adult starts the round by saying, "Marbles please", showing the child how to pour the marbles into the adult's cup. Partners take turns saying, "Marbles please" and passing the marbles from cup to cup. As the child proceeds the game can be played with several cups full of different objects placed upon a small table. Partners take turns requesting "Pennies please", "Checkers please" etc.

Becoming an Apprentice
Level Two

*H*aving mastered Level 1, children are ready to become competent apprentices. Parents are taught to gradually guide their child through the steps of simple role based activities. Children learn to enjoy synchronized activities, to coordinate their movements with parents and later to share in co-regulation. The following table briefly outlines the major treatment objectives for Level 2:

Level 2 Stages and Treatment Objectives

Stage 05: Frameworks

- The child enjoys learning the rules, roles and structure of activities requiring observation for role enactment (role timing).

- The child demonstrates pleasure when he successfully enacts his role under partner guidance.

Stage 06: Variations add the spice

- Partner introduction of variations becomes the highlight of activities.

- The child understands and appreciates activity frameworks, despite rapidly introduced variations.

- The child accepts cues to reverse, modify roles and change actions, when required by his partner.

Stage 07: Face-to-Face and Complementary Coordinated Role Sets

- The child participates as a partner in regulating activities requiring coordination of face-to-face role sets.

- The child co-regulates as a partner in regulating activities requiring coordination of complementary role sets.

Stage 08: Moving Together: Symmetrical Coordinated Role Sets

- The child successfully enacts activities requiring symmetrical role actions (e.g. running, falling together)

Case Study

Manuel was diagnosed with Autism at 23 months of age by a neurologist in his home city in Mexico. At the time of evaluation he had no language. He did not attend to other children, was fascinated with ceiling fans and loved to spin objects. The neurologist noted that Manuel had no social graces such as waving goodbye, making faces or playing simple games. He didn't point to indicate his needs. He threw significant tantrums at which time he would repeatedly bang his head.

At the time of our evaluation Manuel was 32 months old. His parents reported that he was affectionate and close to both of them and to his baby sister, who was five months old at the time. In his pre-school, Manuel followed most of the rules, but did not interact with the other children—even refusing to hold their hands when it was time to leave the room for recess. During free play he often sat and watched. While Manuel liked to be around his parents at all times, he showed indifference to other adults. He enjoyed playing a simple form of "chase" with his parents, but this was his only real game when we met him. Manual showed no evidence of pretend play. However, he displayed many signs of intelligence and seemed fascinated and quite adept at figuring out how things worked and putting them together.

Our Evaluation

Manuel and his mother, Consuela, walk into the playroom hand in hand and begin the free play activity part of the RDO. It immediately becomes clear that they have established the rudiments of a relational partnership. Manuel leads Consuela to explore but doesn't let go of her hand. He takes her hand to open the door and mildly protests when she gently refuses. She leads him to the stack of beanbags and excitedly pats them to indicate where she wants his area of interest, while making excited noises each time she pats. Immediately his face changes from distress to pleasure as he focuses his attention to her area of interest. Manuel takes Consuela's hand and returns to exploring the room. She lets him lead her again to the door which he tries to open and again she gently leads him away. She talks to him in one to three word sentences. This time he doesn't protest. She brings him back to the beanbags, softly chanting in a rhythmic tone. Manuel and Consuela sit side-by-side and he immediately visually references her without any cues. He raptly attends while Consuela slowly crawls her fingers closer to him in a typical infant game of "gotcha." He smiles when she finishes and then looks away, sitting comfortably next to her.

Consela excitedly tells Manuel to follow her and he laughs, makes animated noises and runs to her. Then he runs to the center of the room and laughs when she follows him. Without any formal announcement, they are starting their game of "chase." She tells him to run away, then follows and tickles him. He runs again—all the time glancing back at her—and she follows. She is clearly the center of his focus. Manuel runs clear across the room and looks to her and then they run to the center of the room together and laugh when they meet. He suddenly sits down in front of her, then gets up and runs off and looks back, initiating the game again. He goes to the beanbags, sits and smiles anticipating that she will come over. They sit facing each other; Consuela claps and starts a song. Manuel claps with her several times, all the while referencing her.

Conseula is clearly a natural expert at working with Manuel. She has achieved excellent progress with him, without the benefit of treatment. She knows enough to keep the relational field simple and understandable for Manuel. For example, at this point in the evaluation, Manuel has not uttered one word yet, but Consuela is not disturbed in the least by this. At this point—as she should be—she is much more attuned to teaching Manuel to maintain their Emotional Coordination, than in developing any specific behavior.

The evaluator, Rachelle, enters and Manuel appears comfortable with just a quick glance at mom nearby. When Rachelle walks out through the door he cries and walks to the door. Consuela calls his name and he immediately references her. Rachelle holds the door open and Manuel looks out into the hallway but doesn't leave. She closes the door and he approaches Consuela and tries to initiate the old game. As they are now in segment two of the RDO, she ignores him and starts filling out the form. He stops after two attempts and sits on a beanbag, waiting passively. After a moment, he goes over to Consuela, circles her and keeps looking at her, then sits down right next to her and gets comfortable. For the first time he verbalizes to her. Getting no response, he starts gently banging his head softly against the wall and then slaps the wall. He is no longer exploring on his own. Unlike Patrick, Manuel is a child with few obstacles to coordination. But he is quite passive. He has few relational memories, or means of initiation and repair.

Rachelle returns and brings in the toy box. Manuel immediately orients visually and approaches the box. He goes to open the box, but Consuela stops him gently. She looks in the box and chooses a toy for them. When she requests his attention he immediately references her. He reaches for the balloon she is blowing up. She blows it up and then releases it; he is avidly interested. Manuel quickly involves himself in the interaction, without mother cueing him, by running for the balloon and then bringing it back to her to blow up again. She blows it again and he raptly attends. He reaches for the balloon but she doesn't let him have it. She blows it up and then releases it again. He smiles, gets it, brings it back and puts it in her hand, looking at her face expectantly. Now he is smiling with anticipation. Manuel has rapidly learned to follow the consensual framework established by Consuela. He no longer grabs for the balloon but starts laughing as she blows it up. She allows him to hold it while the air goes out, then switches to a new balloon; he has no problem with the

> **...Manuel has not uttered one word yet, but Consuela is not disturbed in the least by this...she is much more attuned to teaching Manuel to maintain their Emotional Coordination, than in developing any specific behavior.**

change. He shifts his gaze from the old balloon to mom's face. Adding more variation, Consuela blows up the balloon and slowly lets the air out onto his face. Manuel smiles, but moves away. He approaches and she squirts him with air again. He smiles and moves away and then approaches again. Wisely, she returns to the prior game where he gets to hold the balloon while the air is coming out. He clearly prefers this game. After another try, she lets the air out in a way that makes a loud sound. He retrieves the balloon and looks at it with great curiosity as he hands it back to her. Unlike Patrick, Manuel knows that Consuela is the real source of his pleasure, not the balloon. The object is just an enhancement of their relationship activity.

They move into the Peek-a-boo variant. Consuela leads him to the center of the room. She gets a blanket and starts peek-a-boo, covering and uncovering her head. By the second trial, Manuel is smiling but also a bit anxious, so he hugs her. On the third trial Manuel looks on with curiosity and suddenly it is clear he has figured out the framework. He pulls the blanket off and says, "Ah, esta mama." Consuela covers Manuel and says "Donde esta Manuel?" He uncovers himself and hands her back the blanket. She covers herself again and the game progresses with glee. Consuela suddenly shifts the game and goes to hide behind the beanbags. She calls out to Manuel, "Donde esta mama?" and then pops out from behind the beanbags. Manuel sits passively—not understanding the game yet. Consuela does an excellent job of re-organizing Manuel—something that all parents are taught to do when they notice their child is confused. She brings him closer and returns to the prior game, which they play for another several rounds. With Manuel at a much closer distance, she hides again and this time he smiles and runs over and sits on the beanbags with his back to her. He still does not understand the game and is holding the blanket, waiting for her to do something he does understand. She goes back to covering her head. After a few trials Consuela once more hides behind the beanbags and pops out. Manuel is just beginning to understand the game. He is starting to smile and watch her pop out. But he doesn't approach. She crawls to him and he runs away to initiate the game of chase that he does know. Instead of chasing him she hides again. He still doesn't approach.

Next, we ask them to play rolling the ball back-and-forth. Consuela quickly seats Manuel on a carpet square and sits on her own square facing him, about five feet away. He begins to get up and she seats him. This time he waits patiently. Consuela softly rolls the ball to him and he throws it back to her with a big smile. While he cannot do the rolling part yet, this is a game that Manuel can understand! The ball accidentally moves away and without any cue, Manuel initiates a repair action. He goes and gets it and returns to his carpet square, smiles and throws the ball back. Consuela tells him to roll it, not throw. He throws it lower, but he is clearly having trouble with the motor skill of rolling and will need practice. (We would not work on the new motor skill of rolling at the same time we are working on learning the sequence or the role sets. Each piece must first be framed and mastered on its own, prior to being integrated.)

> Consuela does an excellent job of re-organizing Manuel—something that all parents are taught to do when they notice their child is confused. She brings him closer and returns to the prior game...

They move into another new game, Giver-Builder. Consuela moves their carpet squares close together. She takes a block from the box and hands it to Manuel, who takes it and puts it back. She hands him another block. He examines it, but doesn't realize yet that she wants him to build. She shows him stacking and stacks three blocks to model for him. Then she hands him one; he puts it on the ground. She hands him another and it goes on the ground. Finally he puts one block on top and starts to stack. He smiles broadly at his mother when he realizes he has figured it out. While he is building, Consuela is still the center of Manuel's attention whenever she requests it.

Consula's next task is to reverse roles. She asks him to hand the blocks over and points to her hand. He looks at her hand but then starts stacking his blocks. She holds out her hand again and he bangs the blocks, clearly confused and agitated. Again she points to her hand and tells him to give her one. Manuel spreads them out and then builds a tower with three blocks. Again Consuela asks him for one, but Manuel is unable to reverse roles and be the Giver. Later, in treatment, she will need to move him physically through the actions of being a giver by guiding his hand repeatedly to give the blocks to her.

The final task for these two is to try and enact a pretend Tea Party. There are three place settings, a tea set and a big bird doll that can be used if wished. Consuela seats Big Bird at his own setting. She gives Manuel cups to give to each of them. He does not understand the framework. She pours pretend water for each of them and pretends to drink. Manuel watches his mother pour him pretend water but he is confused by the pretense. He is more interested in the cups as objects to stack.

Formulation

Manuel is a child who has clearly met all of the Level I objectives. He visually referenced Consuela for soothing, excitement and to obtain meaning. He accepted his mother's framework and attended to the areas she communicated as meaningful. Consuela and Jim—Manuel's father—were clearly the center of Manuel's universe. While Manuel had almost no language at the time of his RDO, the frequency and type of visual referencing he displayed was a clear sign that he was ready to move on to Level 2. He had learned to play a rudimentary form of "Chase" with his mother and enjoyed it when Consuela added noises and new moves. But Manuel was unable to understand the choreography of the game enough to take a role in its maintenance. Consuela had to set it up and keep it coordinated. Nor was he able to generalize from that game to other relational activities like peek-a-boo, or to enact role reversals. Additionally, he had not yet developed an understanding of pretend play.

Manuel presented few obstacles to progress. His parents were not overly anxious about developing speech or any one specific social skill; they were committed to working on Emotional Coordination. While he did not fully understand how to participate actively in them, Manuel appreciated the simple games that his parents created for him. He did not attempt to add variety and chaos into their interaction—as did Patrick—but had learned to orient to his parents for new information. We predicted this pair would make rapid progress.

By the close of Level 1, children like Manuel have become good novices who accept adults as masters of the relationship laboratory. But, they remain largely passive, relying on the expertise of the adult to provide the structural frameworks to increase excitement and pleasure, create new meaning and decrease distress.

In Level 2, the child starts learning how to be a partner, a co-regulator, although not yet a co-creator of shared experiences. By the close of Level 2, she will enact her own role actions, at the right time and in the correct manner to achieve Emotional Coordination. The payoffs for this increased co-regulation include the enjoyment produced by being an active participant in an interaction and knowing how to add more novelty without making it chaotic. The child completing Level 2 can quickly learn role actions, perform them on cue and is a proficient partner in an activity, rather than an observer.

Level 2 Activities

We introduce the child to **Coordination Action Sequences** in Level 2. These are activities with predictable, highly structured frameworks, clear limits and specific boundaries that require social partners to synchronize their movements to complete the activity. Partners operate from a specified physical perimeter and orient their bodies in a prescribed manner. These ritualistic elements ensure that the child can function as a partner and co-regulator without the sophisticated moment-to-moment observation and regulation that will be taught and required later. Objects are still strictly limited to those that facilitate coordination without creating their own attention demands. Formless objects like beanbag chairs and balls are favored over those that require sustained focus, or provide their own payoff unrelated to the relationship. Role timing and switches are highly orchestrated. The child is not yet ready for negotiation or improvisation.

While activities in Level 2 are still highly structured, in Stage 5 adults begin to carefully introduce variation. In this manner, new elements of coordinated movement can be added without overwhelming the child. When possible, language phrases, self-narration and songs are used to enhance the enjoyment of arriving at a mutual destination or end point: "We're jumping", "We're falling" or "We did it!" Language is also used to aid coordination: "1,2,3, jump!" Ideally, both partners have some ownership in the elements and timing. For example, they might jointly chant, "Ready, set, go," or "1,2,3" before running. This not only heightens the motivation of the child but also prepares her for future co-regulation demands. If pretend skills are in place by the close of Level 2, simple pretend games can be role-played, such as pretend telephone conversations, mommies feeding their babies, or Doctor listening to a patient with stethoscope.

Synchronizing actions requires many different skills. Some activities, like Simon Says, or a board game, require that a child's movements immediately follow the specific actions of his partner. Other activities, like falling down together, require simultaneous role enactment. In some activities one partner's actions are cued by and must be timed to coincide with, a specific action of the partner. For example, when one partner releases a ball, his partner must be prepared to receive it.

When these activities are first introduced, the child is taught to be an observant apprentice, to carefully watch the adult in order to learn specific actions and their sequence and the cues that indicate correct timing. Adults must frequently take control of the child's limbs in order to teach her the correct orientation of her body and the movement, goals and timing of a designated action. For example, when we begin teaching patients to catch and roll a ball, we often have two adults involved—one immediately behind the child directing his actions and orienting his body and the other face-to-face, ready to receive the ball.

Along with proper movement and timing, the child must also maintain his actions within certain frameworks. These include environmental boundaries, physical orientation, a specified range of motion, and limits on vocalization. This prevents too much "noise" from being added that would interfere with working on coordination. For example, when rolling a ball, adults often have to initially teach the child to release the ball in the proper direction, so that the adult does not chase after it. We want to make sure the child does not misunderstand the point of the game, which is about co-regulation. Thus, the ball must eventually move from one partner to the other, with neither having to move to retrieve it.

Manuel's Treatment Plan

Our initial objectives for Manuel centered on teaching him sufficient frameworks to participate with Conseula in enjoyable interactions and that he learned to understand and enjoy the variations that she introduced. On the following page, treatment objectives are outlined for Manuel.

Four weeks after his initial evaluation, our session begins by playing the chase game Manuel knows and combining it with a new game of bouncing on the beanbags. Even after just a few weeks, Conseula is able to introduce variety and to combine two activities into a single, more integrated one. When Conseula runs in one direction, it is a cue for Manuel to run in the other direction. Whoever runs in the direction of the bean-

Manuel's Level 2 Treatment Objectives—Part A

- Manuel will derive enjoyment from learning rules, roles and the structure of activities that require observation for role enactment (role timing).

- Manuel will actively participate in activities that highlight a number of coordination variables such as, your turn-my turn, hiding-revealing, higher-lower, closer-farther away, slower-faster, stop-go etc.

- Manuel will demonstrate pleasure when his role is carried out successfully under his partner's guidance.

- Adult introduced variations will become the highlight of the activities.

- Manuel will maintain an understanding and appreciation of activity frameworks despite carefully introduced adult variations.

bags, lands on them and bounces. The game has a definite starting place, outlined with masking tape and an ending of the round demarcated by one of the partners bouncing on the beanbags. At the end of each round, Manuel, as he has learned, runs back to the start place and waits for his mother's start signal. She cues him with a word to run to the other end and sit down and then she follows and bounces with him and he laughs with glee. Manuel has added a shriek to the game as an enhancement and Consuela has accepted and incorporated it. Consuela has been working 20 hours per week with Manuel on these activities and it shows in the rapid progress they have made. Manuel is already starting to initiate games like Ring Around the Rosie, by pointing to a picture symbol of the two of them holding hands. Now Manuel initiates their current game by running to the starting place and signaling to his mother with a hand gesture, making sure to get her visual attention in the process.

Manuel is having difficulty with his motor control when he bounces on the beanbags, so Consuela stops the running part of the game and slowly and carefully frames that one activity by showing him again how to jump up and down. They practice their bouncing together while she excitedly says "jumping, jumping, jumping!" This is an excellent example of how guided participation—using simple frameworks and working in a step-by-step manner—allows us to isolate a single element the child is struggling with and focus on mastery of it, before continuing to the next step.

Manuel has also become a more active co-regulator. We are already seeing a dramatic surge in his self-development. He is attempting many more initiation strategies and verbalizes directly at Consuela.

They have expanded the Level 1 activity, where Conseula blew up the balloon and Manuel fetched it, into a more complex Level 2 activity, a game of bat the balloon back and forth. She ties up another balloon and bats it away. Manuel tries to bat it back. It is exciting to see how quickly

Consuela can now introduce variation and novelty without confusing Manuel and how much novelty excites him at this point. She is pacing him well and knows how much novelty he craves.

Mother and son start rolling the ball back and forth. Consuela counts— "1, 2...3 and roll". Manuel is learning to wait for her to count to three before he releases the ball back to her. She hesitates for different periods of time in her counting to help him build up his referencing and self-regulation skills. Manuel holds himself back by observing his mother's face carefully, watching for the facial cues that indicate she is going to say "3."

They've been working on the Giver-Builder game and now Manuel looks to see that Consuela is handing him a block; he easily starts building his tower. Even though they are different shapes he is organizing them as she gives him each block. Consuela has turned the stacking game into building a small tower and then breaking it quickly and putting it away. Manuel is able to switch roles from "builder" to "giver" without any problem.

The next activity is falling together onto beanbags. Consuela and Manuel are side by side, holding hands with their backs to the beanbags. She counts "1-2-3." Manuel observes her face raptly for cues that it is time to fall. They land and share excited glances while lying on the beanbag pile. After several successes, Consuela tries the game without handholding. But, Manuel cannot coordinate his actions at that level yet and he protests. She returns to handholding.

Many relationship elements are involved in Level 2 work. Each is taught sequentially and lays the foundation for the activities that follow. On the following page, the list illustrates the primary elements in early Level 2 activities.

Later stages of Level 2

As Level 2 progresses, we expect children to take on more of the responsibility for performing their roles in a coordinated manner. Children learn simple Coordinated Role Sets. These are carefully timed synchronized actions between the child and a partner. They consist of two roles taught as a single interlocking unit. A simple example is illustrated by the role set of "Giver and Builder." I give you a block. You take it and stack it. The Giver is not allowed to build and the Builder is prohibited from selecting a block. Children learn that the completion of the activity depends on the ability of each person to take only his prescribed role actions in a specific, synchronized way.

Three types of Coordinated Role Sets lay the foundation for all future roles: Face-to-Face, Symmetrical and Complementary. Face-to-Face interactions, such as rolling a ball back and forth, require that both partners

Level 2—Treatment Objectives—Part 1

- The child learns to be an apprentice, carefully observing the adult for the activity sequence and modeling the adult to learn his role actions.

- The child allows the adult to temporarily take motor control (e.g. placing her hand over the child's), in order to teach designated role actions.

- The adult acts to limit the variety in the child's actions, to ensure that the child does not add too much "noise" to the interaction that would interfere with proper execution of roles, or destroy the specific structure of the activity.

- The child learns to enact specific role actions at the proper time.

- The child learns to maintain his actions within certain boundaries, to limit his actions within the role constraints that have been taught.

- During the activity, the child learns to shift his focus of attention at predictable intervals, from himself to his partner. The child attends to the completion of his partner's actions, which serve as a signal for the child to take his own action. The child shifts back, in order to perform his own action successfully.

- The parent stops and carefully "frames" any part of the child's action that is causing difficulty, working on this one action until it is mastered.

- The parent introduces variety into the interaction in a careful manner and observes the child closely to ensure that he can still enact his role successfully.

enact identical roles in a sequential manner, while seated or standing face-to-face. Symmetrical, coordinated roles, like falling together while holding hands, or beating drums at the same pace, require that partners enact the same actions in a simultaneous, synchronized manner. Chorus lines and military marching formations are well known examples of adult Symmetrical Role Sets. Complementary roles require that both partners take a distinctively different role, but perform it in a highly synchronized manner, to reach a common end point. Examples of Complementary Roles used in Level 2 are Hide and Seek, Simon Says, Pitcher and Batter and I-Push, You-Fall.

Synchronized Movement

We begin with many different symmetrical role sets of the "on-off," "start-stop" variety. We practice running together, falling together, lifting objects and carrying them to a pile together and racing cars side by side. A common starting place is for partners to count "1,2,3 go" together using the word "go" as the signal to begin an action at the same moment. We use two Paddle Drums and drumsticks to work, in a fluid manner, on "start" and "stop". The child is first instructed to use the paddle drum and drumstick appropriately. Then he is taught the goal of the activity—for partners to start and stop beating their drums at the same time. The adult begins by taking the roll of "caller," verbally indicating when it is time to start and stop beating drums. Early on, adults must be very slow and deliberate and even lead into the "start/stop" command with, "1,2,3, start; 1,2,3, stop!" As work progresses, external cues are eliminated and the timing of "start" and "stop" is varied, until it is unpredictable. Similarly, we may start with lots of supporting language and then quickly move to the use of only facial expression to indicate our readiness to start and stop. This will eventually evolve into teaching the child how body motion determines when we start and stop.

As treatment progresses, the child assumes the responsibility of being the "caller" and synchronizing the starting and the stopping. This enables him to enact the "caller" role and simultaneously function as a drummer. Furthermore, he must be able to vary his calling while beating the drum. As interactions become more fluid, partners rapidly shift turns being the caller.

At a more advanced level, additional dimensions of coordination are introduced. However, we continue using action sequences in which the degree of coordination can be simply and immediately observed: "Are we coordinated or not?" At a more advanced level, Paddle Drums provide the opportunity to work on fast and slow, or soft and loud. Gross

Program Tip
Working on Higher Level 2 Activities

- An adult developed framework provides the opportunity to practice one element of coordination at a time.
- Coordinated Role Sets are introduced. Referencing, communication and self-regulation actions are used for simultaneous starting and stopping and later to determine partners' relative degrees of coordination, while their bodies are in motion.
- Goals of landing together, falling together etc. produce immediate moments of pleasurable emotion sharing, that are heightened by the joy of being an active agent who helps produce the desired outcome.
- Parental guides gradually introduce methods for synchronizing movement and rapid attention shifting for moment-to-moment referencing.
- Adults gradually introduce minor, planned disruptions in coordination that provide the child the opportunity to take regulating actions.

motor activities can be changed from walking to running, one direction to the opposite, or pushing and pulling.

In the final stages of Level 2, the degree of coordination becomes relative, rather than absolute. Evaluations of coordination are much more subjective and made on a "feel" basis. This is a critical, but very difficult step, if a child is to progress towards normal peer interaction. Returning to the Paddle Drums as an example, beating drums "fast then slow" becomes "faster and slower"; "loud-soft" becomes "louder-softer." The caller works through multiple levels of "faster" and "slower" to gradually introduce the concept to the child. Once this is accomplished, we integrate the child's ability to increase his actions in a gradual amount with his ability to judge whether both partners are moving at approximately the same speed. This is the ultimate test of progress at Level 2. The child perceives himself making small relative changes in his actions, while attending to his partner's change of action. Thus, each person approximates the other on one or more dimensions, while continuing to vary the level of activity. Both are at a similar degree of loudness, softness, or speed of banging and both continue to vary their actions to introduce variation and also to remain coordinated. So, if I beat slightly slower, my partner responds by beating slightly slower and attempts to match my pace. Throughout Level 2 a "caller" is still necessary to maintain coordination. However, this action is faded out in Level 3, where activities take on a highly improvisational, fluid quality.

> In the early stages of Level 2, the pace of activities is clear-cut and slow...as Level 2 progresses, activities occur quickly, requiring near-simultaneous attention shifting between self and partner.

Shifting Attention

In the early stages of Level 2, the pace of activities is clear-cut and slow. In a rudimentary activity like taking turns playing a board game, the child must only wait for the end of his partner's turn, to know when to take his own turn. However, in more sophisticated coordinated activities, like Paddle Drums, attention shifting must occur more rapidly. As Level 2 progresses, activities occur quickly, requiring near-simultaneous attention shifting between self and partner.

Co-regulation

A final element introduced during the last stage of Level 2 is the use of regulatory actions to maintain and repair coordination. Uniformly, children with Autism do not notice the gradual loss of coordination that often occurs in their interactions; they continue enacting their roles, even despite a total breakdown. To practice co-regulation, parents must deliberately and systematically create highly amplified coordination breakdowns within a Coordinated Action Sequence and teach the child to perceive and respond to these with appropriate regulatory actions. An example of a deliberate breakdown is the use of hesitation as a parent chants "1,2,..." and stops prior to saying "3." Adults may also introduce deliberate strategic pauses, such as not finishing a phrase, leaving it incomplete and even using exaggerated gaze aversion. Another example, used as a Level 3 measure in our evaluations, is for the child and parent to practice running and falling together, with the parent stopping suddenly in the middle of his run.

Structured breakdowns are introduced as variations to activities a child has already mastered. For instance, during the Paddle Drum activity, a parent may do the opposite of what is called, like speeding up when the caller says "slow down". The child will learn to notice and communicate for increased coordination, "Hey, that's not right. Slow down!" In a systematic fashion, we ask the child to play and react to the role of the deliberate "mistake" maker and to practice self-regulating when we point out that an action has caused a breakdown. Various methods we use to work on co-regulation are described in the table below.

Manuel's Treatment Plan Revisited

Manuel was ready to work on these later stages of Level 2 and learn how to co-regulate his interactions. We developed treatment objectives for him as described on the next page.

Teaching movement coordination in all its facets is a gradual process. It involves several individual actions on the part of the child with Autism, and can be initially confusing. As an illustration of how we work to increase relationship coordination, let us return to our Case Study.

Developing Co-regulation

- Playfully, but deliberately, use gaze aversion until the child communicates or self-regulates for gaze.

- Dramatically stop talking mid sentence, and delay an expected action.

- Perform role actions in a clearly exaggerated, comically incorrect manner.

- Develop activities where, if the child takes his eyes off his parent for a moment, the parent may run away.

- Develop activities where a parent's changing facial expressions provide the key information about what will happen next in the activity.

- Parents learn to wait for longer periods of time when coordination has broken down, to allow the child time to recognize the need for repair actions.

- Require the child to repeat an interaction or start over again, if he acts in a non-coordinated manner. For example, if the child runs to the playroom ahead, without a word, a parent will escort the child back to the waiting room and start over again, until he can walk side-by-side with his parent.

Manuel's Level 2 Treatment Objectives—Part B

- Manuel will experience enjoyment and a feeling of competence from successfully carrying out coordinated interactions.

- Manuel will learn to independently perform his role as part of several different Coordinated Role Sets.

- Manuel will time his actions to coordinate with those of a partner [in performing face-to-face role sets.]

- Manuel will participate as an equal partner in regulating activities that require complementary role actions (e.g. I select and give you the block, you take it and build with it).

- Manuel will derive enjoyment and satisfaction from carrying out simultaneous coordinated actions using symmetrical role actions (e.g. running together and landing on beanbag chairs at the same time).

- Manuel will monitor his moment-to-moment state of coordination with his partner's actions.

- Manuel will regularly engage in communication ("Hey, slow down!") and self-regulation ("I have to slow down") to achieve and maintain coordinated movements.

Manuel and Conseula are practicing running and falling together. Both partners take off from a common starting point, run together and fall simultaneously onto a pile of beanbags. After Manuel mastered the initial framework and role actions, he was taught to attend to information from two different, competing sources. While running next to his partner, Manuel needed to orient his body towards the pile of beanbags; the first part of his role action. While holding hands and running with her son, Conseula initially taught Manuel to notice the tension in his arm when he moved too far ahead of, or behind her. This feeling of tension gave Manuel information he needed to regulate his rate of speed without shifting his gaze, so that he could remain at Conseula's side. As Manuel became more proficient at this rapid joint information processing, Conseula taught Manuel to pay attention to momentary changes in her actions, by deliberately varying her rate of speed as she ran. With these skills in place, they could now move on to visual attention shifting.

Once Conseula let go of his hand, Manuel had to keep referencing her, to ensure that his physical location was approximately parallel with hers, while they were in motion, the second part of his role. Manuel had to rapidly evaluate each source of information and determine its precedence at any given moment. During earlier Level 2 activities, external structure, like holding hands, masking tape on the floor and other signals, take the place of this ongoing rapid attention shifting. However, Level 3 activities require that the child make constant rapid attention shifts and decisions. The transition from external cues to ongoing referencing and momentary judgments often takes place over a period of from several months to two years, depending upon the child.

Conseula and Manuel first worked on visual attention shifting in their start up routine, using a simple 1-2-3-go count. Manuel visually referenced Conseula to determine when she was going to reach 3. She purposefully became trickier by varying the length of her pause and even increased the count to 4 to increase his referencing. This became a co-regulated process, with both partners taking turns counting and varying the start of the activity.

Once Manuel became proficient at visual referencing, the skills were in place for him to learn "on-the-fly" visual shifting. Conseula initially slowed down her running, while still holding Manuel's hand. She made interesting and amplified noises as they ran, as a cue for Manuel to shift his gaze from the beanbags to her. Initially, Manuel looked at his mother to investigate the novel noise, rather than evaluate their level of coordination. As they progressed, Conseula omitted the verbal cues and altered her rate of speed just enough to be out of synch with Manuel as they ran. Manuel became curious about this change and shifted his gaze to his mother. This gaze shift was sufficient to get Conseula to alter her pace and match his, thus reducing the tension in Manuel's arm. They played in this manner until Manuel could shift visual attention from goal to partner while running, with no tension put on his arm. Finally, Manuel discovered that his mother might, at any moment, unexpectedly vary her pace and that keeping pace with her required constant regulation. Conseula exaggerated her pace shifting—running in very slow motion in some trials and very rapidly in others, so Manuel's understanding of his role in regulation was clear.

Manuel and Consuela worked on this task for several months before he was ready to let go of her hand while running. Once Manuel mastered the basic framework of running side-by-side, Conseula inserted a midway stopping point, so that Manuel had to continue monitoring her movements in relation to his own. Eventually, Manuel kept pace with his mother regardless of her movement. He was prepared to run and play simple games like chase, in the erratic, fluid style of his normal peers and as an equal partner in simple play activities.

Program Tip

You can work on coordinated actions often during the day. Each time you are walking with your child, practice walking side-by-side. Lifting a box together that needs to be moved is another opportunity. You will be surprised what a difference this can make in your child's development.

Manuel's Success

Relational Development Intervention can be a slow process. However, the rewards are great. Once children learn the pivotal skills of social referencing, joint attention and emotional coordination, they are well on their way to understanding the intrinsic joy of social interaction.

To measure the effectiveness of our program, we periodically repeat the evaluation process; we did so with Manuel after one year of treatment. The pair enters with Manuel happy and relaxed. Immediately, he initiates play by hiding behind the beanbags and calling to Consuela. He then tries to climb the beanbags and get her to look at him by saying "Mama?" Consuela helps him climb up the stack of beanbags; he falls down and says "Oh fall down." She helps him up again. Manuel offers Consuela a turn. "Mama go up? Mama jump?" He jumps down and starts exploring. Manuel is much more active in exploring now. But, at the same time he shifts his gaze continually to reference Consuela. He initiates with "Play blocks?" Consuela says "No blocks, run?" Manuel says no. They are carrying on a real negotiation, as they have a large shared repertoire of activities to choose from. They agree on a chase game. This is a new format that entails running around the pile of beanbags. They begin to run and suddenly Consuela says, "stop" and they both come to an abrupt halt. Manuel says, "go"—his role—and they both start running again. He runs and looks back at Consuela to make sure she is chasing. When she tries to sneak up on him, he runs in the other direction. She then changes to hopping and the game fluidly continues with both partners hopping. Next they start jumping on the beanbags and yelling "yeah!"

After that, they easily move into running together and jumping. Both partners hold hands; Manuel carefully watches while Consuela counts. They take off together, still holding hands, fall excitedly and scream "yeaaaaah!" With their next round, Consuela teaches Manuel to take part in the counting. She counts "1,2,3" and teaches Manuel to insert the "yeaaah" prior to taking off and running. After falling, Consuela hides herself in the pile of beanbags. Manuel quickly crawls in to join her. She covers him up and he smiles. He uncovers himself and runs off. She covers herself and says "Donde esta mama?" and he immediately finds her and uncovers her. Mother and child are clearly partners at this point, anticipating each other's actions and adapting to each other in a highly fluid manner. Action sequences are beginning to fluidly merge into one another and an improvisational element is emerging—a sign that Manuel is ready to begin working on Level 3 tasks.

They sit, side by side, in front of the toy box. Consuela takes out a spider action figure and pretends that it is walking. Manuel makes it walk just like mother has and gives it a kiss. She takes out a windup toy and starts it up. He watches and goes to grab it. He wants to try it himself and she allows him to do so. Even though Manuel is playing with his own toy,

> Action sequences are beginning to fluidly merge into one another and an improvisational element is emerging—a sign that Manuel is ready to begin working on Level 3 tasks.

each time Consuela brings out a new activity, he immediately stops his activity, references her and uses the new object she gives him in the manner in which she instructs. He is exploring his environment under her guidance. Each time she goes into the box, he briefly shifts his gaze to see what she is doing. She is sitting behind him and to the side a bit—a perfect position for introducing new objects to a child who references on his own. At this point in his development she does not want to be the center of his attention, but rather his guide to increased enjoyment.

Next, they throw the ball back and forth. Rolling was mastered long ago. They are about eight feet apart. Manuel signals that he wants the ball. To make the game more exciting, they both move from place to place while throwing it. This desire to introduce higher levels of novelty and change is another sign of fluid coordination of actions, which indicates readiness to move into Level 3. When Consuela abruptly switches to rolling the ball instead of throwing it, he adapts immediately, without effort.

This desire to introduce higher levels of novelty and change is another sign of... readiness to move into Level 3.

As the evaluation continues they decide to play with blocks. Manuel requests blocks verbally now and pats the table. Consuela explains the framework of the activity with words and he listens carefully. She hands him a block, then a second one. He protests because it's not the same size. She hands him a third. He rubs them together and then lines up the three blocks. He has decided to put them together in a sort of construction and mom allows it. At this stage, the interaction between builder and giver is more important than his compliance with a specific goal, like building a tower. Because of his progress, Consuela permits Manuel to inject much more novelty into an activity's framework. It appears he is making a road or track of some kind. He verbalizes about what he is doing while he works. She asks him if he is building a house. He smiles and says "no." He shifts his gaze from his creation to his mother several times and finally smiles and says, "It's a train." He completes his train, a signal to Manuel to switch roles and become the Giver. Consuela asks for his blocks and while he effortlessly lets her build her own creation, he does choose the order of the blocks he wants to give her. Manuel is very interested in what she is building—clear indications of budding Joint Attention. He asks, "A tower?" She excitedly agrees and they finish. He puts away the blocks on his own.

It is time for falling together backwards onto the beanbag pile. They have worked on each piece of the framework on a step-by-step basis. They hold hands, count together and look into each other's eyes while they fall. Without any cueing, they vary the counting in the next round. Manuel's referencing skills are strong enough that he knows that by watching Consuela, success will be achieved each time they play.

The final task is the pretend tea party. Manuel watches mom pour the pretend water into three cups—a pretend bear is joining them. Consuela demonstrates how to be the "pourer." Manuel quickly takes on the role, pretends to drink the water and says "mmm" while gazing at his mother.

She indicates to him to give the bear some water; he does and says "mmm" while the bear drinks. She gives each of them rice and he pretends to eat the rice. Consuela says, "It's hot, blow." Manuel blows on his pretend rice and then feeds the bear with an "mmm." Manuel has moved into the first stage of pretend play.

The evaluation indicated to us that Manuel was beginning to understand how to coordinate his actions fluidly, within a number of different structured activities. There were many indications of his readiness for Level 3. He was realizing that co-regulation was a matter of degree and not always an all-or-nothing proposition. He could bang his drum a little bit harder, when his mother increased her own pace of banging and yelled out "harder." He could quickly soften his blows when he observed Consuela had softened her own. Manuel had even learned to take the lead in many games. He would signal to Consuela to join him at the start line, look at her and signal to her to jointly count "1,2,3" with him—the first step in their running and falling together. He demonstrated a desire for novelty and liked making new discoveries with his mother. He enjoyed arriving at a common goal with her and experiencing the feeling of "we did it." He loved co-creating new elements of games with her. The next step was to take this new understanding of co-regulating actions and teach Manuel to apply it in more fluid, improvised activities.

Sample Level 2 Activities

Hats on/off in front of a mirror: Children practice parallel, synchronized actions, in front of our one-way mirror. The mirror provides self and other feedback to the children, reducing the need to shift gaze.

I Push, You Fall: A variant of Falling Together is I Push, You Fall. This activity has two distinct roles: the pusher and the faller. Partners stand face-to-face, with one partner's back to a pile of beanbags. The pusher asks "Are you ready?" and when the faller says "I'm ready", pushes him carefully onto the pile of beanbags. Partners switch roles each turn.

Building Beanbag Mountain II: (Can be played with two or three). One child is the giver and the other two are builders. The builders must agree on the color beanbag they want. Then they request it from the giver, who provides it. The boys work together to carry the beanbags to the opposite corner of the room and stack them so they create a mountain of beanbags. When the beanbags are stacked, adults spot the children as they climb to the top of the mountain and slide down.

Running Together: Runners begin by holding hands at a pre-designated, marked starting line. They coordinate their start by counting to three together prior to leaving the start line. They remain side by side while moving towards a pile of beanbag chairs. Just prior to the chairs there is a designated "falling line" which indicates where they should coordinate their falling actions. Falling should occur so runners land facing each other on the cushions. Partners return together to the start line and join hands for a second round. Options for adding complexity, variety, and fluidity include eliminating handholding and/or removing the falling line. At later stages the adult will try to trick the child by looking away just prior to starting. This ensures that the child is actively referencing his partner. Partners can also try to trick each other by varying their running pace, to practice regulating their speed to stay together.

Paddle Drums: Each partner is given a paddle drum and a soft drumstick. Partners practice beating small drums at the same time. Initially the adult is the "caller" and both partners beat their drums. The partners first practice coordinating "stop and go" with the verbal cues of the caller. Next the caller adds Loud and Soft while they are beating and then Fast and Slow. At an advanced level, the caller stops providing verbal cues and members start alternating their roles.

You & Me: Working Together as Partners

Level Three

$\mathcal{B}$y the close of Level 3, we expect the child to function as an equal partner in highly fluid, action based encounters, where movements do not have to be controlled by rule based structure, but by the momentary desires of the participants. Normal children's play consists of spontaneous decisions like "Let's go that way" or "Let's skip and then hop" made and agreed to by peers with minimal

---

Level 3 Stages and Treatment Objectives

Stage 09: Co-variation

- The child enjoys the shared introduction of novelty while engaged in fluid, coordinated actions.
- Child and partner share in the addition and regulation of variations.
- Variations are made in a well-communicated, careful manner (in contrast to the later stage of Improvisation where variations are introduced rapidly, with little warning).

Stage 10: Fluid Transitions

- The child enjoys and participates as a partner in mutually chaining activities into a fluid sequence.
- Actions remain coordinated while merging elements from one activity to another (e.g. moving from running to climbing, to jumping. Moving from Beanbag Mountain to falling on beanbags, to hitting with beanbags).

Stage 11: Improvisation

- The child enjoys activities where partners collaborate to continually modify rules and roles while maintaining coordination.
- Child and partner maintain coordination without specific structural elements in place (e.g. counting to three, agreement on destination).

Stage 12: Co-creation

- The child enjoys creating new games, where partners contribute to rules and themes equally.
- Child and partner readily acknowledge the joint nature of their creation by communicating verbally and/or non-verbally the element of joint ownership of the game. They jointly label and/or acknowledge the unique pattern of shared, improvised elements as their own new game.

---

discussion. Once a child has mastered coordination in the face of continual improvisation, peers—who introduce a great deal more variation—become much more attractive social partners. Primary objectives for Level 3 treatment are presented on p. 113.

Case Study

Neil, Peter and Matt

Neil, Peter and Matt spent over five years together, from ages four to nine, in a small group at our clinic. All three boys were diagnosed with Aspergers Syndrome when they were three; all were very verbal, intelligent and inquisitive. Neil, the child who participated in the unfortunate "knock knock" joke incident, was quite even-tempered, but also quite rule-governed. Peter was also vested in following rules, was more affectionate, but had a quicker temper. Matt was the most flexible of the three but highly fearful. After each boy had worked intensively with his parents and was ready for Level 3 work, the three were placed together in a group. Each had learned to enact their roles in the same activities and so shared a common framework, leaving little room for confusion or conflict about roles and rules. While they were getting accustomed to each other, they did not have to attend to any new information about activities.

Group Work Begins

Level 3 is a common entry point for peer dyads and small groups. The central role of the adult as the primary regulator of interaction gradually changes to that of facilitator. It is important that the adult gradually move to the periphery of attention and that the children perceive each other as their primary source of enjoyment and as sharing responsibility for co-regulation. We often use visual structures to take the place of verbal prompting during the initial phase of group work. For example, for these three boys we designed "I go first" cards, task sequence cards, and similar visual signs to aid them in deciding what they were going to do and how to interact in each activity, allowing the therapist to move to the sidelines.

When we begin working with groups, we replicate many simpler activities that the children have already mastered with adults. These activities require minimal adult structure, because the children have already learned to perform their roles independently. Neil, Peter and Matt started each group with a familiar joint activity. This was followed by a series of varied gross motor coordination activities like falling together and jumping and running together. They built Beanbag Mountains together and played their version of the "Save me from the monster" game.

> **Program Tip**
>
> When transitioning from adult-child to child-child interactions, always begin with activities one level below the child's proficiency with adults. Children provide much more unpredictability and require much more co-regulation and repair from each other.

Developing a "We-go"

A primary goal of RDI is to make sure that children value their group time, not for the interesting activities or toys, or adult therapists, but for the opportunity to work, play and form a genuine reciprocal relationship with same-age children. One way we enhance the value of peers is to provide experiences that help children feel the power and satisfaction of working together to reach a common endpoint.

Researcher Bob Emde refers to this experience as developing "We-go"— the group equivalent of an Ego. Building a mountain of beanbag chairs is one such example of working together towards a common goal. Many other tasks like "Farm-to-market" and "Builder, Architect, Parts Department" described at the close of this chapter, or even a task as basic as lifting and carrying boxes together from one location to another, reinforce this experience.

Another variation of cooperative effort is found in activities that teach children that keeping an activity going—"keeping the ball in play"— through joint effort, is more fun and rewarding than winning or taking your turn. We use many variants of this type of activity. Most have the goal of seeing how long children can work together as a team to keep an activity in play. For instance, children hit balloons back and forth with paddles and see how many times they can keep the balloon in the air.

One of our favorite cooperative activities is Two Ball Toss. The rules are very simple. Two children face each other, each holding a ball. The object is to throw and catch their balls simultaneously. Initially, children with poor motor skills stand next to each other and simply hand their balls to one another. We then gradually move them apart as they become more proficient. Even physically able children with Autism have trouble with this task. It requires that children coordinate several variables: their count, their release and their rate and height of throw. They have to not only throw their balls simultaneously, but also to adjust their throws based upon the success or failure of their prior throw.

The following vignette depicts a practice session with Neil and Matt, when they were eight years old. The boys had practiced this activity for

> **Program Tip**
>
> When they are ready, children can add variation to the Two Ball Toss activity in several ways. The partners can co-vary the activity and decide to move in the same or in opposite directions along parallel lines, as they toss their balls. They may use two balls of different weight and size. At it's most sophisticated form, the children can move in unpredictable directions while they coordinate their throws.

a number of sessions, and became invested in achieving greater mastery. In fact they told me that they wished to set the world record and be listed in the Guiness Book of Records as the greatest team in history. Luckily neither of them possessed the book, so I set a "world's record" goal of 19 successive tosses, which seemed a hard but not impossible goal for them. The boys went for the record in our playroom, standing on carpet squares, about six feet apart. They each had a small, soft nerf ball. They were given instructions for the game and told that they had to remain on the carpet squares for a caught ball to count.

> They start and both throw too hard. Matt's throw is off. He exclaims, *"Oh shoot."*
> They are not counting together. But, they do complete the next throw successfully and laugh together.
> **Dr. G:** *"If you don't do it exactly together it doesn't count."*
> They are still not counting together and saying, "go" at the same time.
> **Dr. G:** *"Start again, you're not saying '1' at the same time."*
> They make another attempt. *"Sorry, you didn't say 'three' at the same time. You have to start all over."*
> On the next round they manage to count at the same time.
> **Dr. G:** *"That was an official one."*
> But then they immediately lose their coordination.
> **Dr. G.:** *"Oh you started too early. You have to start at the same time."*
> They now count at the same time and release their balls together. But on the very next round they forget to say '3' together.
> **Dr. G.:** *"Oh, you have to start again."*
> Both boys are getting frustrated. But, by now they are used to my challenges and get right back to task. On the next round they count and release together, but unfortunately Neil drops his ball.
> **Dr. G:** *"Good form. You're getting it."*
> Now they count together but miss. On the next round

they count together and release together but throw too hard.

Dr. G.: *"Gentler!"*

On the next round they finally have both the timing and gentleness right and they are starting to be successful.

But after six successful trials, they slip back and do not say '3' together.

Matt looks to Neil and says, *"Well at least we made six in a row."*

Neil asks me *"How many are we supposed to make to get the record?"* Both boys look at me expectantly.

Dr. G.: *"The world record is 18."*

They seem unfazed by their distance from the Guinness book and get back to work.

Their form looks excellent and they are starting to get results. On the 5th trial, despite their good efforts, their balls collide in mid-air.

Dr. G.: *"You hit the balls in mid-air. That's a two point bonus."*

The boys seem very relieved and get back to throwing. Both are raptly attending to each other, using identical arm motions and releasing gently.

Neil is keeping count and excitedly exclaims to Matt *"That's 14. We only need 5 more."*

I stop them when they reach 20 in a row, shake both of their hands and inform them that they just set the new world record for Two Ball Toss. They whoop and holler and spontaneously hug each other, jumping for joy while holding each other.

> **Another important element in "We-go" development is the experience of strength felt from working together to overcome a common foe or obstacle.**

Another important element in "We-go" development is the experience of strength felt from working together to overcome a common foe or obstacle. We refer to this phase of work as "United we stand, divided we fall." Typically, the therapist will play the role of adversary, obstacle or even enemy, once the children can grasp the concept that this is a role and not the actual stance of the therapist.

With Neil, Peter and Matt, I began our work by becoming a human obstacle, preventing them from getting to the cabinet in our playroom that held all their favorite toys. Try as they might, any one of the boys functioning as an individual could not get past me. I repeatedly explained to them that they had to work together if they ever wanted to get to the cabinet. But, in the excitement of the moment, they continued to lose their coordination. Finally, I hit upon a simple repetitive song that they sang during this interval: "It takes three to open the door." Once they learned to chant this song, it became a useful reminder and immediately the boys were operating as a threesome, working together to push me physically out of the way to get to their well-earned treasures. The song was employed in future activities with equal effect, even when these didn't involve opening doors.

Treatment Objectives for Co-variation

1. Neil will enjoy sharing in the introduction of novelty, while engaged in fluid, coordinated actions.

2. Neil will share as an equal partner in the addition and regulation of variation.

3. Neil's variations will be made in a well-communicated, careful manner.

4. Neil will conduct ongoing referencing of self-partner coordination following introduction of variation.

5. Neil will reference his partners for understanding, acceptance and comfort.

6. Neil will take self-regulatory actions to maintain coordination following introduction of variation by either partner (e.g. slowing down, speeding up, shifting position, waiting an extra second).

7. Neil will communicate for clarification of partner-introduced variations and to make sure of partner acceptance and enjoyment of variation.

8. Neil will rapidly stop or modify variations that confuse or bother social partners. Neil will use effective repair actions when coordination is lost.

Co-variation

Armed with a solid desire to remain united, the boys were ready to begin work on introducing novelty and variation into their encounters. They had sufficiently learned the importance of continually referencing their state of coordination, to keep their activities in progress and to balance the degree of novelty and structure. While the following table indicates the treatment objectives we designed for Neil, the same objectives applied to each member of the group.

One of the group's first new activities was an expansion of the Giver-Builder game we call Farm to Market. Each week the three boys started the activity by constructing a road from wooden blocks. Following this they chose (with the help of choosing cards) one boy as the farmer, another as the grocer and the third as the trucker, who transported the produce to the store. The farmer assembled his small container of plastic fruit and vegetables and set it up at one end of the road. The grocer built his small store out of more blocks and set up a grocery sign.

To start the activity, the trucker retrieved his yellow plastic truck and drove it to the grocer. The grocer called the farmer on his cellular phone to determine what was available that day. He then placed his order. The farmer requested a delivery and so on. As time passed, the group gradually added many new elements to this activity. For example, the boys decided that the road should be a toll road and so a tollbooth was added. The truck would repeatedly fall off the highway, so the boys introduced a tow truck. Trucks were breaking down and needing repair, so a repair shop was added. In time, the grocery store was running special sales and the farmer was rotating his crops. The boys were quite invested in the process and ran it smoothly as a cooperative effort for many months.

Fluid Transitions

Once co-variation was soundly in place, we began teaching the children that they could remove some of the artificial structures that separated one ritualized activity from another, allowing them to blend into one another, as they do in typical peer play. The treatment objectives corresponding to this stage follow.

Beanbag Mountain and The Tunnel turn into a Clubhouse

The boys rapidly became quite proficient at blending one activity into a completely new one and combining elements of several activities. Building Beanbag Mountain turned into using the beanbags to build a clubhouse. The tunnel they had crawled through in Level 1 was incorporated as the entrance to the clubhouse; one so narrow only a child could go through it.

Treatment Objectives for Fluid Transitions

1. Peter will enjoy and participate as a partner, in mutually chaining activities into a single more integrated activity.

2. Peter's actions will remain coordinated with his partner's, while they fluidly transition from one role set to another.

3. Peter will conduct frequent visual and verbal referencing of self-partner coordination.

4. Peter will transition with his social partners from one activity to another using rapid nonverbal referencing for acceptance.

5. Peter will communicate to obtain social partners acceptance, before or just after transitioning.

6. Peter will quickly stop or modify any transitional actions that confuse or bother social partners.

7. Peter will communicate for clarification, when confused about partner variations. (e.g. "Do you want me to stop too?)

8. Peter will communicate appreciation for his social partner's transitions.

9. Peter will use self-regulatory actions to maintain coordination (e.g. slowing down, speeding up, shifting position, waiting an extra second) during periods of transition.

10. Peter will notice when activity coordination between himself and his social partners is lost.

11. Peter will use effective repair actions when coordination is lost.

At the beginning of each session they would carefully rebuild their clubhouse and all climb into it through the tunnel. They'd ask me to turn off the lights and flashlight in hand, they would conduct "secret time" in their sanctuary.

The Clubhouse, Paddle Drums and the Monster get Connected

As Neil, Peter and Matt progressed in their group work, we re-introduced the Monster. Once they have an adequate understanding of pretense, all children love the excitement of defeating an evil monster that is threatening to eat them. When we first played the game in our group I played the monster. The clubhouse—sans tunnel—became the monster's cave. I would wait until the children were not focused and suddenly leap out, snatch one of the children, while making monster noises, and drag him or her back into the cave, ostensibly to be devoured. The victim was taught to scream "Save me, save me" which served as the cue for the other two members to come to his rescue. If the other two boys worked in unison, the rescue attempt was always successful.

After a while the monster, now costumed in a bed sheet, arrived not from under the table, but from outside the playroom, at unpredictable moments. In one hand he carried a fork and in the other a ketchup bottle. By now, the monster's cave had gone through several transformations, all created by the boys. First it was a secret hiding place where the monster could not find them. Later it became a fortress, from which the boys would emerge to attack the monster. Finally, in a complete reversal of roles it became the boy's lair, where they would drag the monster, kill and bury him.

> **Program Tip**
>
> Level 2 activities are adapted for Level 3 by allowing the child to perform them in more improvisational ways. For example, Running and Falling can be varied by direction, speed, running backwards, etc.

Improvisation

At this stage of Level 3, our children are learning that they can rapidly insert completely new elements into their activities, without losing their coordination with partners. They have also learned to maintain their

Treatment Objectives for Improvised Actions

- Peter will participate in and enjoy activities where he and his partners collaborate to continually modify rules and roles while maintaining coordination.

- Peter will insert elements from prior activities in a highly fluid manner and allow his peers to do so as well.

- Peter will maintain the coordination of his actions with his peers, without specific structural elements in place.

- Peter will conduct frequent visual/verbal referencing of his degree of self-partner coordination, on a moment-to-moment basis.

- Peter will obtain partner acceptance before enacting new elements.

- Peter will communicate appreciation for new elements contributed by social partners.

- Peter will communicate appropriately for clarification, when confused about partner actions (e.g. "Do you want me to stop too?)

- Peter will use self-regulatory actions to maintain coordination (e.g. slowing down, speeding up, shifting position, waiting an extra second) on a moment-to-moment basis.

- Peter will rapidly stop or modify any actions that confuse or bother a social partner. Peter will use effective repair actions when coordination is lost.

coordination without most of the external structural rules we had previously imposed to clearly define limits and boundaries on activities. Improvised activity is a key element in preparing children for the normal "free" play they will encounter in a typical school recess period.

Improvisation within Structure

When we work within the realm of sports, games and similar win/lose endeavors, we run the risk of our children becoming overly focused on winning, or in everyone following the rules as they interpret them. Therefore, at the point in our program when we enter these areas, we do so with the knowledge that we also need to teach the children to appreciate that winning is not as important as enjoying the game—a lesson that even children without Autism have problems with. Equally important, children learn that there is room to enjoy improvisation, even in a structured activity like soccer or baseball.

Neil and Peter were playing soccer against Matt and me. Soccer games in our playroom are structured two-on-two, with each team possessing a goalie and a fielder. In this game, Matt was the goalie and I was the fielder. Neil was fielding for the opposition. Each team scores a goal only when they exhibit good coordination—like a good pass from goalie to fielder.

Neil and Peter's team was losing. As usual, Peter got caught up in winning and became angry. Matt noticed this and started playing a silly game with Neil. After every goal, I was the designated "counter" who would count to three and then drop the ball for the face off. My job was to count 1-2.. and then pause until one of the boys was caught off guard, then suddenly count 3 and drop the ball. During one of my long pauses, Matt decided that he was going to do anything to make Neil laugh. He made every ridiculous face and noise he could think of until Matt was falling to the floor in laughter.

It wasn't long before this improvised moment became the most important part of the game for the two of them, even though they were on opposing teams. Neil called Matt "tricky Matt" making the two of them laugh even harder. At one point, in the unintentionally profound way he sometimes has, Neil said to Matt, "Having fun and scoring goals is like a balance. When you're not winning, you have more fun. When you are winning, you feel good but you can have less fun. It's like the balance of justice."

Perhaps the crowning moment in competitive sports for this little group was the year they spent working on baseball. Getting ready for even the simplest form of a baseball game—even in our small playroom—took months. Each child came to the sport with different individual deficits that had to be addressed. For Neil, it was dealing with not winning all the time. For Matt, it was working out all of the motor skills needed to stand on the correct side of the plate, swing the bat at the right time and run the bases. All the boys had difficulty deciding what constituted a bad pitch, one not worth swinging at and how to understand the relationship of the different positions. And, they all had a torturous time working out decisions about what to do in all the different types of fielding and base running situations that occur in the game.

To help them, we recruited a "coach"—a boy, two years older, who was working on higher Level 4 skills. When our children move into more advanced levels, they benefit greatly from the self-esteem and practice that coaching provides. The coach practices putting himself in his players' shoes and seeing things from their perspective. This young man turned into a caring and compassionate but disciplined coach, who showed great patience in gradually developing the individual and cooperative skills of his players.

The goal of all this training was a tournament between the group and two of the therapists who had challenged them for the office trophy. The boys were determined once again to work together and defeat their adversaries.

The following vignette illustrates the progress the children made in working together as a team, coming to grips with their own strengths and weaknesses and feeling the excitement and challenge of being part of a group activity. While these skills may be commonplace in nondisabled children, they are monumental achievements for children with Autism. They depict the pivotal changes that can occur when we teach children social relatedness rather than rote social skills.

It is a tense moment in our league opener; the game is about to begin. Richard, the coach, sets the batting order for the boys. Matt is up first. He still needs some work positioning his body correctly to face the pitcher, but he gets a hit and remembers to run to first base and stop there. His teammates shout "safe." Richard tells him, "Matt don't run, stay there." Matt points to second base "I need to go there." Peter is at the plate. He tells the pitcher—me—"Dr. Steve don't throw that hard. I can't hit that good." I reassure him and deliver a gentle pitch. Peter swings and hits a line drive. In the excitement Matt forgets to run and Peter has to push him to second base. As a result of his sacrifice, Peter is called out. Peter, with his notorious temper yells out "I hate baseball and I quit." Their coach warns him, "If you don't apologize, you won't get the trophy." Immediately Peter is contrite and says "OK, I'm sorry. I don't quit. I changed my mind I want to be on the team again."

It's Neil's turn at bat. Following up on their soccer experience, Neil and I have developed a ritual where we tease each other when one of us happens to be pitching and the other one batting. I try and make him laugh with strange faces and noises. But Neil is determined and remains focused. He hits a line drive, scoring Matt from second base (with a little help from Richard, pushing Matt around the bases).

We move to the last inning, the bottom of the 4th (we only have time for four innings). Richard, the coach, is warming up Neil who is coming in as the new relief pitcher. The boys are winning by a score of four to three. Peter is watching intently as he knows his turn to pitch will be next week. Neil is jumping up and down with excitement as he waits for the first batter to arrive at home plate. Matt is playing combination shortstop and third base. Peter is the first baseman.

Richard, who also serves as umpire, deems Neil ready and says "OK, Dr. Gutstein. You're up to bat." Neil pumps his arm and delivers his first pitch. Strike one. The boys are jumping with excitement. In short order we arrive at "Strike three. You're out." Both Matt and Peter go the mound to congratulate Neil. There's one out. My co-therapist is up. He takes a bad pitch and it's ball one. Two quick strikes follow. You can feel the excitement in the air, as evidenced by some mild hand flapping from the fielders. "Strike three!" He strikes out swinging. The fielders are jumping for joy. That was the second out; one more and the game will be over. I return to the plate. I swing and connect with the first pitch—a grounder to third. Matt fields the ball cleanly, but in all the excitement forgets to throw to first, so I am safe. Now my co-therapist grounds the second pitch to Peter. He fields it cleanly and this time makes an accurate throw to first. Unfortunately, Matt has forgotten he is a fielder and thinks he's a base runner and has taken off for second base so there is nobody to field the throw from Peter and we are both safe. My co-therapist scores and the game is tied. I take off from first and head for second with what would be the winning run. In desperation Peter reaches down, grabs second base and throws it into the outfield. It is clearly cheating, but the team considers him a hero nonetheless as time runs out on the session. Peter has redeemed himself and saved the day with his quick thinking and he is mobbed by his teammates as they leave the playroom.

Co-creation

The final objective of Level 3 is to introduce the function of co-creation as the heart of relational encounters. While children start creating new games as variations of prior activities, they eventually move into the realm of spontaneous creations combining imagination and the joy of shared invention. The treatment objectives at work during this stage are presented below.

> The final objective of Level 3 is to introduce the function of co-creation as the heart of relational encounters.

The games that partners co-create are initially quite basic but nonetheless constitute real breakthroughs in relational development. For example, at age eight, our three boys began creating what became a highly complex beanbag war game. It started at a very simple level, with the boys taking turns flinging the beanbags at each other. Peter launched his beanbag from a distance. Neil defended and then flung his own. The boys quickly learned to twirl around several times to build momentum. One boy's twirling quickly became a signal for the other boy to hold up his bag in defense. In short time, they moved from flinging their beanbags to using them as battering rams and colliding in the center of the room. The game evolved with charging, twirling, and defense all mixed together with a great deal of laughter and joy.

We were initially startled that the same children who could so creatively improvise ways to defeat the monster and win the critical baseball game would choose to create at such a primitive level when allowed to develop their own frameworks. But, the reality is that no matter how intelligent and how much they have progressed, they seem to want to start this way. Apparently the children first feel the need to return to an

---

Program Tip

Children love to videotape their new co-created activities. Recently one of our dyads proudly produced their own aerobic workout video.

earlier developmental stage—one that they previously enacted with the help of adult scaffolding, in order to re-experience mastery, this time with their peer partners. After several months the children are able to add much more sophistication. But initially, our partners and small groups are quite content with lots of repetition. They beam with pride at the jointly created frameworks—recognizing that, for the first time in their lives, they belong only to them.

Sample Level 3 Activities

Two Ball Toss: Two children each with a ball, face each other. The object is for them to throw and catch their balls simultaneously. Initially, if needed, we start with just one ball. The children may need to stand within visually demarcated boundaries, so they know they cannot regulate their interaction by moving to catch the ball, but by adjusting their throws and timing. There are many ways this activity can be varied and improvised, including distance, movement while throwing, type of balls etc.

Paddle Drums II: In the Level 3 variation of this activity, members vary their stop and go, loud and soft and fast and slow in a fluid, improvised manner. There are no distinct roles and verbal cues are phased out.

Relay Race for Referencing: Colored papers are divided into four equal piles and shuffled. Empty baskets are placed some distance from the starting place. Two complete sets of colored slips of paper are each placed on a different table, behind where the communicator stands. Runners start out next to their respective baskets. The Communicator holds up a colored paper and each Runner must go past his Communicator to their pile, get the needed color and return it to the basket. Then he references for the next color. The first team that gets all of the colors wins. Variations: Distances between objects. Number of slips of paper, colors, amount of verbalization allowed, using facial expressions, pictorial signs on papers etc. You can place different colors or shapes in different locations in the room that the team has to find.

Farm to Market: This is a good cooperative work game for young children. The children can be provided with pretend cellular phones for more realism. The game features several interlocking roles. There is a "producer"—who can be a farmer or manufacturer, located at one end of the toll road. There is a "buyer"—like a supermarket owner—located at the other end. A final role is the trucking company—who transports the merchandise from producer to buyer. Roles can be combined if there are fewer children. Other roles that can be added later are the toll road operator—who collects the tolls at a designated toll location and the road builder-repair crew—who constructs the road and does the entire wrecker and repair work.

Builder, Architect, Parts Department: There are three roles. The children have to work on negotiating their actions and coordinate their roles. The Architect is not allowed to touch any blocks, but he is totally in charge of the design. The parts department must supply the blocks to the builder. But, they must be the blocks that fit the architect's needs. Finally, only the builder is allowed to actually build with the blocks. However, he must reference the architect for design and use the Parts Department for any additional blocks.

Sharing Our Worlds

Level Four

$\mathcal{A}$s children develop through Levels 1, 2 and 3, they learn that the topics of Experience Sharing interactions are behaviors like facial expressions, sounds, gestures and movements, that can be directly referenced, compared and coordinated. Level 4 marks the beginning of a permanent, dramatic change in the primary reference point for Experience Sharing. Rather than overt "public" behavior, children learn to understand and value the inner, "private" experience and exert enormous energy learning to coordinate their unique perceptions, ideas, and feelings with those of their social partners.

Level 4 Stages and Treatment Objectives

Stage 13: Joint Attention

- The child enjoys visual and verbal emotion sharing, following joint perception of an external stimulus.

- The child rapidly shifts attention from a shared stimulus to a partner's facial expression for emotion sharing (not to obtain an object or gain information) without being cued to do so.

Stage 14: Perspective Taking

- The child actively seeks to compare and contrast perceptions of: 1) the same object, "How do you see it?" 2) differences in the same visual field, "I see a face in that cloud. What do you see?" and 3) different visual fields, "What are you doing?" What are you looking at?"

Stage 15: Unique Reactions

- The unique reactions of our partners becomes the highlight of the joint attention experience.

- The child realizes that her partner's emotional reactions and unique perceptions are as interesting as her own.

Stage 16: Adding Imagination

- Shared addition of imaginative elements becomes the highlight of the joint attention experience.

- The child enjoys pretend role-plays and games where each partner equally collaborates in the creation.

In the early stages of Level 4, our patients make the startling discovery that other people see the world differently. This discovery prompts an earnest inquiry into the perceptions, thoughts and feelings of other people. What do they see that I don't? Do they perceive it differently than I do? Is the information they provide useful to me? Does it help me better understand myself and the world around me? The culmination of Level 4 is the ability to find joy by sharing unique perceptions of any environment in which our children and their social partners jointly find themselves. They learn to share not only what they see, but also their unique emotional reactions and imaginative embellishments.

Case Study

Brian was diagnosed with Autism several months after his second birthday. As part of our evaluation, we still remember watching a videotape of Brian and his family celebrating Christmas together when Brian was 19 months old. His family was gathered around the Christmas tree, laughing and showing each other their presents. Brian was off to one side by the fireplace, oblivious to his joyful family members, smiling oddly and playing with some wrapping paper.

Brian began his work with some Level 1 skills already in place. His language was quite slow to develop, but as with Manuel, Brian's parents were more concerned with the quality and appropriateness of his language, rather than the number of words he spoke. Following his initial evaluation with us, Brian's parents converted their garage into a version of our playroom and for the first year spent over twenty hours per week working on assigned activities. Brian made excellent progress in developing his desire and ability for Experience Sharing. By age four, he had completed Level 2 and was ready to begin working in a dyad with a matched peer. Brian was one of the relatively few children with Autism we work with whose understanding of the various functions of Emotional Coordination soon began to surpass his repertoire of skills for sharing his experiences. When this disparity occurs, it is always a sign that the child is poised for rapid progress. By the time Brian was five, he had mastered all of his Level 3 objectives and was ready to work on Joint Attention.

We were already seeing signs of higher functioning in his Level 3 activities. The following vignette with Brian and his mom, Julia, describes one such activity we call Crashing Cars. Two partners sit about five feet

Program Tip

The Crashing Cars activity can be modified in many ways. You can vary the distance between partners, the size of the cars, the amount of structural cues provided, etc. The spectacular collisions make for an exciting activity that few children can resist. However, be prepared to replace your cars frequently!

> ## Program Tip
>
> Even though an activity might be designed to highlight a lower level of functioning, (for example, Crashing Cars is a Level 2 activity) we find that when a child is functioning at a higher level, he will demonstrate abilities appropriate to that higher level no matter what the task.

apart, each holding a small metal toy car. Midway between the partners is a center area marked out with masking tape. The object of the activity is for both partners to release their cars at the same moment so they crash together in the middle area.

As you read through the vignette, note how much responsibility Brian takes for regulation and repair. This is an excellent sign that he has learned and is employing the essential elements of Level 3. Also, while Brian's language is quite limited, notice how high a percentage of his words serve the function of Experience Sharing, and how much "mileage" he gets from such a small language repertoire.

> **Julia** (pointing): *Do you want the blue or beige mat?*
> **Brian** (pointing and making sure his mother notices): *Here's some neat cars. Wow!* (A good example of Joint Attention).
> **Julia** (indicating where he should sit): *You sit on the carpet.*
> **Brian** (getting seated): *Cool!*
> **Julia:** *Are you ready?*
> **Together:** *1,2,3, go. Aaaaah!* (The cars crash successfully in the middle).
> **Brian:** *Again! Again!*
> (They count and release together again but this time the cars pass by each other).
> **Julia:** *We missed.*
> **Brian:** *What happened?* (Communicating for regulation).
> **Julia:** *We missed.*
> **Brian:** *Let's try again.* (This is a great example of repairing their coordination).
> They count together again and this time the cars meet with a resounding crash.
> **Brian** (holding the car in his arms): *But it's crying.* (Brian is introducing a novel element by pretending that the crash has injured the car)
> **Julia:** *It needs to go to the doctor.* (Brian pretends to fix it).
>
> (The examiner enters to instruct them in Running and Jumping, which Brian has practiced many times before).

Brian (pointing): *We are going to play this. Right there!*
(Mother and son count together while looking at each other raptly. They leave at the same moment, hold hands and run at the same pace. They land together on the bean-bags face-to-face and laugh uproariously. They walk back to the start line together, with Brian even stopping to help his mother up from the beanbags. The next time they fall Brian initiates a "wheee!" noise and Julia imitates him. When, after the third attempt, she walks back at a faster pace, he makes sure to run to catch up with her).

Julia—*"Let's count to 4."* (Brian adapts without any prob-lems. They complete a round).
Brian—*"One more time."*
(This time Julia pauses while they are running. They are still holding hands and Brian immediately stops with her as he feels the tension in his arm).

(They try running without holding hands. In his excite-ment during their initial trial, Brian, for the first time, runs ahead of his mother. They return to the starting point.)
Brian: *Mom, are you ready?* (Clearly a repair attempt after running ahead of mom the last time. On the next trial, Brian matches his mother's pace and they fall and land together. On the third trial, Julia abruptly stops running midway to the goal. Brian runs past her and falls on the beanbags).
Brian (realizing the loss of coordination): *Whoops. I'm sorry.*
Julia: *What are you sorry about?*
Brian: *Let's try again.*
(She stops again and he runs ahead and—realizing his error—laughs).
Julia: *Did momma stop? Let's try again.* (This time, while they run, he watches her all the way and times his stop to match her stop exactly.)

Brian's Treatment Plan

Brian clearly was ready to work on Joint Attention. We developed the seven treatment objectives outlined on the next page.

Brian became adept at Joint Attention only after many months of careful guidance, where we systematically broke down the elements of this process and then gradually integrated them. In the beginning, Julia was taught to just show him objects. Our goal was to teach Brian to swiftly shift his attention from the object to Julia's face, to share the emotional meaning of her discovery. Children with Autism find this rapid shifting between an object and a partner's face very difficult. We typically spend several months working on this one objective.

To help children with Autism appreciate Joint Attention, we instruct parents to use highly amplified vocalizations and exaggerated movements to cue children to shift back from an object to their face, to experience the shared excitement of the discovery. For example, Julia would point and say, "Look, it's Big Bird!" Just as soon as Brian's gaze locked onto the doll she would gasp loudly, make highly excited noises and shout "Wow!!!" while flapping her arms wildly. If even more amplification was needed, we taught her to fall to the floor, or perform almost any exaggerated action that would motivate Brian to look back to her.

We also taught Julia ways to reinforce with Brian that the joy they shared together was the real reason for their interactions. Julia would show Brian a picture from a book. Suddenly, she would close the book and do something extremely silly, something that would result in shared laughter. Then she would turn to another picture and repeat the sequence. It was interesting to note that when Brian was finally placed in his group, he imitated Julia's actions. He would show something to a group member, then suddenly stop and do something hilarious to get him to laugh.

Brian first learned to imitate the sequence of pointing, shifting attention and sharing excitement in a symmetrical role set, alongside Julia. Once these skills were familiar, we taught him how to use them in a

Treatment Objectives for Joint Attention

- Brian will enjoy visual and verbal emotion sharing, following the joint perception of an external stimulus.

- Brian will learn to rapidly shift attention from a shared stimulus to his partner's facial expression, solely for the purpose of emotion sharing (as opposed to requesting an item or gaining information about the situation) without being cued to do so.

- Brian will carefully observe to make sure he accurately perceives what his partner is indicating.

- Brian will communicate (e.g. use distal pointing, showing, gesturing, verbalization) to direct his partner's attention to interesting objects for the purpose of sharing an experience.

- Brian will communicate to better perceive objects that his partner is trying to point out (e.g. ask for clarification, ask his partner to move the object or show it to him again).

- Brian will self-regulate to help his partner attend to the things he wants to point out (e.g. pointing instead of gesturing, moving object closer to his partner).

- Brian will self-regulate to better perceive the objects that his partner is pointing out (e.g. he'll move closer, shift his position).

complementary manner, where he would point out his own unique discoveries to her. However, accomplishing this goal required that Brian grasp two important things: 1) his perceptions were unique and could be different from those of his partner; and 2) there was an emotional payoff for sharing his personal world.

By mastering Joint Attention, Brian made a crucial breakthrough, one that would make it much easier for him to initiate and sustain interactions with other people and form friendships with peers. Just about every parent of a child with Autism can recite stories about times they have arranged for a peer to come over to play, only to watch as their child ignored his "pal" and focused completely on his Nintendo or a favorite video. Brian had reached the point where the lure of interesting objects and toys was no longer an impediment to Experience Sharing. When his pals came over, they received his undivided attention for good reasons. He knew that no matter how exciting a Nintendo game or TV show might be, it didn't produce the joy and excitement that could occur within his interaction with people.

After three months of working on Joint Attention, we assessed Brian's progress. The first evaluation activity involved reading a book together. Julia was instructed to let Brian have the book and to sit adjacent to him, acting receptive but not initiating any interaction. Brian opened the picture book and started turning pages. He pointed to items on the page as he told Julia interesting things he noticed. He referenced Julia as he talked about them, and at times emphasized his discovery with exclamations of "Look at that!" Julia was a crucial part of his interaction; he wanted to share his enjoyment with her. This is an example of early Joint Attention. But, Brian did not yet realize his mother could not easily see what he was seeing, because of where she was sitting. As he had not yet developed Perspective Taking, he made no attempts to reposition the book to make sure she could see the pages.

> **As he had not yet developed Perspective Taking, he made no attempts to reposition the book to make sure she could see the pages.**

As we progressed through the Level 4 evaluation, Julia and Brian engaged in an activity called "Junk Boxes." In this activity, the examiner brings out two plastic boxes, each filled with small interesting items. The partners are seated, facing each other, with their boxes about two to three feet apart. The partners are instructed to take turns showing one item at a time to each other. Parents are asked not to cue the child to show them anything, but to notice what happens naturally.

Examiner: *Guess what? I have a box for you and a box for mommy.*
Brian (alternating his gaze between his mother's face and the box): *For me?*
Examiner: *Yes, for you.*
Brian: *Ooooh wow!!!*
Brian (holding up a small toy car to show her): *Look at this car momma!* (He smiles with her.)

> **Program Tip**
>
> When beginning Joint Attention instruction, adults may have to take the child's arm so they point to the referent with their hands together. Continue pointing while walking up to and actually touching the object. The pair can then practice backing away while still pointing and then again approaching the object, in order to establish the connection between pointing and the object. If the child is still having difficulty, try using a more visual structure, like a line of masking tape between the object and the child.

(Julia holds up an object.)

Brian (looking at Julia's object and then at Julia): *Pretty neat!* (This is one of Brian's favorite phrases. It is amazing how much popularity Brian has achieved among peers with just a few phrases such as this, used with genuine enthusiasm and good timing.)

(Brian holds up a small plastic red bear and shows it to Julia. Julia finds a blue bear in her box and holds one up too. They share in the laughter of their coincidence.)

Brian: *You too? Bear!*

Brian (holding up yet one more bear): *Look at this! Wow! Pretty neat!*

(They now take turns in a highly fluid manner, showing each other their discoveries, without ever being told to do so. The examiner walks in the room and—without a pause—Brian includes her in sharing his discoveries.)

The examiner brings in two dinosaurs, some baby diapers and some bottles and dishes for the pretend play activity. They sit face to face on the carpet. Brian loves dinosaurs.

Brian (pointing): *Yeaah that's pretty neat.*

(They each take dinosaurs. Brian takes two and pretends they are biting each other).

Brian: *Hi yah dinosaurs. Mom, it's a Barney! I will teach you, Barney.*

Brian watches Julia pretend to mix food to feed her baby dinosaur. He rapidly switches his attention back-and-forth between his mother's activity and his own two dinosaurs who he still has fighting.)

Brian (pointing to one of his dinosaurs): *Mom, what should it say?*

(Julia is now diapering her dinosaur.)

Brian (pointing to Julia's dinosaur): *It's a baby! Momma, give me a diaper.*

(Julia points to one for him and he begins to diaper his baby dinosaur, just like she has. He stops midway in his diapering because it gets too hard and then tries again. Julia continues to feed her dinosaur quietly, not disturbing Brian. She knows when she should not introduce any more information, nor does she rush in to do too much for Brian).

Brian: *Mommy, would you help me?*
(Julia gives him just minor help. Brian tries again and fails and she gives him a bit more help and finally shows him how she fastened her diaper. He works independently and finally figures it out.)

In our last Level 4 activity, each partner is given a toy to play with. Parents are instructed to focus on their own activity and not look over to the child, unless the child initiates interaction. Julia and Brian were seated about five feet apart. Both were provided with a coloring book and crayons (one of Brian's favorite activities).

Brian (offering Julia a crayon): *One for you?*
Julia: *Thanks, I have some.*
Brian (struggling to get his crayons out): *Hey. I can't get it out.*
Julia: *Need help?*
Brian: *Yeah.* (but finally the crayon comes out).
Brian: *I got it.* (Even though Brian has his own activity and Julia is quite involved in coloring, Brian is continuing to find ways to keep her involved with him without disturbing her. Brian moves over to Julia's activity.)
Brian: *What's that?* (Julia tells him. Brian returns to his own coloring book but continues a non-stop narration of what he sees in the coloring book. He closes his book and looks at what she is doing. Then he opens his book again.)
Brian: *Look—a dinosaur. It's O.K. It's a baby.*
(Brian—despite his limited language—is doing almost all of the talking. He wants to maintain their coordination and knows that Julia is not doing much to engage him, as each time he doesn't initiate, she goes back to work. Not more than a 10 second interval passes during the whole five minutes they spend coloring without Brian saying something about either of their activities.

Seeing Another's Perspective

As he moved into the second stage of Level 4, Brian was ready to learn that other people's perspectives were not necessarily the same as his own. Julia began to communicate to Brian that she could not always see what he saw. Brian quickly learned—even without formal instruction—to re-orient pictures and objects to provide her with a better view.

Among the many perspective-taking activities we practice, one of our favorites is The Blindfold Obstacle Course. Two children work together in this activity. We set up a safe series of barriers forming an obstacle course. One child acts as the sighted guide, while the other child is blindfolded. Their objective is to maneuver through the course together without knocking anything over. The guide, to be effective, has to take the perspective of his unsighted partner and carefully direct him verbally around the obstacles.

Sample Objectives for Perspective Taking

- Brian will actively seek out possible differences between his and partner's perceptions (e.g. "I see a red car. What do you see?")

- Brian will actively compare and contrast his perceptions of the same object with partners (e.g. "I think that plane is huge. Do you?")

- Brian will carefully observe and communicate with partners to ensure that they understand his perspective.

- Brian will self-regulate so that his partner better shares his perspective (e.g. noticing that his partner's view of an object is obstructed, although it is plainly visible to him)

- Brian will make appropriate adjustments to facilitate a shared perspective, such as turning a book so his partner can better see a picture.

Unique Reactions and Adding Imagination

As Level 4 work progresses, external perceptions and the unique meanings of these perceptions blend more smoothly together. By the close of Stage 14, our children notice all sorts of objects and events in their environment and actively share these with their partners. In the latter stages of Level 4, children with Autism are not only coordinating their tangible discoveries, but are beginning to share their emotional reactions and unique interpretations of these objects as well. Once they reach this point, language becomes the major vehicle for Experience Sharing; it will henceforth remain.

In the latter stages of Level 4, we work on treatment objectives similar to those outlined on page 137.

We believed that Brian was ready to move to more advanced Level 4 activities. He loved to look out the window and share his joyful emotional reactions with his partners as they jointly pointed out their discoveries of cars and trucks on the freeway. He enthusiastically came prepared each week to show off photographs of his home, family and favorite community landmarks. He made sure to turn his photo album

Program Tip

Determine the most minimal way to provide scaffolding for the child to reach the next developmental stage. This form of adult guidance is the most effective as it allows the child to take ownership and feel the positive results of his own discoveries.

so that his group partner, David, could see the pictures. He was more than happy to answer any of David's questions about the pictures.

We were then surprised when Brian suddenly became a reluctant participant as we moved into the latter part of Level 4 work. For us, it became a critical part of our understanding of how relational development progresses in children with Autism. We were working on elaborating our perceptions, adding a little bit of imagination to what we agreed was out there. Clouds could also be castles. Red toy trucks could be fire engines for mice. Brian's group partner, David, found these interchanges highly appealing. Of course, he was not without difficulties, as he would become so enamored with his own imaginative creations that our responses ceased to matter to him.

We realized that by the end of Level 4 children are still primarily concerned with sharing perceptions. However, the way they define a perception changes significantly. Children are no longer concerned only with showing, pointing out or labeling objects or events. Sharing perceptions of everyday objects no longer holds the excitement it once did. At this stage, the real joy is derived from the unique ways in which we use our minds and our imaginations to shape what we see.

> **...we all have our own unique internal reactions to things we see, hear, smell, taste, or touch—an understanding quite different than merely labeling what we experience.**

Our work had left behind the concrete, real and visible and evolved into joining that external world with the invisible, internal parts of our minds, and herein lay the difficulty for Brian. While he had mastered the skills involved with joint attention and truly felt the joy and connection inherent in these types of interactions, sharing internal worlds required a new set of skills. Brian, and other child with Autism working at the advanced stages of Level 4, often overlook the fact that we all have our own unique internal reactions to things we see, hear, smell, taste, or touch—an understanding quite different than merely labeling what we experience.

Once we understood the giant leap that takes place within these stages of Level 4, we noticed the specific difficulties Brian was having. Brian lacked an awareness of the way his own mind could function as a chalkboard to creatively modify his perceptions. He had never considered that he could put his own 'spin' on the objects and events around him. Brian needed to be able to think on a representational level, to appreciate that a thing, such as a red car or a cloud, does not have to always be itself, but can symbolize something else. A cloud had always been a cloud and was nothing else. A picture of a house in mid-air being lifted by a tornado might be really funny to him—but his level of thinking prevented him from imagining that it could be a house-plane going on a vacation. Even if he could imagine such things, Brian could scarcely express them in a manner his partner could comprehend. By age 10 he spoke in well-formed, full sentences. However, when he moved away from well-rehearsed phrases, his capacity for inventive language dropped off considerably.

Brian's Level 4 Treatment Objectives

- Sharing emotional reactions will become the highlight of the joint attention experience.

- Brian will act as if his partner's emotional reactions and unique perceptions are as interesting as his own.

- Brian will communicate to determine similarities and differences between self and his partner's emotional reactions, to ensure that he understands them accurately and to ensure his partners accurately understand his reactions.

- Brian will find ways of personally appreciating and validating his partner's reactions.

- Brian will understand that his partners may not share his own unique reactions and will accept these differences.

We designed a treatment segment that would help Brian notice he had unique perceptions, feelings and ideas, and that he could adjust his thinking to incorporate imaginative elements without causing him an undo amount of stress and anxiety. Initially, we limited our language output. We removed full sentences and long statements and restricted our reactions to, at most, four well-chosen words, coupled with amplified joy and excitement. For the next several weeks our time with Brian and David was spent leafing through magazines—mostly National Geographic—to find odd, absurd photos to cut out and place in a "Silly Pictures" photo album. We found a photo of two men in India, with one man's feet sticking out of a hole and the other man's head poking into a second adjacent hole in the ground. We found a picture of a house in the grips of a tornado, bike riders racing on glaciers, men posing with large stacks of books on their heads.

At first, our therapists provided the captions to the photos. The men in the hole were labeled: "Come back feet!" The house in the tornado was deemed "Wake up, you're flying." The intrepid bicyclists were told "Hey, get some skis!" The men with novel hats were called "Book brains."

As the weeks went by, we began our group sessions with a review of our Silly Pictures albums; they never failed to bring forth hilarity. We continued to scour new magazines to add to our collection: to be accepted, a photo required unanimous agreement and someone had to add a silly enough caption to rouse our laughter.

After several weeks we introduced a change in the game. As we reviewed the pictures, we each had to take turns giving the photo a new caption. David was limited to using no more than four words. Likewise, Brian was not allowed to merely re-state the previous caption by slightly varying the words. He had to come up with an original caption, even if he used only one word that was all his own, or even if he merely made a new noise, without a real word. Brian's initial efforts were not especially profound—but they were his. More importantly, though, was the sense of pride and accomplishment that emerged as Brian created on his own. His interest in Experience Sharing was renewed and he once again became an active participant. Having tasted the joy of sharing his internal world, Brian was on his way to a much richer and rewarding quality of life.

Sample Level 4 Activities

Silly Pictures: Cut out interesting and odd pictures together from magazines like National Geographic and put them in a photo album. While looking at each picture together, have each child make up an interesting noise or phrase that connects to the photo. For more advanced work, children can take turns pointing to objects in the photo and sharing what they see, followed by them together making ridiculous noises specifically tied to the perception. For example, a child can point to a picture of a thunderstorm, say that it makes a loud noise, and together the children can shout "Kaboom." A sister activity is Silly Captions: Make up new interpretations of silly pictures, pretending that something is there that is really not. For examples, writing captions that illustrate the opposite of what they see, or captions that express highly ridiculous points of view.

The Barrier: Two students play this game. Each student stands on an opposite side of a barrier, tall enough for neither to look over. On one side of the barrier is a box or a ring that a soft nerf ball must be tossed into. The goal of the game is for the two students to work together, using communication to coordinate their efforts. Since the thrower can't see the goal, he must depend on the student on the other side of the obstacle to direct him.
There are many, many variations of this game, which is a great beginning exercise to promote cooperative learning. For example, the teacher can keep moving the goal, so that extra communication is needed. This is a good game for teams to play against each other as well, if the students can positively manage the extra stress of competition.

Inkblots: Have the children make their own inkblot using some ink or paint, putting it on a piece of paper, then folding the paper in half and opening it again. Several activities can be generated from the inkblot: sharing with each other what each child sees, discovering which things you both see, helping your partner see something in the blot that you notice and he can't see, etc.

The Blindfold Obstacle Course: One student is blindfolded. The other student is the guide. Students switch roles each time they get through the obstacle course. Set up a safe indoor obstacle course, where you have the ability to shift objects and obstacles on each trial. One student dons a blindfold. The other has to use verbal communication to guide the blindfolded student through the course as quickly as possible (time bonus points), while knocking over as few obstacles as possible (obstacle deduction points). This is a game that begs to be played on a competitive basis against another team. However, it can be started by the single team trying to best its own record. Adults can alter the course on each trial. They can also make it more complex or simple depending on the needs of the team.

Sharing Our Minds: The Inner Game

Level Five

*A*t the close of Level 4 work, we notice the emergence of true "mind-sharing" developing in children with Autism. The referent, or topic of interest within interaction, has shifted from objects in

---

Level 5 Stages and Treatment Objectives

Stage 17: Sharing Ideas

- Enjoyment is obtained through sharing ideas, opinions and feelings.

- The child and peer partners co-create new ideas and themes to communicate and share their inner worlds.

- The child has developed a good understanding of shared pretense. He uses pretend characters and actions in collaborative role-plays without external props. He fluidly creates and shifts pretend roles.

Stage 18: Exciting Differences

- The child demonstrates a high level of interest in comparing and sharing his different ideas, viewpoints and opinions.

- Relationship excitement is enhanced by the different ideas and themes brought into play and conversation by social partners.

Stage 19: The Inside and Outside Worlds

- The child differentiates between internal and external reactions and places more importance on the internal state of her partner.

- The child recognizes that outward reactions may not accurately represent her partner's true emotional state and actively attempts to determine the internal state of her partner.

- The child understands pretense and deception. She can pretend to have an emotion different from her actual feelings; she reacts appropriately when a partner pretends to have an extreme emotion.

Stage 20: The Primacy of Minds

- The child recognizes that thoughts, feelings and ideas are the critical elements of Experience Sharing and is highly motivate to share these internal states.

- The child demonstrates an active interest in determining what his partners are really thinking and feeling.

---

the external world to the partners' thoughts, feelings and opinions about these objects. Sharing common and different reactions to the external events becomes the highlight of interaction, coupled with a growing interest to explore the minds and imaginations of their partners. However, these conversations are still limited by the child with Autism's need to maintain some common external anchor. As children work through Level 5, their interactions become freed from the constraints of a tangible reference point. They develop the ability to talk about anything at anytime. Their imagination blossoms into the realm of things that could never exist, as opposed to adding imaginative elements to familiar objects or events. Children with Autism develop the awareness that they need no other props—just themselves—to carry on this type of interaction with other people in their environment.

Case Study

Porter, a delightful teenager with Autism, first came to treatment with us when he was eight. Although he already possessed all Level 1 and beginning Level 2 skills, he knew little about co-regulation. For example, Porter would routinely greet me in my waiting room with great excitement and then run right past me, bolting into the treatment room without a backward glance. Like Brian, Porter was a child with delayed language who was motivated to be a good apprentice and learn meaning from adults, a more important predictor of success than language.

After four years of steady progress, Porter was ready to move to Level 5. His initial treatment objectives are outlined below.

As happened with Brian, our work quickly stalled. We first looked to Porter's limited language as a potential obstacle to development, but determined the problem was not Porter's language, but his lack of self-development. While Porter was language delayed, he had developed

Treatment Objectives for Sharing Ideas

- Porter will obtain enjoyment through sharing and integrating ideas with social partners.
- Porter and his partners will co-create new ideas, themes and objects using novel imaginative elements.
- Porter will develop a good understanding of shared pretense. He will use pretend characters and actions in collaborative role-plays without external props.
- Porter will fluidly create and shift pretend roles.
- Porter will frequently reference, communicate and self-regulate to ensure a mutual understanding of the ideas and feelings of his social partners.
- Porter will modify his own ideas to maintain the integrity of the interaction.
- Porter will rapidly discard and discontinue any ideas or pretend elements that cause discomfort to social partners, or impede their Emotional Coordination.

> ### Program Tip
>
> Within the autism community, most parents and professionals associate more language abilities as "higher functioning," with the resultant notion that Aspergers Syndrome is a less severe diagnosis than Autism. However, within the arena of relational development, language facility does not always equal success. Social referencing and the willingness to accept adult instruction do.

sufficient expressive and receptive skills to be able to share simple ideas. Much like Brian, Porter was really not conscious of having his own mind, one with unique thoughts and feelings. His Experience Sharing could not progress until he first developed a greater awareness that he possessed his own unique personal experiences. It was unrealistic of us to expect Porter to understand the unique contents of other people's minds, if he didn't even understand that he had his own.

We returned to one of the cardinal principles of our program: when teaching becomes confusing for a child, we simplify the environment so that the child can concentrate on only one segment of treatment at a time. For Porter, we needed to completely separate his problems with oral language from his lack of self-awareness.

When we work with persons with Autism who have language-processing delays but can read fluently, we find it highly effective to introduce true reciprocal conversation by sitting side-by-side at the computer keyboard. Unlike oral language, which must be processed quickly and through auditory channels, working on the computer allows the person to process language visually, and at a speed more comfortable for him.

As we started communicating via computer with Porter, we discovered we could be much more elaborate and challenging with him that we could on a verbal level. We quickly moved into framing the variable of "mind" by using a method of poetry instruction developed by Kenneth Koch, author of *Rose Where Did You Get that Red?* Koch's basic method is to provide a series of simple structured themes—similar to what we call frameworks—from which children can communicate their unique ideas and images, without becoming overwhelmed and discouraged by having to write from scratch.

Porter responded well to this methodology. We would choose a particular poem framework, with Porter adding the title and the creative part of the material. In the following poem, simply entitled "Color Poem", the framework is italicized, with Porter's text following it.

Color Poem

Red is like JELLO in the spring.
Yellow is like the sun that rises all the way up in the morning.
Blue is like a frozen penguin in the winter.
Green is like salad in the afternoon.
Orange is like dropping down a palm tree in the fall.
Purple is like violets that blur out in the night.

Our initial success spurred us on to a frenzy of poetic activity. As we progressed together, we had Porter work with elements such as outcomes, colors, place and feelings within his creative responses.

In oral discourse, Porter was still relegated to simple phrases and more scripted conversational questions and responses. However, in his writing, Porter was learning that he could use language creatively to express himself—his inner ideas, feelings and thought, even about things that could never exist in the real world.

Koch also outlines an exercise called "In my movie" that Porter enjoyed. Children learn to use their imaginations to create improbable stories. They experience the thrill of inventing scenes that set the stage for later playful co-creations with peers. Notice how the poetic framework allows us to focus entirely on the playful, imaginative use of language to evoke mental images, with no concern for grammar, syntax or whether the scenes make sense.

In My Movie

In my movie someone throws dinner at police officers
And the hero arrests the dinner blaster.
In my movie someone steals the gameboy
And the villain is pushed to the pole.
In my movie the evil father plans to find bullets
And the hero puts the father in the trashcan.
In my movie someone steals the pizza delivery
And the villain got cheese on his face.
In my movie the jumpy boy breaks the movie
And the hero twists bubble gum at him.

Co-creating Minds

As Porter became more aware of his own self and his unique inner world, and was expressing it more fluidly in his written communications, we decided it was time to move Porter back into the arena of shared communication with a peer. Towards the end of the year, we began working on Porter's ability to share his newly discovered ideas and imagination with his partner, Craig. We created a game called "Silly Questions," in which we posed a question and the boys took turns formulating absurd answers. Like the Silly Photos exercise in the preceding chapter, at first we provided both the questions and the answers. But very quickly, the boys started taking over the answers and soon had mastered the entire structure, leaving us with the role of amused audience. Examples of work they created entirely on their own follow.

Silly Questions

What do you get when you mix an elephant with a blueberry?
Answer—A Blue Elephant
Answer—A Belephant
Answer—A Dark Blue Elephant
Answer—A giant blueberry
Answer—A blue mammal!

Who invented the balloon?
Bob Float
Fred Hotair
Gary Gas

Once I ate the telephone!
Yum!
Did your tummy ring?

Once I ate the stapler!
Good taste!
Did your tummy get stuck to your lungs?

Once I ate the building!
Did you burp up an elevator?

We were ready to move into a more complex format for sharing minds—the co-creation of stories.

We were ready to move into a more complex format for sharing minds—the co-creation of stories. Unlike poems, the prose format is less forgiving when it comes to coherence. When we read stories, much like conversations, we expect the meaning of one sentence to flow in a highly coordinated manner into the next one.

For Porter to co-write stories, he had to care about his partner's ideas, as well as his own and figure out how to coordinate his thoughts. Porter was not ready to begin this task with his dyad partner Craig, so as is often the case when we introduce a new level of complexity, we resumed a guided participation role with him. Our first joint story attempt—"The Boy who Tracks the Road"—was very difficult for him. We had to maintain full responsibility for cohesion of the story. Porter, at this point, was fairly oblivious to how the direction of our ideas affected the work. He remained focused on a highly rigid progression of his own ideas. At one point, under the clear threat of death, his character refuses to build the road, because it is 9 PM and thus "too late for building." The fluidity he expressed in play and poetry had not yet entered his dialogue. There was little Experience Sharing or co-creation of a common story. It was as if we were sharing two unblended, disparate experiences.

On a positive note, by the end of the story Porter had already began moving into a more emotionally descriptive plane, noted especially by his comment "The boy was lonely." Loneliness was a new emotion for Porter, something he had never considered until the previous year. His awareness that someone could feel lonely was a real sign of progress in his understanding of a mind adrift and set apart from others.

During the three-week interval between Part 1 and Part 2 of the story, Porter wrote short phrases and worked on recognizing when a sentence fit the ideas that preceded it. The result of this effort is clearly evident in Part 2. Notice that while responsibility for maintaining Emotional Coordination still remains with the therapist, Porter's lines are fitting together nicely and the emotional tone and story line are more coherent. (Lines presented to Porter are in italics.)

> **His awareness that someone could feel lonely was a real sign of progress in his understanding of a mind adrift and set apart from others.**

The Boy Who Tracks the Road—Part 2

Just when he was about to give up, he heard a strange voice calling him from outside the door. It wasn't the prince. It was someone else. It sounded like a girl's voice.

But it is not the boy's sister.

It's not the boy's mother either.

"We need you back."

"But, I can't come back, because I am locked in this dungeon and the evil prince stole the keys!"

"He stole the keys?"

"Yes. He stole the keys. Can you help me?"

"Yes! I can help you out!"

"If you want to help me, you must go kill the prince and get the keys!"

"All right! I can kill the evil prince!"

So, the girl left the dungeon and went out to find the evil prince.

The boy waited for her.

After several hours, the boy heard the girl's voice. She said,

"I killed the evil prince! Now I can let you out of this dungeon!"

The girl got the keys.

And she opened the dungeon door and let the boy out.

The boy was happy to be out again.

He kissed the girl and said "Will you marry me?"

The girl said, "Yes!"

So the boy and the girl went home and found a minister of a church. And they said to the minister

"We want a wedding!"

The minister said, "O.K. But, if you want a wedding, you have to give me 100 gold coins. Do you have 100 gold coins?"

The boy said, "Yes!"
He gave the minister the gold coins and said "Hurry up and marry
*   us. I have to go and build a road. There's not much time left."*
The boy heard the wedding music.
The boy and the girl were married right away.
So the boy built a road.
And his wife helped him build it, because she knew all about road
*   construction.*
The boy finally finished building. The boy can't wait until the
    race starts at 9:00 am.
And everybody lived happily ever after.

Porter and I continued to write stories at a prodigious clip. He was immensely proud of his efforts and always rushed out of my office at the end of our sessions to excitedly read his latest work to family members. Porter experienced the excitement and competence of knowing he could express his inner creative world. The stories themselves became an important memory that bound us together, as we frequently re-read them and compared their various themes and characters.

The next story entitled "The Boy Who Ran Around the World", was written about a month later. Notice the playfulness and creativity that has entered Porter's contributions. Porter is clearly a co-creator of the emotional tone of the story and introduces new themes at a regular rate—albeit with fewer words. Porter is also co-regulating to make sure the new ideas fit into a coherent story line. By Chapter 2, we are almost completely coordinated and the story is flowing quite fluidly—almost as if it is emerging from a single mind!

> **Porter had left the absolute world of black and white thinking, where there could only be one right answer, and had entered a world where he could use his mind to create solutions as needed.**

Also note a major breakthrough related to Porter's thinking and problem solving abilities. At one point in the story, we are trapped at the tip of South America and Porter's response is a flexible, "Suddenly there is a bridge." This was a far cry from his initial story where the head of the road building crew rigidly declared that everyone would just have to die because it was 9 PM and road building had to stop. Porter had left the absolute world of black and white thinking, where there could only be one right answer, and had entered a world where he could use his mind to create solutions as needed. Porter's world would never be the same!

The Boy Who Ran Around the World—Chapter 1

(Therapist's words are in italics.)

Once upon a time, there was a boy who ran around the
    world.
He started running in Texas on a hot July day.
Next, he ran to California.
Luckily, California was a lot cooler than Texas.
Then, the boy ran to Phoenix, Arizona.
When he got to Phoenix, he realized he was running backwards.

Then he went to Denver, Colorado.

But, if he kept running back and forth he would never get around the world. He realized that he had to keep running in one direction only.

Then, he ran to Mexico.

He decided to keep running south for as long as he could.

He is in South America.

Finally, he got to the southern most part of South America. He had to decide what to do, because the next southern place was Antarctica.

Suddenly, there was a bridge.

It was called the Bridge to Antarctica and it was owned by a flock of penguins that collected the tolls.

Then, he crossed the ocean to Antarctica.

After he threw a few snowballs, he decided that he was too cold and he needed to go to Africa to warm up.

Chapter 2

The boy was still in Antarctica.

How was he going to get to Africa?

He decided to take a boat.

Luckily, he spotted a beluga whale who owned a sailing ship.

The boy said, "Can I have a ride?"

The whale replied "Yes, but you have to give me your Nintendo Game Boy to pay for the cruise to Africa."

The boy gave the Game Boy to the whale.

Then, the whale told the boy to get on the ship and they sailed to South Africa.

Suddenly, there was a stampede of elephants and rhinos.

The boy quickly climbed a high tree and narrowly escaped from being crushed.

The charging rhinos made the tree break apart.

The boy fell off the tree, but luckily he fell right onto the back of one of the charging elephants.

And the elephant let the boy have a ride.

The boy and the elephant rode together all the way to Algeria in North Africa. While they were on their journey in Africa they met Tarzan the king of the jungle.

Suddenly, Tarzan had a sword.

He said to the boy "I am going to kill you, if you don't give me your Nintendo Game Boy."

The boy said, "No, you're not."

The boy took out his Laser Pistol and shot Tarzan.

Finally, Tarzan exploded.

All of the animals in the jungle cheered and said to the boy "Now you are the king of the jungle."

The boy said, "Thanks, but I'll be back later." First, I have to finish running around the world. But, after that, I will come back to be your king."

His final destination was Europe. He had to figure out how to cross the Mediterranean Sea.

So, he telephoned the whale.

And the whale agreed to give him a ride across the Mediterranean Sea.

And the boy reached Europe.

After he went across Europe he called the whale again to take him across the Mediterranean Sea so that he could return and be king of the jungle.

So, the whale let the boy have a ride across the Mediterranean Sea. When the boy got back to the jungle, all the animals cheered and had a big celebration. And so, the boy finally became king.

He lived the rest of his life in the jungle and never again returned to his home in Texas.

About six months after we began writing stories with Porter, he was ready to try the activity with his peer partner, Craig. Within another three months, both boys' desire and skill in coordinating their inner worlds had progressed to the point that they wrote with one mind.

Conversations

Once Porter had gained a greater understanding of self and had acquired the ability to use language to share his inner thoughts and feelings with others, it was time to transition him to reciprocal conversation. Conversation is, of course, the ultimate medium for sharing in our society. Within our program we define conversation in a very specific manner. It is a form of communication whose sole purpose is to link some aspect of our mind with the mind of another person. Conversations require that both parties be equally curious about the other person's internal world. To maintain conversation, each person must take on the responsibility of co-regulating their feelings, ideas, bodies, voices and other related variables.

To teach children with Autism about conversation, we first define what a real conversation is and suggest reasons why they might choose to have one. One of the most frequent games we use to teach conversation is "Who Wants to Have a Conversation?" adapted from the popular television show, "Who Wants to be a Millionaire?" The game is a real hit with our clients and comes complete with two lifelines: 50/50 and Phone a Friend. Segments from the our game are illustrated below.

Who Wants to Have a Conversation?

For $100: Why do people have conversations?

A: To talk with the animals

B: Because they can't dance

C: To Fight

D: To share their ideas

Program Tip

We distinguish "true" conversation from other forms of verbal exchange observed in even the brightest, most socially adept people with Autism and Aspergers. The following four types of "pseudo" conversations may function as obstacles to the development of true reciprocal conversation:

- Scripts are emotionless verbal interchanges where the child is repeating rote dialogue he has been taught—"Hello, what is your name? Where do you go to school?"—with no real interest in the answers. The lack of affect and rote nature of the interaction is a giveaway;

- Random communication occurs when the child believes it is acceptable to say whatever comes into his head, and the people around him adjust their responses to keep the dialogue coordinated;

- Data Collection is a verbal exchange that occurs when a child desires information and uses his partners as data banks to obtain this information; and lastly,

- Invasions are highly animated verbal onslaughts, often seen in children with Aspergers Syndrome, where the child bombards listeners with facts and trivia, regardless of the interest, or even the comprehension of the listener.

For $200: When someone starts a topic the right thing to do is:
A: Ignore him
B: Talk about something else
C: Sleep
D: Try to be curious about his ideas

For $300: When you start talking about something, the right thing to do is:
A: Just keep talking until you are finished
B: Look to see if your partner is interested
C: Talk with your eyes closed
D: Walk away while talking

For $400: In a conversation, if your partner acts interested in your topic, you should
A: Poke him with a stick
B: Keep talking about yourself
C: Act interested back. Return the interest
D: Burp

For $500: If you are having a conversation and you do not understand what your partner is saying, you should:
A: Chew gum
B: Point at his nose
C: Tell him you are confused
D: Say something silly

For $1000: The right time to change the topic of a conversation is:
A: Never
B: After your partner's first sentence
C: When your partner is finished talking about his topic
D: When your mother tells you to

When we start teaching conversational formats, we are careful to take into consideration the chronological age of the child or adult with Autism, and teach what would be peer appropriate conversation for that age. With Porter and Craig, other 14-year olds, like themselves, did not go around saying, "How are you? What is your name? Where do you go to school?" when encountering one of their peers. The conversation of young adolescent males is more creative and fluid—less scripted and sequential. It is much simpler and quite unlike the formal adult conversational structure we often attempt to teach in social skills training.

Our work in developing meaningful conversation among our clients moves in many different directions. We work on age appropriate slang, expressing emotional reactions (ER's, for short), verbalizing feelings (both positive and negative), sharing opinions and preferences and many other functions and means of mind sharing.

The Enjoyment of Differences

Relationships would quickly become boring if the participants all had the same ideas, emotional reactions, preferences and opinions. Sharing differences becomes a critical part of enhancing the excitement of conversational interchange. Most people with Autism, even those who progress to this level, sometimes find it odd that we would want to know about the differences that separate us from each other. In working with our clients, we have to make sure that they not only acquire the skills of sharing differences, but understand why someone would value differences as much as commonalities in their relationships.

Most of the people with Autism we work with, even those who appear to have excellent vocabularies, are sorely deficient in being able to describe and communicate their feelings. They tend to think of emotional reactions as black and white—happy or sad, angry or pleased, without many shades of gray. This tends to severely limit their ability to experience the myriad of subtle emotional reactions that inhabit our minds on an almost constant basis. Therefore, we usually spend quite a bit of time with our clients teaching them to recognize degrees of emotions: "I feel a bit tired; I am a little worried; I had a bad day, but now it's better. "

Porter and Craig practiced role-playing feelings and emotions. They took emotions quizzes and played our feelings version of "Who Wants to be a Millionaire?" using multiple choice answers to questions like "What emotion would you feel if your little brother is making too much noise and it's hard for you to listen to your TV program?" Once they had their emotion vocabulary in place, we spent the next two months comparing and contrasting the boys' emotional reactions to everything and anything from dogs (Porter felt terrified, Craig felt cheerful) to little brothers (Porter was excited, Craig was usually irritated).

After the boys understood the basic aspects of sharing emotions, we introduced them to games and exercises that explored their opinions and preferences. They spent several months compiling and contrasting all of the preferences they could think of: favorite foods, restaurants, activities etc. as well as comparing their opinions about issues such as the value of homework, whether Houston should host the Olympics and which sport is more interesting, baseball or basketball. These activities gradually turned into lively respectful debates that became a primary source of conversation initiated by the boys.

The Inside and Outside Worlds

During the time we spent working on sharing and contrasting our feelings, it became apparent that Porter had difficulty understanding that someone could express a feeling that did not necessarily correspond to how he really felt. For example, during role-plays, when I pretended to be really angry with him, even for a blatantly ridiculous reason like blaming him for blowing up the moon, Porter would be confused and try valiantly to convince me that he was not responsible for the deed. While Porter now understood that we each had an inner world containing emotions, opinions, preferences and imaginative ideas, he did not yet know that this internal world did not have to correspond to the external image we portrayed to others. We developed several treatment objectives, described in the following section to help Porter understand this critical difference between how we feel and the external appearance we present to other people.

We went back to Koch's poetry method to work on the areas of pretense and deception. For the first time, Porter was able to explore himself from an imagined "what if" context. A whole new exciting world opened up for him. It whetted his appetite for acting and puppetry, which he pursued with great passion at school.

It is important to note that we started working on pretense in a similar manner as when we began work on imagination—progressing from the

---

Distinguishing Internal/External Selves

- Porter will recognize that outward reactions may not accurately represent a person's true emotional state.

- Porter will perceive internal reactions as different and more important than external reactions.

- Porter will reference to determine the internal state of his partner.

- Porter will be able to tell the difference between good-hearted teasing and cruel name-calling, using voice tone and facial expressions of the teaser as a reference point.

- Porter will demonstrate an understanding of pretense and deception. He will be able to pretend to have an emotional reaction that is different from his real feelings and will react positively when his partners engage in such pretense. (e.g. "I want to kill you and eat you up!")

---

world of the concrete and visible into the internal feelings and emotions. Our initial games of Pretend Facts gave way to the boys adopting pretend identities in a game called, "Who Am I?" Each boy took turns interviewing the other as he assumed his new personae. 'Becoming another person' helped Porter and Craig better appreciate degrees of pretense and deception, especially at the internal level.

As the boys became more comfortable with these new concepts, we focused on blending deception with imaginative silliness. This helped both Porter and Craig start to understand the difference between pretense and deception that occurred "on purpose" versus deception that was mean spirited and possibly harmful.

Once the ideas of pretense and deception were firmly ingrained in Porter and Craig, we wanted them to understand that people sometimes pretended on not only a physical level, but an emotional one as well. We have found that when introducing broad, conceptual ideas, like deception, to children with Autism, it is effective to start with examples from the physical plane and gradually move into the realm of feelings, emotions and thoughts, as the child's understanding develops.

The Primacy of Mind

The final developmental stage in Level 5 occurs at the point where sharing minds becomes a child's primary motivation for interaction. While it would be helpful to be able to pinpoint the specific moment when this occurs, we have found that it normally develops over a several year period in a gradual manner. However, as mind sharing becomes a primary motivator, it is usually apparent in the way conversation flows. It takes on

---

Level 5 Treatment Objectives for Primacy of Mind

- The person recognizes that thoughts, feelings and ideas are the critical elements of Experience Sharing and is highly motivated to share these internal states.

- The person reflects on personal thoughts and feelings for purposes of sharing them with others (self referencing).

- The person recognizes the importance of determining other people's reasons for acting (intentions) to better understand them. He also recognizes the importance of explaining his motivations to help partners understand his intentions.

- The person relates other people's experiences to similar events in his own life and shares these reactions with someone who has had a similar experience.

- The person distinguishes between actions that occur "on purpose" or "by accident". He reacts to the same action in drastically different ways depending upon the person's motivation.

---

a fluid rhythm, similar to a jazz duo, jamming together for fun. Once the child reaches this stage, our treatment focuses on the following objectives:

The following examples pertain to Roger, the brilliant but despairing young man briefly mentioned in Chapter 3. At the time of these examples, Roger was beginning his junior year of High School. He was a brilliant student and talented musician, but he had never had a friend and was growing desperate for real emotional contact. Roger's talent for generating conversation, witty responses and "psuedo" caring replies that he believed his social partners wanted to hear, was truly uncanny. Ironically, the very ability that had helped him escape ridicule and gain safe anonymity and superficial acceptance, left Richard with no energy to reflect on his own ideas and feelings, or to really consider his reactions to what his partners were saying, beyond figuring out his next correct response. Roger and I began the difficult work of removing this obstacle and focusing instead on simple, but genuine ways of sharing minds. For a period of several months we limited our conversations solely to what we referred to as UP's and ER's—Unique Perceptions and Emotional Reactions. We temporarily removed all the typical conversational niceties that Roger had mastered so adroitly, as well as any questions, statements or any other language that didn't qualify as what we considered pure mind sharing. Our conversations sounded like the brief sample that follows.

> **Roger:** *I'd like to live on a tropical island.*
> **Steve:** *Sometimes I just want to go live on another planet.*
> **Roger:** *I want to find out if there is life away from Earth.*
> **Steve:** *I want to get a pet dinosaur.*
> **Roger:** *That's strange.*
> **Steve:** *Yes. Weird!*
> **Roger:** *I'd really love to find the perfect woman.*

Steve: *I'd really like to find the perfect ice cream cone.*
Roger: *Food is the best invention ever.*
Steve: *While we're at it, I'd find the perfect book to read.*
Roger: *Yeah.*
Steve: *To tell the truth, I want my own personal bomber.*
Roger: *I'd borrow him for personal use.*
Steve: *I want a B-1 bomber with a full load of bombs.*
Roger: *I'd like to run the world.*
Steve: *I think I'd load my plane with ice cream bombs.*
Roger: *With all 31 varieties.*

Even now, years after this work, Roger continues to experience highs and lows in his relationship development. He makes breakthroughs, yet at the same time despairs that he cannot yet realize his dream of deep emotional connection with other people. Roger realizes he is socially still a young child, albeit one with an adult mind. He is frequently depressed that the process of relationship development must be so slow. Roger sent me the following email after he had started college.

"I had another breakthrough tonight that I think you should know about. There was this girl I recently met. She was part of a club that for some reason, was dressed up really weird outside of my dorm. Anyway, I stopped to ask her what was going on, and something in the way she answered caught my attention. It sparked something instinctual, like I couldn't control it. I decided I wanted to talk to her more. I asked her her name, something I would have been too paralyzed to do normally, but my desire overrode my fear. We went our separate ways, and that was OK. Because the point was that I initiated social contact based on MY OWN desire to know a person, not by knowing it was the right thing to do. Even further, I started to think about the conversation and I started to think of ways in which I could present myself to other girls in the future. Do you see what that means? Social functioning! Like when you told me that other children spent thousands of hours processing other people and figuring out ways to make themselves fit with other people. I started to see that the routines I design to protect myself from the world are really mundane and boring. Plus, just for a brief moment, no one scared me anymore. And everyone made a little bit of sense. I'm becoming less worried about each little thing I say or do. Even if I do or say something strange, at least it's something I said. At least I can try and tell myself that.

Roger is hungering to connect on an emotional level with other people. Yet, at the same time, he is terrified that when he tries, the other person will be repulsed or, even worse, will mock how little he has to give. Despite his fears, Roger's intense need for real human connection, what he refers to as "something instinctual", overcomes his fear and propels him to risk rejection, to reach out into the unknown.

Sample Level 5 Activities

Mindfulness through Poetry: Kenneth Koch's poetic activities are well described in his wonderful books; most notably *Rose Where did you get that Red.* If the child can read, I highly recommend, at least initially, working at a computer keyboard. The therapist can do all of the typing, if the child is not a skilled typist.

Conversational Tennis: This is a simple activity that provides our patients with an understanding that conversations require both participants to co-regulate the coordination of topic and theme to maintain coordination. It also provides our children with a feel for the basic rhythm of back-and-forth conversation. Here is how it works:

Explain the game of tennis, emphasizing that the object of the game is not to beat the other person but to keep the ball in play. When the ball (the conversation) is kept in play for 5 minutes you win! Make a score sheet for keeping track of earned points. Typically, three people are needed for this game—two players and a judge.

1. A child gets to "serve" first. He will tell and ask something to the opponent. He wins a point if he asks something that the other person is interested in. He loses a point if he asks or tells something that the other person is not interested in.

2. The second person gets to "volley". He has to answer the first person's question. He does not win or lose a point for answering. S/he next gets to "serve" with his own telling and asking. He earns points if he tells and asks something that is relevant and interesting to the other person.

3. After simple "serves", exchanges will progress to a volley. The "ball" remains in play. The person to drop it loses the point. Conversational Volleys must be related to the opening serve topic. A response that is off the original subject costs the player the point.

Practicing Deception: As described in this chapter, there are a number of frameworks for helping children explore the different aspects of Pretense and Deception. These are excellent tasks, not just for social development, but also for the development of flexible thinking. One good starting activity is "Can you tell how I really feel?" Children practice portraying one feeling with their words, while they communicate an opposite emotion with their non-verbal behavior (e.g. Saying "I hate you", while speaking gently and smiling in a friendly manner.) The other child has to guess which emotion is the real one.

Board Games with Captions: In Level 5 we want children to learn that they can engage in games and other activities, but that they are only the background for having a conversation. For the first time in our program, we re-introduce board games, checkers, chess (but still not electronic games) and teach our children to play these games while engaging in a primary conversation. One way we begin is to play a board game like Monopoly, where each time a player draws a card or makes a move, he has to draw a special "Conversation Card" that cues him to be verbally curious about his partner. While this activity can certainly be conducted with children in lower levels, if the real curiosity about one's partner is missing, the activity becomes a dead-end, performing no real function outside of the treatment room.

11

True Friends
Level Six

There is nothing we like to see so much as the gleam of pleasure in a person's eye when he feels that we have sympathized with him, understood him, interested ourself in his welfare. At these moments, something fine and spiritual passes between two friends. These moments are the moments worth living.

Don Marquis

What makes Life worthwhile? When we are questioned about the quality of our lives, most of us would answer that it is our mutually caring, enduring relationships that bring us true pleasure and contentment. These may be with a spouse, children, family, friends, organizations, clubs or co-workers. People become an integral part of our identity; we become bound to them by a shared past and a hoped-for future. We cannot imagine our lives divested of these important relationships. Yet, that is what it is often like to have an Autism spectrum disorder.

Level 6 relational functioning is different from the other levels. It is more nebulous; a highly individualized process that varies from person to person. Once our patients learn to share their minds in different ways, our role becomes one of a mentor or guide, rather than a teacher. We seek to help them understand the value of integrating their lives with others, in many different ways. This type of relational binding allows them to feel a new sense of shared experience; one so powerful that even when they are alone, they can still feel emotionally connected to others.

Some of our patients may never reach Level 6 functioning. However, this does not mean their lives will be completely deprived of attachments to and deep caring for others. On the contrary, our treatment approach provides them with the reasons for and means of sharing themselves with others. They not only acquire the skills of relationship development, but also come away feeling and understanding the intrinsic reasons we reach out and connect to others. Their lives will continually unfold socially for them.

While we have developed broad treatment guidelines for Level 6 (on the next page), each person progresses in a unique manner. The teenagers with Autism you will read about in this chapter are each struggling with different parts of Level 6. Each has his or her unique history of years of courageous work and perseverance to reach the ultimate discovery of intimacy. As you read through their stories, these people may remind you of other people you know—other teens without Autism, struggling to make their place in the world, to understand who they are, where they fit in, working to define their personalities and find other people who understand them. Level 6 work is not just about Autism. It is a journey we all go through, one filled with highs and lows, achievements and failures. Many of us happily embark on this path; for others, it becomes a continual struggle. And so it is for people with

Level 6 Stages and Treatment Objectives

Stage 21: Unique Selves

- Enjoys finding commonalities and differences with others for purposes of better defining a unique sense of self.

Stage 22: Belonging to Groups

- Values his membership in specific groupings as a critical part of his identity.

- References group members frequently to determine if his actions are having the desired positive effect of strengthening membership.

Stage 23: Pals

- Values pal-ships that involve shared interests, activities and history.

- Works to determine actions that will increase his friends' desire to be with him.

- Frequently references his friends to determine the status of their friendship.

Stage 24: Enduring Friendships

- Friendships are primarily based upon abstract principles.

- Knows the difference between superficial playmates and close friendships, based upon history of shared experience, trust and loyalty.

- Has an accurate understanding of what it takes to make and keep friendships. Has valid reasons for trusting and valuing friends.

- Frequently references friend's feelings about the friendship.

- Anticipates friends' needs and desires, outside of the interaction, in order to strengthen friendship bonds.

Autism. At Level 6, we all share common ground as we seek to discover who we really are and how we fit into the world around us.

Self-Identity

As we discussed at the end of Level 5, individuals with Autism functioning at this level of Emotional Coordination need an organized and cohesive self-concept. Our patients often reach this stage understanding bits and pieces about themselves, but with no real cohesive sense of identity. Often they report it feels impossible to distinguish their own ideas, beliefs and preferences from what parents and others have told them is right, or what they have observed. We don't want our patients to learn to base their relationships on responses designed just to please their partner. Therefore, rather than striving for Coordination, we begin Level 6 work helping them understand the unique ways they are different from other people. They learn to reflect in ways that allow them to extract a sense of unique identity and determine the enduring attributes that make them who they are.

We continue using writing and conversation to help spur this discovery of self. Our clients explore the deeper realms of feelings, preferences and morals. As they progress, we introduce Executive Functioning—the ability to use our minds to reflect back on our prior actions and project ourselves into the future. Autism researchers like Bruce Pennington have presented convincing evidence that lack of Executive Functioning is a major impairment for most, if not all, people with Autism. Porter's first "executive" poetic adventure was into the past and is entitled Life Poem. Here, for the first time, Porter reflects upon what he used to be like in prior periods of life and encounters the experience that he continues to change over time.

> **Life Poem**
> *I used to* be an actor.
> *But now* I am a puppeteer
> *I used to* be in elementary school.
> *But now* I am in junior high school.
> *I used to* like spinach.
> *But now* I don't like it.
> *I used to* have a sitter.
> *But now* I don't have a sitter.

Often the past/present relationship is easier for people with Autism to grasp and understand. There is a concrete nature to it. The past event has a tangible quality, as does what exists in the present. However, the present/future relationship is often filled with doubts and insecurities for people with Autism. In the next poem, Porter tries projecting himself into a potential future. He attempts to think about what it would feel like to work at different occupations. The humor evident in this piece reflects the joy, self-assuredness and use of imagination that Porter has developed in less than a year's time. If you read more deeply, you may recognize that the poem also reflects Porter's growing awareness and concern about the challenges he faces, as a person with Autism, finding success in his future life. Notice how each potential career choice is fraught with disaster.

> **Going To Knocked Out Places**
> (the poem's framework text is in italics)
>
> *I went to* an Italian restaurant.
> *And* I was a cook.
> *And* I stirred too much spaghetti.
> *I went* to the supermarket.
> *And* I was a shopping man.
> *And* I crashed the carts.

The past event has a tangible quality, as does what exists in the present. However, the present/future relationship is often filled with doubts and insecurities for people with Autism.

I went to junior high school.
And I was a principal.
And students were throwing food at me.
I went to the dental building.
And I was a dentist.
And someone was biting my fingers.
I went to the department store.
And I was a salesman.
And someone got me fired.

With some of our patients, this self-discovery advances to where they are ready to confront a major part of their identity—their Autism. For Craig, Autism crystallized as more than just a label, when two years ago he decided to write an article on PDD for our newsletter. Craig wrote his essay in order to provide encouragement for other teenagers with the disorder. In it he traced the history of his difficulty and the strides he had made in learning to value relationships with family and friends.

For Brian, the self-realization of his disorder came one day, when he and his father were walking through their favorite playground. They came upon a boy Brian's age—he was 11 at the time—who exhibited many of the stereotyped behaviors of Autism, like hand flapping and echolalia. Brian—who had never seen someone like that before—asked his father, "Dad, what is wrong with that boy?" His father carefully, but honestly, explained to Brian what was wrong with the boy and the diagnostic label. Brian—seeing behind the superficial odd behaviors—replied to his father, "Dad, so that's what's wrong with me, isn't it?"

> **Once people with Autism have confronted their disability, we find that they enjoy talking about it, the personal meaning it has for them, and reflecting back on progress they have made.**

Once people with Autism have confronted their disability, we find that they enjoy talking about it, the personal meaning it has for them, and reflecting back on progress they have made. Three teenagers we work with, Carter, Jed and Benjamin, were asked to be part of a panel discussion on Asperger's Syndrome. In the following segment they reveal their attempts to understand their disorder, underscored by their willingness to participate as a panel at a recent meeting of a local support group. Notice the self-discovery that has, and continues to take place.

Ben: *I was so nervous on that panel. I was watching all these adults giving me all these questions and it was just like...*
Carter: *I'm up here telling them about my past life and what I'm planning on doing. I've told this to people so many times and all of a sudden I'm telling people things I've never told anyone before. I had a great time anyway. Everybody said I did a good job. We all did.*
Jed: *And you forgot to tell them you're going to be an Eagle Scout.*
Carter: *I didn't want to brag.*
Jed: *There is one nice thing about Aspergers. When you walk into something and see it a lot, every day, you can pick it up.*

Benjamin: *I kind of see patterns; once I see patterns, I can figure it out. I figure out what to say, when to say it and when not to say it.*

Carter: *You figure out the pattern and then follow it. Now I can get things quickly. Before when I thought I saw a pattern, I'd continue to follow it through. I didn't look for anything that was sort of a block in the situation—a little bit different that turned out bad. I got kicked in the butt a bunch of times until I figured out that things never stay exactly the same.*

Benjamin: *You learn how to figure it out. It's this way once, it's this way the other time and you figure out the basic things that stay the same.*

Jed: *And you adjust.*

Roger, with his characteristic penchant for over-analysis and drama, has spent more time and effort than anyone else we've worked with trying to figure out which of his actions are the result of Aspergers Syndrome and which are simply his personality. While he dreams about what his social relationships would have been like without his AS, he is dedicated to overcoming the obstacles that hold him back from emotional relationships. Roger has taught us more about the experience of Autism than we've learned in all of our years of reading and research combined.

In the following passage, Roger discusses his struggle to become an authentic person and free himself from the social scripts that have dominated his interactions. In his first year away at college, Roger is discovering the degree to which his years of scripting interactions to avoid ridicule have deprived him of emotional connections.

> *Well, the important part of that story is that I haven't learned how to stop being afraid of people. It preoccupies my mind so much that I stop being myself, and I never say a word. Worse, sometimes I start scripting everything, depending on what type of person I'm with, so I won't stand out as somebody different. The last thing I want to be is different; I don't want to be weird. And sometimes I take extreme measures to make sure I'm not. Like acting like something I'm not, which I've discovered destroys any ability for me to grow and develop a self.*

> *The problem is, as I've discovered, that there is so much excess stimulus bombarding me, that I can't tell what's fun and what isn't, so I don't learn to manipulate situations to my liking. That's when I start to go on routine, because I am in la-la land, and I know that people are expecting certain things of me. More important is that I WANT to contribute to the people around me, so I make desperate, and often inappropriate attempts at joining a conversation.*

The last thing I want to be is different; I don't want to be weird. And sometimes I take extreme measures to make sure I'm not.

I guess what I haven't realized is that when I finally do act as myself, somebody somewhere is going to think I'm weird. Since I magnify that 10,000 times, I never pay attention to the people who say, "Wow, that's pretty interesting." I somehow tell myself that because they think it's interesting, they are deficient in some way, just like I am.

Even while Roger was away at school, we were able to keep in touch via email and regular phone sessions and work with him on better understanding his own identity. Much of our work with individuals who are no longer in a school setting, who have jobs or have gone off to college, occurs on this one-on-one basis with a schedule tailored to their specific needs. While our work in earlier levels consists largely of games and exercises, helping individuals work through Level 6 concepts usually comes through ongoing process groups, written communications, poetry, story creation or in personal sessions.

We worked with Roger on finding the courage to take the risks to become emotionally authentic, even if it meant Roger might be seen as a "weird freak," something he has spent his life trying to avoid. Notice the uncertainty, the depression, and the confusion Roger feels—not unlike any other teenager trying to form his or her own identity. However, for individuals with Autism, the task is even more of a challenge because of their difficulties with social relatedness.

> **Roger:** *Last semester a couple of girls got physically aggressive with me. I'd be out with them alone, but I wouldn't act on their advances. Then I started hearing things said about me. I just don't want people talking about me. One day I reached down and scratched my leg walking down the hall. This guy went on and on about me being a dork. You live in the dilemma of either working hard to 'fit in' and winding up empty or being yourself and some people seeing you as a weird freak. What am I supposed to do?*
>
> **Dr. G:** *Wake up every morning and say 'Today somebody is probably going to think that I'm a weird freak and I don't care.'*
>
> **Roger:** *How do I get depressed about something I want?*
>
> **Dr. G:** *You used to want it (to fit in), but no more. It's an old defense.*
>
> **Roger:** *Instead of telling the person who thinks I'm a weird freak 'screw you', I give up myself so I don't stand out—and become nothing again.*
>
> **Dr. G:** *I would like you to wake up each day and make a choice: to go unnoticed, be scenery or to be who you really are and risk being seen as a weird freak.*
>
> **Roger:** *I think that maybe you really do understand what's happening to me even more than I do. And I thank you for giving me the warnings you did, because now it's so easy for me to see that it's all true. Maybe I am pursuing people for the wrong*

You live in the dilemma of either working hard to "fit in" and winding up empty or being yourself and some people seeing you as a weird freak.

reasons. I can't even pursue relationships on the foundation of emotional experiences; I really see that now. The question is, do I have the guts to do anything about it? And I think I do. I'd be willing to go through any kind of hell if it meant I'd come out with genuine feelings, feelings that I won't allow myself to have now. This is going to be the highest order of 'a search for the self', because I realized just yesterday, that I don't know anything about the self I might be. For all I know, I'm a mad scientist, a starving artist, an athlete—it could be anything—a bluegrass musician, a classical musician, a hard rock musician, there's a million different possibilities. And since I wasn't 'all there' in my younger years, I never got to explore my feelings about these things. Well, it's time to act. And I mean NOW!!!

Belonging to Groups

Participation in treatment groups can be a major source of shared identity for many of the individuals with Autism with whom we work. Group members develop a strong sense of loyalty and shared history. They also plan parties and frequently go out to dinner together. Of course, as therapists we also share a very close lifelong bond with them; we have worked with many of our patients for well over 10 years.

The individuals we work with who reach Level 6, clearly value the close emotional relationships they have painstakingly made over the years. Each person finds slightly different ways to form enduring connections. Craig, who is adopted, basks in his extended family relations and never fails to keep in touch with his uncles, aunts and cousins. He recently came to the realization of what it must have been like for his younger sister, during the many years his Asperger's kept him oblivious to her existence, or actively hostile towards her, and has resolved to find opportunities to make this up to her.

Some of our patients find other traditional ways to develop their shared identity through group participation. For Craig, it was his decision to become an orthodox Jew. Religion was something that his parents first perceived as an obstacle to Craig's relationships. At points in Craig's development, that was certainly true, like when he decided to play only Jewish religious music during car-pool rides with his secular classmates. However, at other times, religion provided Craig with a framework for better understanding who he was. It gave him a common culture and common rituals that he could share with others. Eventually, Craig's enactment of his sense of belonging to the Jewish faith, epitomized by his flawless Bar Mitzvah service, won him the respect of those around him.

Both Craig and Carter found a sense of identity in their affiliation with the Boy Scouts. Carter, now 18, has recently completed his Eagle Scout badge and Craig, three years younger, hopes to reach it soon. Carter, in a poignant speech at his awards ceremony, sincerely thanked all the people who had helped him reach his goal. He expressed a real awareness of the effort and sacrifice it had taken from many people to help him achieve his badge, and that he was truly grateful and proud to belong.

Pal-ships

Our therapy groups are often the first opportunity for some of our patients to develop real pal-ships—where the child understands and feels a special bond with a peer who has shared interests and ideas. At this stage, we begin actively working on what is termed Social Cognition. We encourage our patients to realize that:

- pal-ships require continued work and maintenance, or they will be lost;

- pals make an effort to figure out what their pal likes and dislikes;

- pals actively show interest and enthusiasm;

- pals keep communicating about their common bonds; and

- a pal will even think about his pal when he is not around—"I'm going to save this piece of candy for Johnny. He really likes this kind."

Children who reach this stage experience not only the fun of having an ally and compatriot, but also the loneliness of watching other kids play with their pals without having one of their own. It is one of the sad truths of Autism treatment that often the individuals who make the most progress are also the ones that become most acutely aware of—and sometimes depressed by—their differences and shortcomings.

Carter and Jed are two teens who have been together in a teenage Aspergers groups for several years. They have become pals. Last summer they worked together as counselors in our summer day camp for children, many who have Autism. As with working colleagues, they often bonded by sharing the common travails of their jobs.

Jed: *Most of these kids have a lot of what we have and lots of verbal disorders.*

Carter: *Mine are the obsessive type. It's like, they'll be working on something and get fixed on that for hours. You can't get them away.*

Jed: *We deal with that, too. We have one kid who is that way for puzzles and the other for blocks.*

Carter: *For the kids in my group, it's about everything.*

Jed: *There's this one kid, Brad. If he brings a car in and we take it away, he cries for 30 minutes. We even timed him.*

Carter: *It's like that for us. George will cry and scream when we go outside. Jordan will cry when he upsets everyone and they are annoyed at him. That's basically how my group is.*

Jed: *That sounds like mine, too.*

Roger is struggling at college with his relationships. He can't allow himself to trust his fellow students and let them become his pals. In the following passage, he shares his excitement at learning that he can have his own authentic emotions, followed by despair that he is not yet able to share them with his new pal in the spontaneous, fluid way he most desires.

My best friend here, Jim, had a childhood a lot like mine, but for other reasons. He didn't play with other kids; he used to be mean to them. At some point, he just realized that he was being mean to people and started being nice to them. He's not at all concerned with impressing people. I go to his room a lot, but when I go over there, I feel like I am invading their space. I am scared they are going to say, 'How come you are over here so much?' Jim gives me the sense that I am an interesting person. He expresses awe at some of the things I can do. He's totally baffled by my memory. He's brought to attention some of the abilities that I have. But I don't know if I feel that we are friends. I have doubts that I have any feelings at all. I don't know if I can form friendships.

Jim, he always did this male bonding thing—insulting everybody. He said I took it so seriously when I was younger, but now I just had to learn to take it. I began to see what he meant. When I started to let the other guys know I could really take it [their teasing] that's when they related to me more. I acted more myself; that was easier. That's when I could see the individual differences in the people in the dorm. I always thought they were a mass and I was on the outside. This time, instead of focusing on what they were thinking about me, I started thinking about what I wanted and what I could contribute to them.

The time when I felt most attached to Jim was when he downloaded a bunch of Nintendo games. We played Nintendo together, talking non-stop until 5 am. I was flooded with this experience of total wonder. I opened up. I had a love for something that I remembered.

You've asked me to think about what I give back to my friends. I feel like I'm nice to others—but is it fear? I'm very curious about Jim, but not when I'm with him. I met with him before he left for home, and not once did I try to fake anything, or mimic what other people thought. That was the good part. The bad part was, I could FEEL that he was a real person with his own thoughts and as he talked, I could feel him reach out to me, like I've never felt before. It made me uneasy, and I found that I actually could not be myself in his presence.

I could FEEL that he was a real person with his own thoughts and as he talked, I could feel him reach out to me, like I've never felt before. It made me uneasy...

In the next passage, Roger relates his first experience with a different kind of pal-ship, in describing an encounter with Sheila, a young lady he was briefly involved with in a romantic way. Roger experienced desire and jealousy for the first time. Uncharacteristically for Roger, who over-analyzes everything, he reacted emotionally, with tears, although not understanding why.

> *I talked to Sheila again. This time I had decided to not withdraw myself and get into the discussion, whatever it was. She was telling me about some of the frustrations she was having. We started talking about that, and I gave her a helping hand. It felt great to do that. Today, right after school, I saw her with another guy and he was putting his arm around her. For some reason, I just felt extremely depressed, even though I knew that our relationship was long gone. Something came over me. I sat down on the couch and for the first time I cried; I couldn't control it. I was crying and I don't know where it came from. It just happened. All of a sudden, I just felt tears rolling down my cheek.*

Enduring Relationships

When we reach the final stage of Level 6, relationship work focuses on more abstract principles like loyalty, trust and integrity. The teens and adults we counsel begin to think of a friendship as having more to do with a shared past and potential future together than about what they are doing at the moment. We use several methods to help them distinguish between different levels of intimacy; from playmates, to pals, to good friends, to best friends and even beyond, to more intimate relationships. As therapists who have worked with many of our clients for many years, some view us as close friends. Craig loves to talk about how awful he used to treat me when he was young. Porter and I write stories about events in our group that took place years ago. Carter, preparing to leave therapy, reminisces with his friends and me about our 10 years of relationship work together.

While Roger is off at college, struggling on his own to understand the relational world, Carter, Jed and Ben have had the comfort of each other for mutual support. In the following conversation, note the ease with which their relationship is developing. Ben is the oldest of the three—a college sophomore—while Jed and Carter are both graduating seniors, soon to go off to college. The younger boys look to Ben—their more experienced friend—for assurance that people with Aspergers can survive this right of passage and that relationships—especially with girls—will not be as torturous for them as they have been in the past.

Carter: *Judy thinks that I'm trying to go for her again.*
Jed: *Oh boy.*
Carter: *She said 'I love you' over the phone. I told her I thought we were just friends. She said 'Yeah we're still just friends.' And I go 'Yeah.'*
Jed: *Oh man. I feel sorry for you.*

Ben: *I know. With girls, it's required that you have to listen to them and solve their problems.*

Carter: *When I get to college it will be a whole different matter.*

Jed: *My parents are saying I'm going to break up with my girl-friend when I start college. I said I didn't think so. If I was going to break up with her, I would do it by now, because we've been going out a month.*

Carter: *I say you're better off going into college without a girl-friend.*

Jed: *Yeah.*

Carter: *I don't know what the major difference will be between high school and college.*

Jed: *In high school, if you didn't have a girlfriend, you were nobody.*

Ben: *In college it's a different level. They stop looking for that crap and it doesn't become such a status issue.*

Carter and Ben simultaneously: *Great!* (They exchange 'high fives')

Ben: *You can still be considered a good person if you don't have a girlfriend.*

Jed: *I didn't care about girls until I was fifteen. In high school I happened to get in with one guy who taught me how to flirt.*

Carter: *In 11th grade I sort of picked it up, real quick.*

Jed: *It took me virtually all of high school to handle the social stuff.*

Ben: *It took me until I was out of high school to figure it out. It was kind of a gradual thing, with me just getting better and better at it. I think I've always been able to associate better with guys than girls. It used to be the opposite way for me until my sophomore year when everything switched.*

Carter: *It kind of made sense in high school. Coming up from 8th grade into high school, the girls didn't have any sort of heavy cliques or anything. Everyone just hung around. Coming into high school, they developed this 'secret knowledge', you know, 'We know all the stuff that you don't' and they started to sec-tion people out. All of a sudden, when I was hanging out with girls I was just scared, because it was like I was going to get hurt even if I tried to talk with them.*

Ben: *My dad told me that high school was going to be easier than middle school, but I didn't see that at all.*

Jed: *I think middle school may have been a bit easier. You still did-n't have as many cliques as in high school.*

Carter: *It was harder for me in middle school because I wasn't totally with it. In high school I had to straighten up fast. I just toughened up. It's a hard adjustment. My freshman year was the worst and then after that it had to go up.*

Jed: *Some people love high school.*

Ben: *But they're the ones that already know the stuff.*

Carter: *Those people frustrated the heck out of me.*

Ben: *Same thing in the beginning of college. I don't study as much now as I used to because I'm better adjusted. You'll probably*

I think middle school may have been a bit easier. You still didn't have as many cliques as in high school.

have to readjust when you get to college. I wrote this English paper and thought it was the best paper in my life. I turned it in and got a D in it, and I thought, 'Man, what is this?' The teacher was considered to be dead easy. I thought, 'Do I really belong in college?' and I went through a whole crisis. Eventually I recovered and wound up with a B in that class, but I did a few extra essays to compensate for the D.

Carter: *Is it because they taught something for one major test in high school and then it was totally different in college?*

Ben: *As far as the writing goes, I could do stuff like make a few grammatical mistakes on my papers and it wasn't a main deal. In college, it was completely different. If you have a weak link in your essay they will tear it apart, even if they know what the weak link is.*

Carter: *I'm kinda scared of college.*

Jed: *Me too.*

Carter: *Yeah. But you know, I don't know how, but I know some way, we are going to stay together, like know each other forever.*

Jed: *Yeah. I know what you mean. Like even if we don't see each other for the next 20 years, we will be connected in some way.*

Carter: *Yeah. I know what you mean. It's like we share something that ties us together.*

Jed: *Yeah. That's all right!*

While the boys express their fear of going off on this unknown journey, at the same time they know that no matter where they are, they will not be totally alone. Their bond with their close friends feels permanent to them, even if they do not yet know exactly why. Jed and Carter, each going off to a different college, reaffirm their enduring bond with one another and by doing so, realize that they have created a special type of emotional connection that transcends time and space.

Undoubtedly, there are further stages of relationship development that follow Level 6. In typical development, adolescents continue learning about their varied roles and responsibilities. Young adults venture into the world of intimate relationships. And so it will be with any of our patients who reach Level 6. We derive much joy knowing that they will be able to keep up the work of relationships without much guidance from us. They leave us with social and emotional development building blocks in place, well equipped to fully experience the myriad of human emotional experience throughout their lifespan.

Sample Activities

Group parties and celebrations are a normal part of Level 6 activities. Teenagers develop their own meeting places and activities apart from their therapists, who sometimes get invited, if they are lucky.

Group Journals: We encourage our group to keep a journal of their shared experiences. When a new member arrives, we like to do a brief reading of the group's history.

Personal Reflection Journals: In a similar vein, we often encourage our group members to maintain personal journals.

Future Dreams: We often ask groups members to share various future scenarios with one another. An example would be "What do you think will happen if the two of you meet in 20 years?" Group members are also encouraged to share and contrast their personal dreams for their futures, as well as work on how they will maintain their relationships once their formal membership in the group ends.

The Friendship Test: As an introduction to distinguishing Friends from Playmates and Pals we sometimes use a formal quiz format. Children list their best friends and then provide evidence that the friend is able to pass the 'test. Our Friendship Test, Part II is shown below. It requires the person with Autism to demonstrate that he or she is fulfilling the requirements of being a good friend.

The Friendship Test, Part II

How do you decide if you are a good friend? Which of the following ten items can you honestly say you do as a friend? Which do you not do? Why? Do you have any items, not on the test, that you use to decide if you are a good friend? What score would you get if your friends were rating you? (a passing score is a 7). Talk about times when you have passed the test and times when you have not. When it's journal time, write about a specific memory you have of acting like a good friend. You can include some or all of the 10 items. If you can't recall a memory, write about the type of friend you would like to be, using the 10 items in the test.

	That's Me	Not Me
1. I enjoy doing the same kinds of things as my friend.		
2. I don't mind that my friend has other friends, as long as we still spend time together.		
3. I feel good when my friend is successful. I am not jealous or envious of my friend's success.		
4. I can keep my friend's secrets.		
5. I know special, personal things about my friend that everyone else may not know, like what makes him/her sad or scared.		
6. Our friendship has lasted a long time, even though sometimes it's not easy to keep being friends.		
7. I never lie to my friend.		
8. I never talk badly about my friend to other people.		
9. I try to be real interested in my friend's ideas and feelings.		
10. I do things my friend likes, just to make him/her happy.		

Your Total Score

12

Afterword

*I*t is an old literary cliché to end a work such as this by stating that the ending signifies only the beginning. Cliché or not, even for our "stars" who progress all the way through Level 6, their relationship development is only starting. As magnificent as are the accomplishments of Roger, Craig and Porter, they still have a long way to go before they reach the level of their peers. However, they have felt the intrinsic joy of personal connection. They will never take their ability to share emotions and experiences with others for granted. Because they can remember the devastating effect their lack of social development brought to their lives, they will continue to find avenues for developing meaningful relationships. They understand what it takes to make a friend, be a friend and keep a friend—concepts that many people without Autism think about only in the most superficial way throughout their lives.

We have no real idea how far they can progress. I like to think their future is unlimited. Will there be roadblocks along their path in forming enduring close friendships, romantic relationships, marriage and family life? Probably so, but no worse than those we all face in our quest to belong and fit into our world. For Roger, Craig, Porter and the other teens and young adults we have followed for so long, we believe their path will be filled with the highs and lows that are a natural part of life. But, only time will tell.

In a similar vein, I hope this book is just the beginning of a new wave of interventions that will thoughtfully improve the quality of the social and emotional lives of people with Autism. If I have launched you on a journey of discovery that leaves you approaching the business of relationships with a great deal more wonder and appreciation, then my work has been a success.

While this book does not present any systematic evaluation of the success of our methods, my hope is that it might spur interest in students and researchers to undertake an analysis of our approach. Our evaluation instruments and treatment methods are sufficiently structured to make it fairly simple to determine whether our patients make the progress we claim they do. It needs just time and people resources. In the years since our work began, we have concentrated on using the little manpower we have in direct instruction and work with people with Autism, rather than in research. Somehow, helping a child learn to reference his mother's face, to feel the delight in their interaction, to experience the intrinsic joy of real social interactions with real friends, was always more important than recording data.

One of the most crucial research issues is distinguishing the factors that separate patients who make the most rapid progress from those who seem to move at a snails pace through our treatment program. One obvious factor is the degree of relational development they attain at a young age, prior to ever beginning therapy. We see this factor as much more significant in predicting later outcome than early language development or measured IQ. A related factor is parental willingness to make relationship development the primary objective for their child and for both parents to do the sometimes tedious work of practicing the exercises—especially in Levels 1 and 2. This work often requires a leap of faith that other skills (like language) will develop in time, as well as a strong will to resist their child's demands. Lastly, we should formally determine, as we should in any treatment method, who is most suited and who is unsuited for this treatment. We find that children who begin therapy after the pre-school ages and who, at that age, are still deficient in Level 1 Functions and Means, may be better served by other modalities.

An issue that impedes qualified research is the extensive time and effort that our treatment requires. As described throughout the book, many of our children work with us from pre-school ages until they go off to college. Initially, parents are required to spend at least 20 hours per week at home practicing therapeutic activities. Can we shorten the duration and intensity of treatment? Can we isolate those elements that are most effective and develop methods to speed up the process? These issues beg for intensive research study.

It would be exciting to determine whether we could distinguish children with different forms of relational disorders, based upon the model presented in this book. In our clinical experience, we see children who seem to inherently strive to form unstable systems, by constantly expressing random ideas and engaging in disruptive, disorganized activity. Similarly, we work with children who have a penchant for creating Static systems, demanding that others follow rigid rules and seeking to control everyone's actions within any system they enter. Neil originally presented many of these characteristics. Other children we work with vary in their actions from overly chaotic, to overly rigid functioning, seemingly without rhyme or reason. A final group of children we see are those who—like Manuel—appear initially to be more passive and present fewer initial obstacles to treatment.

Another interesting question involves comparing the relational disorders of children within the Autism spectrum, to those with other disorders, like ADHD. Our clinical experience indicates that a good portion of more severe ADHD children fail consistently to demonstrate co-regulation for Emotional Coordination, especially at the higher levels, and tend to rapidly create unstable, chaotic interactions. Unlike people with Autism, the problem for many people with ADHD appears to be the inconsistency of their actions, not the total lack of social ability. In the right circumstances and at those moments when they stop to focus on a relationship, most people with ADHD appear to have the capacity for fairly complex Experience Sharing.

The trade-off for me, in moving from my prior career as a researcher, to my last 15 years as a clinician, has been the opportunity to so fully share in the lives of my patients. Recently I went along on a several day camping trip with a number of students attending our therapeutic school—several of whom are long standing patients of mine. On the third day of the trip, I suddenly found myself surrounded by three mean-looking adolescent males. They were all children with Autism I have treated since a young age, but none of them had been in any groups together. I had noticed them "conspiring" earlier in the trip, but had placed no significance in their interaction. Now they appeared to be seriously out to inflict pain and I was clearly their intended victim. As a unit, they grabbed me and put me on the ground. As they loomed over me, one of them said, "Dr. Steve. Do you remember when we were young and got out of control and you sat on us? Well, we've been talking and the three of us feel it's time that we finally got our revenge on you. Say your prayers Dr. Steve, you're history!" With that, the three boys suddenly let go of me and fell to the ground themselves, rolling around in hysterical laughter. "We sure got you going this time, didn't we, Dr. Steve?" They surely did and I hope they always do.

Glossary

Asperger Syndrome: Asperger (AS) is a diagnosis named for Hans Asperger, the Viennese physician who along with Leo Kanner in the U.S. initiated the systematic study of Autism beginning in the early nineteen forties. AS falls under the Pervasive Developmental Disorders broad classification of disability, as does autism, in the Diagnostic and Statistical Manual, 4th edition (DSM-IV). The diagnosis of AS is quite similar to that of Autism, with the exception that children with AS must have a near-normal development of early language and intelligence measured within the normal range to receive the diagnosis. Many professionals and lay persons alike believe that people with AS have a better prognosis than either Autism or PDD. In some areas of life functioning, this is true; however, within the realm of relationship challenges, this idea is questionable.

Autism: Officially, Autism is classified as one of the Pervasive Developmental Disorders. Unofficially the term is used to describe the entire spectrum of conditions under the PDD label. Autism is characterized by a severe impairment in social, communication and language functioning. A high percentage of individuals with Autism also have other severe developmental disorders resulting in severe cognitive dysfunction.

Behavior modification: An intervention approach that focuses on developing specific skills in a rote, scripted manner. Behavior modification typically begins by breaking a specified skill down into a number of very small steps and then reinforcing the child's use of each step, until behaviors are chained together to form a skill. Like RDI, Behavior Modification requires many hours of weekly practice and repetition. It is very useful for eliminating aversive behaviors that can be obstacles to developing Experience Sharing. It is also a major way in which we teach Instrumental skills.

Co-regulation: Alan Fogel describes co-regulation as the essential part of a relationship. Individuals in a social encounter are constantly evaluating the degree of novelty that is entering their shared system and regulating this flow of new information; at times increasing it to add more excitement and interest and at other times limiting it to prevent misunderstanding and chaos. People with Autism do not learn co-regulation without intensive intervention. Co-regulatory actions include communications and self-regulatory actions, like slowing down or speeding up, which are enacted to increase the level of coordination.

Complementary Role Sets: These are role actions, which, though different, must be linked together to successfully complete an activity. Common examples are the "hider and finder" in Hide and Seek and team positions such as Quarterback and Wide Receiver in football.

Conversation: Within the RDI model of intervention, conversation is defined as a carefully co-regulated exchange of ideas, feelings, and perceptions, where both parties are involved for the sole purpose of understanding their partner's mind. We contrast true conversation from pseudo-conversations in which one or both parties either does not work to co-regulate, or participates for some purpose other than mind-sharing.

Coordinated Action Sequences: These are actions performed by two people simultaneously in a prescribed sequence. Coordinated Action Sequences are the building blocks of Level 2 relationship development. They provide children with Autism with clear frameworks and rules that allow them to feel comfortable when adults gradually add variation and novelty.

Coordinated Role Sets: These are role actions, which must be linked together in a specific order to successfully carry out an activity. CRS's can be complementary (two different roles which fit together) or symmetrical (two similar roles which must be performed in a coordinated manner). They can also be Sequential—with one person's action following another, or Simultaneous—with both partners needing to act at the same time.

Emotional Attunement: Daniel Stern defined Emotional Attunement as the first task of the newborn infant and mother. Both parties are motivated to become highly emotionally sensitive to each other. Attunement is a pre-cursor for all further relationship development.

Emotional Coordination: Emotional Coordination is the desire and ability to maintain a state of highly synchronized actions, perceptions, feelings and ideas for the sole purpose of sharing experiences. R. Peter Hobson believes that a deficit in Emotional Coordination is a hallmark of Autism.

Executive Functioning: The pre-frontal cortex is the "executive" part of the human brain. It allows us to reflect back on prior experiences and to use that information to anticipate and prepare for potential future situations. Executive Functioning deficits have been found in people with Autism and AS and are clearly a critical aspect of the disorder.

Experience Sharing: Experience Sharing occurs when we interact with no endpoint in mind other than sharing some part of our mutual world with others. People engaging in Experience Sharing are motivated by the potential for new discovery and creation, through careful, mutual, introduction of novelty. We believe that a deficit in Experience Sharing is one of the hallmarks of all forms of Autism. Experience Sharing is one of the two major reasons for social interactions, the other being Instrumental interactions. Often, they may be difficult to differentiate from one another.

Fluid Systems: One of three types of social systems that describe the overall structure and functioning of different types of interactions. Fluid Systems permit the introduction and creation of novelty in a meaningful context. They are highly flexible and adapt to change easily.

Functions of Experience Sharing: Functions are the reasons why we choose to engage in various actions. Coordination Functions are actions that we take for the sole purpose of strengthening some part of our emotional connection with social partners. The only payoff or reward of Coordination Functions is the emotional experience of closeness.

Guided Participation: This is a term, coined by the Russian Psychologist Lev Vygotsky, to describe the natural role of parents in early development. It has also been used to describe any "master-apprentice" or "teacher-student" relationship in which the more competent individual initially assumes most of the responsibility for structuring and maintaining the interaction and gradually helps the less capable partner to function on an equal basis.

Impression Formation: This is a term from Social Psychology, referring to our desire to want to influence the way that other people view us. Children begin to consciously engage in Impression Formation by the age of six, when they grasp that they can deliberately affect their social partner's mental state.

Instrumental Interactions: This is the second major type of human social encounter. They are actions deliberately taken to achieve some specific endpoint. When we engage in Instrumental interactions we desire to reach our goal in the most efficient manner possible. Novelty and variation are not valued or desired.

Joint Attention: This refers to a form of Experience Sharing in which we desire to share a perception of some external object or area with another person. Joint Attention appears to develop by 18 months of age in the typical child. Peter Mundy and other Autism researchers have conclusively demonstrated that people with Autism have a severe deficit in their initiation of Joint Attention encounters.

Means of Experience Sharing: These are the methods that we use to achieve and maintain our Emotional Coordination with social partners. In typical development, Means follow Functions. Each new Function or reason to coordinate typically spurs the child on to develop methods to more reliably achieve that Function.

Obstacles: Factors—behaviors, characteristics, beliefs, conditions—that may impede or prevent the development of Functions and Means of Experience Sharing. Obstacles may exist as a result of the child's disability, may be habitual actions unrelated to the disability, or may arise from environmental factors that create interference.

PDD: Pervasive Developmental Disorder is the technical medical term for the class of syndromes which involve a severe deficit in Experience Sharing development. The PDD's include Autism, Aspergers, Rett's Syndrome, Childhood Disintegrative Disorder and PDD NOS—Not Otherwise Specified. A person diagnosed with PDD-NOS still has a severe impairment in relationship development but does not possess *all* of the other characteristics associated with the disability in a severe enough form to warrant an autism or AS diagnosis.

Perception Sharing: This is another term for describing Joint Attention, where two people experience an object, feeling or event at the same time or in the same manner.

Perspective Taking: This is an initial form of understanding that another person's inner experiences may be different than one's own. By age two, children know that their social partners may not see objects in the same manner that they do. When children learn perspective taking they make specific accommodations, like turning a photo album around to make sure their partner can see a picture that excites them.

Pseudo-conversations: A form of talking that characterizes most of the verbal activity of people with Autism and Aspergers. Pseudo-conversations are initiated to fulfill *an instrumental need* of the person with Autism. In pseudo-conversations, one of the social partners has to do all of the co-regulation and repair work to maintain coherence and coordination.

RDA: Relational Development Assessment is the evaluation protocol used as part of the RDI treatment model. Intervention service plans are based on the RDA. The RDA includes intensive structured observation of the child as well as detailed interviews with parents and other important individuals in the person's life.

RDI: Relational Development Intervention is the model program outlined in this book to teach people with Autism spectrum disorders to fully participate in Experience Sharing relationships. RDI uses information from the RDA to develop clear, specific, developmentally appropriate treatment objectives and customized activities.

RDO: Relational Development Observation is the structured observational instrument we employ to carefully analyze a child's level of relationship development. The RDO takes about 1.5 hours to administer and requires careful analysis. Typically the RDO is videotaped and reviewed.

RDQ: The Relational Development Questionnaire was developed to evaluate the perceptions of parents and other adults of the child's Experience Sharing development. The RDQ is always followed by a careful interview to clarify responses.

Repair: These are actions that we routinely take when we perceive that relationship coordination has broken down. Repair actions are typically offered by one partner and accepted by the other. People with Autism are unaware of the need to engage in repair actions.

Scripts: Pre-planned, systematic instructions for how to respond to a given event. Scripts can be either actions or verbal expressions, or a combination of both. Instrumental interactions can often be successfully taught via scripts and social stories. These methods provide the person with autism with a socially acceptable response to situations that do not vary from one instance to the next. For example, waiting in line at the bank can be taught with a script. Scripted methods are ineffective, however, when the person is involved in Experience Sharing encounters, which by definition involve the introduction of novelty and variation.

Self Regulation: Actions taken for the purpose of keeping oneself coordinated with a partner during a social encounter.

Sequential Role Sets: An activity where one partner takes an action, which serves as a signal for the other partner to take his or her action. Coordination between partners can be attained by enacting one's role immediately following the actions of a social partner. Sequential Role Sets are the initially taught in Level 2. They require less difficult social referencing and much less rapid attention shifting than do Simultaneous Role Sets.

Simultaneous Role Sets: These are the more advanced form of action role sets taught in Level 2. Social partners are enacting their roles at the same time. They must maintain physical coordination while at the same moment making sure that they are continuing to act in their prescribed ways. Walking and running together are two simple forms of Simultaneous role sets. Even high functioning people with AS and Autism have great difficulty enacting Simultaneous Role Sets.

Social Referencing: This is a critical process, beginning during the first year of life, where children learn to actively utilize the facial expressions, reactions and actions of their social partners as an essential reference point to determine their own behavior. In later years. social referencing takes on a more "mindful" component as children strive to know the real feelings and thoughts of their social partners, rather than just their external manifestations.

Social Skills Training: A behavioral approach that teaches different types of social actions. Social Skills Training is typically conducted using a scripted approach and has value in preparing people for Autism to successfully participate in Instrumental interactions.

Static Systems: These are social systems designed to efficiently provide end products to their participants. Static systems are based upon unvarying rules and structure. Novelty and variability are perceived as disruptive. Individuals in Static systems are largely interchangeable as long as they follow the prescribed rules and enact their role actions at the appropriate time and in the correct manner.

Symmetrical Role Sets: These are role sets in which the participants enact largely the same actions in a coordinated manner. They can be either sequential or simultaneous. Riding bicycles together, or dancers in a chorus line are examples of people enacting Symmetrical Role Sets.

Temptations: Temptations are objects, activities or settings which enhance the child's desire and ability to participate in Experience Sharing interactions. For example, with a child who enjoys numbers, counting 1-2-3 before running may increase his interest in the activity, and be used as a temptation. However, for the same child a book of number puzzles may divert his attention away from Experience Sharing and therefore, becomes an obstacle. External reinforcements are rarely temptations as they distract the child from the real inherent emotional payoff in Experience Sharing.

Theory of Mind: Dr. Simon Baron-Cohen and his associates at the University of London defined Theory of Mind as a person's ability to appreciate that other people have internal experiences that are different from his/her own. Their research clearly demonstrates that this deficit is one of the distinguishing characteristics of Autism spectrum disorders.

We-go: Dr. Bob Emde coined this term to describe the excitement and power felt through participation in a larger group entity. We-go development is characterized by children with Autism using the words "us" and "we" in referencing their plans and memories.

The Six Levels of Experience Sharing

Level 1 Summary

What we share

- First three months—Emotional attunement via coordination of child and parent's nervous system.

- Second three months—introduction of large amounts of novelty, at the edge of the child's excitement/distress threshold.

- The excitement of anticipating climaxes of simple games.

How we share it

- Parent carefully regulates the input of excitement and novelty by referencing the child's reactions.

- Child raptly attends to parent for novelty and soothing.

- Child learns to anticipate exciting climaxes of simple games.

- Child's early communication provides additional data to parent for regulatory decisions.

Level 2 Summary

What we share

- Learning the essential structural framework of sequenced games.

- Enjoying novel variations added to structured games, while still understanding the framework.

- The joy of acting together as a single synchronized unit.

How we share it

- Children learn to use the structure of games to reference and anticipate the sequence.

- Parents can add ongoing variations to games without the child losing perception of the basic framework and sequence.

- Parent engages in careful guided participation.

- Child becomes an active participant in simple role-taking games.
- Parents gradually guide child's learning of moment-to-moment regulating actions.
- Child learns to maintain coordination in an activity by co-regulating his own actions based on the prior action of his partner.
- Child learns referencing and co-regulating in simultaneous coordinated actions.
- Child learns to evaluate and modify his actions in subtle ways, to remain coordinated with his partner.

Level 3 Summary

What we share
- Rapid introduction of variations
- Improvised encounters
- Co-creating unique activities

How we share it
- Coordinating our actions without structured rules and roles
- Careful evaluation of the effect of added variations
- Rapid repair actions to maintain the coordination of partners

Level 4 Summary

What we share
- Unique perceptions
- Different perspectives
- Unique reactions
- Adding imaginative elements to perceptions

How we share it
- Initiating Joint Attention
- Accepting Joint Attentional invitations from partners
- Understanding perspective taking
- Formulating subjective reactions
- Combining objective perceptions with imaginative elements

Level 5 Summary

What we share

- Common and contrasting ideas, feelings and viewpoints
- Appreciation of other's ideas
- Co-creating new ideas
- Our inner feelings

How we share it

- Co-created imaginary play
- Playful integration of ideas and fantasies
- Distinguishing outer from inner emotions
- Understanding deception
- Understanding intention
- True, reciprocal conversation

Level 6 Summary

What we share

- The search to find elements of our unique identity; commonalities and differences
- The power of group membership
- Memories of enjoyable encounters with playmates and pals
- Sharing our inner selves with others in more intimate, enduring relationships

How we share it

- Referencing for social comparison
- Adopting various roles for group acceptance and participation
- Impression Formation
- Developing pal-ships based upon common interests
- Evaluating relationships at different levels of closeness and trust

A Summary of Research
on the Social Development of Children with Autism

Emotion Sharing and Regulation

- Don't seem to display a differential preference for maternal speech (Klin, 1991; Klin, 1992).

- Much less likely to smile in response to another's smile (Dawson et al., 1990).

- The human face holds less interest for autistic infants (Volkmar, 1987).

- Less engaged with and affected by other people's expression of feeling (Hobson, 1993).

- Don't appear to engage in the coordination games of infancy like peek-a-boo with as great a frequency (Volkmar, 1987).

- Rarely look and appear unconcerned when adults pretend to be frightened or hurt. Adultís emotional expression doesnít change the child's play with an object (Sigman, Kasari, Kwoon & Tirmiya,1992).

- Exhibit a deficiency of positive affect when making communicative bids to others (Dawson et al., 1990; Snow et al. 1987).

- Don't seem to use gestures of embarrassment, consolation or apology for communicative repair (Attwood, Frith and Hermelin, 1988).

- Less likely to combine their smiles with eye contact (Le Couteur et al., 1989; Dawson et al., 1990).

- Tend to be more flat and unclear in emotional expressions (Yirmiya, Kasari et al 1989; Langdell 1981; Macdonald, et al., 1989).

- Don't develop babbling in a socially directed, contingent manner (Lord, 1991).

- Don't attempt to coordinate topic, turn taking, interest etc. (Tager-Flusberg, 1989; 1991).

Joint Attention

- Rarely engage in "referential looking" between an active mechanized toy and an observer (Mundy et al., 1986; Sigman et al., 1986).

- Young autistic children don't show objects to an adult in a spontaneous way (Curcio, 1978).

- Failure to initiate joint attention alone discriminates 80–90% of young children with autism from children with other developmental delays. This deficit is present in young children with autism regardless of developmental or intellectual level. (Lewy & Dawson, 1992; Mundy et al. 1986; Baron-Cohen, 1989; Landry & Loveland, 1988; Loveland & Landry, 1986; McEvoy et al., 1993; Mundy, Sigman & Kasari, 1994; Wetherby, Yonclas & Bryan, 1989).

Theory of Mind

- Specific deficits in pretend play about the mental states of characters (Lewis & Boucher, 1988).

- Low frequency of spontaneous pretend play with social themes (Baron-Cohen, 1987).

- Show a variety of Theory of Mind deficits in understanding beliefs of others, understanding others goals, perspective taking, pretense and deception (Baron-Cohen, 1993).

- Impairment in empathic responses (Sigman, Kasari, Kwon & Yirmiya, 1992).

- Significantly less able to understand that they manipulated the beliefs of another person, by predicting the outcome of their deceptive act (Yirmiya, Solomonica-Levi & Shulman, 1996).

Peer Relationships

- Spend much less time observing peer behavior in a classroom (Hauck, 1995).

- Interactions of 8–11 year olds with Autism with peers are much more impaired than interaction with adults (Sherman, Shapiro & Glassman 1983; Hauck 1995; Stone and Lemanek 1990; Stone & Caro-Martinez 1990; Ungerer 1989).

- Initiations with peers are more about giving information and greeting, while initiation of matched controls are more about inviting to play and sharing personal information (Hauck, 1995).

- Older children with Autism were unable to describe what a friend is in a satisfactory manner, even though they listed many people as "friends" (Lord et al., 1989).

References

Attwood, Frith and Hermelin, 1988. The understanding and use of interpersonal gestures by autistic and Down's Syndrome Children. *Journal of Autism and Developmental Disorders.* 18,2, 241–257.

Baron-Cohen, Simon. (1987). Autism and symbolic play. *British Journal of Developmental Psychology,* 5, 139–148.

Baron-Cohen, Simon (1989). The autistic child's theory of mind: a case of specific developmental delay. *Journal of Child Psychology and Psychiatry,* 30, 285–298.

Baron-Cohen, Simon, Tager-Flusberg, Helen, Cohen, Donald, J. *Understanding Others Minds: Perspectives from Autism.* Oxford University Press. 1993.

Bates, E. Camaioni L., & Volterra V. (1975). *The acquisition of performatives prior to speech.* Merril-Palmer Quarterly, 21, 205–226.

Bruner, J.S. (1983). *Child's Talk.* Oxford: Oxford University Press.

Curcio, F. (1978). *Sensorimotor functioning and communication in mute autistic children.* Journal of Autism and Childhood Schizophrenia, 8, 281–292.

Dawson, G., Hill, D., Spencer, A., Galpert, L., & Watson, L. (1990). *Affective exchanges between young autistic children and their mothers.* Journal of Abnormal Child Psychology, 18, 335–345.

Dennett, D. (1991). *Consciousness Explained.* Boston, MA: Little, Brown.

Emde, R.N. (1989). The infant's relationship experience: Developmental and affective aspects. In A. J Sameroff and R. N. Emde (Eds), *Relationship disturbances in early childhood: A developmental approach.* Basic Books, New York.

Fogel, A. *Developing Through Relationships.* The University of Chicago Press, Chicago Ill. 1993.

Gottman, J.M. The world of coordinated play: Same and cross-sex friendships in young children. In J.M. Gottman and J.G. Parker (Eds.), *Conversations of friends: Speculations on affective development* (pp 139–191). New York: Cambridge University Press.

Gottman, J. (1994) *Why Marriages Succeed and Fail.* Fireside, New York.

Hadwin, J., Baron-Cohen, S; Howlin, P. and Hill, K. Does Teaching Theory of Mind have an Effect on the Ability to Develop Conversation in Children with Autism? *Journal of Autism and Developmental Disorders,* Vol 27, No. 5, 1997, pp. 519–537.

Hauck, M., Fein, D., Waterhouse, L. & Feinstein, C. (1995). Social initiations by autistic children to adults and other children. *Journal of Autism & Developmental Disorders,* 25, 579–95.

Stone, W.L. and Lemanek, K.L., (1990). Parental report of social behaviors in autistic preschoolers. *Journal of Autism and Developmental Disorders,* 20, 513–522.

Hobson, R. P. *Autism and the Development of Mind.* Lawrence Erlbaum Associates. Hover (UK), Hillsdale (US). 1993.

Klin, A. (1991). Young autistic children's listening preferences in regard to speech: a possible characterization of the symptom of social withdrawal. *Journal of Autism and Developmental Disorders*, 21, 29–42.

Klin, A., Volkmar, F.R., Sparrow, S.S. *Asperger Syndrome.* Guilford. New York. 2000.

Klin, A. Volkmar, F.R. and Sparrow, S. (1992). Autistic social dysfunction: some limitations of the theory of mind hypothesis. *Journal of Child Psychology and Psychiatry*, 33, 861–876.

Landry, S.H. & Loveland, K.A. (1988). Communication behaviors in autism and developmental language delay. *Journal of Child Psychology and Psychiatry*, 29, 621–634.

Langdell, T. (1981). Face Perception: An approach to the study of autism. *Unpublished Doctoral Dissertation*, University College, London.

Le Couteur, A., Rutter, M., Lord, C., Rios, P., Robertson, S., Holdgrafer, M., and McLennan, J.D. (1989). Autism Diagnostic Interview: a semi-structured interview for parents and care-givers of autistic persons. *Journal of Autism and Developmental Disorders,* 19, 363,387.

Lewis, V. & Boucher, V. (1988). Spontaneous, instructed and elicited play in relatively able autistic children. *British Journal of Developmental Psychology*, 6, 325–39.

Lewy, A. & Dawson, G., (1992). Social stimulation and joint attention in young autistic children. *Journal of Abnormal Child Psychology*, 20, 555–566.

Lord, C. & Magill, J. (1989). Methodological and theoretical issues in studying peer-directed behavior and autism. In G. Dawson (Ed.), *Autism: Nature, Diagnosis and Treatment* (pp 326–345). New York, Guilford.

Lord, C. (1991). Follow-up of two-year-olds referred for possible autism. Paper presented at the Biennial meeting of The Society for Research in Child Development. Seattle.

Loveland, K. & Landry, S. (1986). Joint attention and language in autism and developmental language delay. *Journal of Autism and Developmental Disorders*, 16, 335–349.

McEvoy, M.A., Nordquist, V.M. Twardosz, S., Heckaman, K.A., Wehby, J.H., and Denny, R.K. (1988).Promoting autistic children's peer interactions in an integrated early childhood setting using affection activities. *Journal of Applied Behavior Analysis*, 21, 193–200.

Mckean, T. (1995). *Soon Will Come the Light.* Future Horizons. Arlington.

Miller, A & Miller, E. (1990). *From Ritual to Repertoire.* Wiley, New York.

Mundy, P., Sigman, M., Ungerer, J., & Sherman, T. (1986). Defining the social deficits of autism: The contribution of non-verbal communication measures. *Journal of Child Psychology and Psychiatry*, 27, 657–669.

Mundy, P. (1998). Joint Attention and Early Social Communication: Implications for research on intervention with autism. *Journal of Autism and Related Disabilities.*

Mundy, P., Sigman, M. & Kasari, C. (1994). Joint attention, developmental level and symptom presentation in young children with autism. *Development and Psychopathology*, 6, 389–401.

Osterling, Julie, and Dawson, Geraldine. Early recognition of Children with Autism: A study of First Birthday Home Videotapes. *Journal of Autism and Developmental Disorders*, Vol. 24, No. 3, 1994. pp247–257.

Parker, J.G. & Gottman, J.M. (1989). Social and emotional development in a relational context: Friendship interaction from early childhood to adolescence. In T.J. Berndt & G.W. Ladd (Eds). *Peer Relationships in Child Development* (pp95–131). New York: Wiley.

Prizant, B.M. & Wetherby, A.M. (1987). Communicative intent: a framework for understanding social-communicative behavior in autism. *Journal of the Amercian Academy of Child and Adolescent Psychiatry*, 26, 472–79.

Rubin, Zick. *Children's Friendships.* Harvard University Press, Cambridge, Mass. 1980.

Sacks, O. (1995). *An Anthropologist on Mars: Seven Paradoxical Tales.* Alfred A. Knopf, N.Y.

Sherman, M., Shapiro, J., & Glassman, M. (1983). Play and language in developmentally disordered preschoolers: a new approach to classification. *Journal of the American Academy of Child Psychiatry*, 22, 511–24.

Sigman, M. Mundy, P., Sherman, T., & Ungerer, J.A. (1986). Social interactions of autistic, mentally retarded and normal children and their caregivers. *Journal of Child Psychology and Psychiatry*, 27, 647–56.

Sigman, M., Kasari, C., Kwon, J.H., & Yirmiya, N. (1992). Responses to the negative emotions of others by autistic, mentally retarded and normal children. *Child Development*, 63, 796–807.

Sinclair, J. ëPersonal Essays.' in E. Schopler and G. B. Mesibov, (Eds.). *High-Functioning Individuals With Autism.* Plenum Press. New York, 1992.

Snow, M. Hertzig, M., and Shapiro, T. (1987). Expression of emotion in young autistic children. *Journal of the American Academy of Child Psychiatry*, 26, 836–8.

Sroufe, L.A. (1989). Relationships, self and individual adaptation. In A.J. Sameroff and R.N. Emde (Eds.), *Relationship Disturbances in Early Childhood: A Developmental Approach* (pp70–94). Basic Books, New York.

Stern, D. (1971). *The First Relationship.* Harvard University Press. Cambridge, Mass.

Stern, D. (1985). *The Interpersonal World of the Infant.* Basic Books, New York.

Stone, W.F., and Caro-Martinez, L.M. (1990). Naturalistic observation of spontaneous communication in autistic children. *Journal of Autism and Developmental Disorders*, 20, 437–54.

Tager-Flusberg, H. (1989). An analysis of discourse ability and internal state lexicons in a longitudinal study of autistic children. Paper presented at the biennial Meeting of the Society for Research in Child Development. Kansas City.

Tager-Flusberg, H. (1991). Semantic processing in the free recall of autistic children: Further evidence for a cognitive deficit. *British Journal of Developmental Psychology, 9, 417–30.*

Ungerer, J.A. (1989). The early development of autistic children: Implications for defining primary deficits. In G. Dawson (Ed.), *Autism, Diagnosis and Treatment* (pp 75–91). New York: Guilford.

Volkmar, F. (1987). Social development. In D.J. Cohen and A. M. Donnellan (Eds). *Handbook of Autism and Pervasive developmental Disorders* (pp41–60). New York: Wiley.

Wetherby, A., Yonclas, D. & Bryan, A. (1989). Communication profiles of preschool children with handicaps: Implications for early identification. *Journal of Speech and Hearing Disorders,* 31, 148–58.

Williams, Donna. *Autism: An Inside-Out Approach.* Jessica Kingsley Publishers. London and Philadelphia. 1995.

Yirmiya, N., Kasari, C., Sigman, M., & Mundy, P. (1989). Facial expressions of affect in autistic, mentally retarded and normal children. *Journal of Child Psychology and Psychiatry,* 30, 725–35.

Yirmiya, N., Solomonica-Levi, D., and Shulman, C. (1996). The ability to manipulate behavior and to understand manipulation of beliefs: A comparison of individuals with autism, mental retardation and normal development. *Developmental Psychology,* 32, 62–69.

Steven E. Gutstein, Ph.D.

Dr. Steven Gutstein received his Ph.D. in Clinical Psychology in 1980 from Case Western Reserve University. From 1980 to 1987 he was on the faculty of the Baylor College of Medicine and the University of Texas Medical School, where he conducted research, developed innovative programs and published extensively on helping children and their families cope with medical and developmental crises. As well as conducting his clinical practice, Dr. Gutstein is currently the Co-Director, along with his wife Rachelle, of The Connections Center for Family and Personal Development. He is also the Clinical Director of The Monarch School, an innovative therapeutic day school in Houston and is on the clinical staff of Texas Children's Hospital. Drs. Gutstein and his wife have been married for over 20 years and have two daughters, Hannah, who is 20 and Esther, who is 18.

The Connection Center for Family and Personal Development

The Connections Center for Family and Personal Development began in 1995 as a multi-disciplinary program to develop innovative evaluation and intervention programs for people with relationship disorders. Since that time, their work has focused on children, adolescents and adults with Autism, Aspergers Syndrome and PDD. Connections staff provide a full range of evaluation and treatment services including Relational Development Assessment, Relational Development Intervention, neuropsychological and educational assessment, speech and language services, parent and professional training and school and home based services. They routinely provide consultation and workshops to families and professionals throughout the United States, Mexico and Canada. For further information browse The Connections Center website at **www.connectionscenter.com,** or contact them at:

The Connections Center
4120 Bellaire Blvd.
Houston, TX 77025
Telephone: 713.838.1362
Fax: 713.838.1447

The Monarch School

Monarch began in 1997 as a joint effort by Dr. Gutstein and Dr. Marty Webb, an experienced educator, to provide a much-needed therapeutic day school for the Houston metropolitan area. Students range in age from 6–16. Monarch accepts children with a variety of disorders such as ADHD, Tourettes Syndrome and Non-Verbal Learning Disorder. About 20% of the students are diagnosed with disorders in the Autism spectrum.

Monarch's mission is to provide each student with the fundamental Functions and Means to participate in meaningful relationships and to take ownership for their own learning and independence. The curriculum is largely based on the Relational Development Intervention model described in this book. Monarch's innovative Executive Functioning Program teaches students the value and methods of meaningful reflection, organization, planning and preparation—critical factors in predicting life success. For information about The Monarch School, browse their website at www.monarchschool.org or call 713.479.0800.

New Books by Dr. Steven Gutstein
in the
Relational Development Intervention Series

Activities Workbook

Step-by-Step instructions for designing
and implementing an RDI program
at home or in the school
Hundreds of ideas and activities!

Assessment

A complete manual for assessing
social relationship skills
in individuals with Autism/Aspergers/PDD

Anticipated Release Date: Fall 2001